On Same-Sex Marriage, Civil Unions, and the Rule of Law

Constitutional Interpretation at the Crossroads

Mark Strasser

Issues on Sexual Diversity and the Law

Westport, Connecticut
London

Library of Congress Cataloging-in-Publication Data

Strasser, Mark Philip, 1955–
    On same-sex marriage, civil unions, and the rule of law : constitutional interpretation at the crossroads / Mark Strasser.
      p. cm.—(Issues on sexual diversity and the law, ISSN 1539–0918 ; no. 1)
    Includes bibliographical references and index.
    ISBN 0–275–97761–7 (alk. paper)
    1. Same-sex marriage—Law and legislation—United States.   2. Same-sex marriage—Law and legislation—Vermont.   3. Same-sex marriage—Law and legislation—Hawaii. I. Title. II. Series.
    KF539.S769   2002
    346.7301′6—dc21   2002025204

British Library Cataloguing in Publication Data is available.

Library of Congress Catalog Card Number: 2002025204
ISBN: 0–275–97761–7
ISSN: 1539–0918

First published in 2002

Praeger Publishers, 88 Post Road West, Westport, CT 06881
An imprint of Greenwood Publishing Group, Inc.
www.praeger.com

Printed in the United States of America

∞™

The paper used in this book complies with the Permanent Paper Standard issued by the National Information Standards Organization (Z39.48–1984).

10 9 8 7 6 5 4 3 2 1

Contents

Acknowledgments

I have discussed some of these subjects in various law reviews:

"*Baehr* Mysteries, Retroactivity, and the Concept of Law," 41 *Santa Clara Law Review* 161–201 (2000)

"Equal Protection at the Crossroads: On *Baker*, Common Benefits, and Facial Neutrality," 42 *Arizona Law Review* 935–63 (2000)

"*Loving, Baehr,* and the Right to Marry: On Legal Argumentation and Sophistical Rhetoric," 24 *Nova Law Review* 769–91 (2000)

"*Loving* in the New Millennium: On Equal Protection and the Right to Marry," 7 *University of Chicago Law School Roundtable* 61–90 (2000)

"Mission Impossible: On *Baker*, Equal Benefits, and the Imposition of Stigma," 9 *William & Mary Bill of Rights Journal* 1–27 (2000)

"The Privileges of National Citizenship: On *Saenz*, Same-Sex Couples, and the Right to Travel," 52 *Rutgers Law Review* 553–88 (2000)

"Same-Sex Marriages and Civil Unions: On Meaning, Free Exercise, and Constitutional Guarantees," 33 *Loyola Chicago Law Journal* 597–630 (2002)

"Sex, Law, and the Sacred Precincts of the Marital Bedroom: On State and Federal Right to Privacy Jurisprudence," 14 *Notre Dame Journal of Law, Ethics & Public Policy* 753–89 (2000)

"Toleration, Approval, and the Right to Marry: On Constitutional Limitations and Preferential Treatment," 35 *Loyola Los Angeles Law Review* 65–99 (2001)

"When Is a Parent Not a Parent? On DOMA, Civil Unions, and Presumptions of Parenthood," 23 *Cardozo Law Review* 299–324 (2001)

I thank each of these law reviews without whose help this book would not have been possible. I also wish to thank Michael Hermann of Praeger Publishers and George Cronheim for their help in seeing the project through to completion.

Introduction

On April 26, 2000, Governor Dean of Vermont signed into law a civil union statute affording to qualifying same-sex couples all of the rights and benefits that the state affords to married couples. Reactions to this newly created status ranged from (1) disappointment that same-sex couples were not simply allowed to marry to (2) joy and exultation that same-sex couples could have their relationships legally recognized and that they would thereby be entitled to the same state benefits and protections that different-sex couples receive to (3) anger and disgust that same-sex couples would be permitted to enter into legally recognized relationships that seemed to have all of the benefits if not the name of marriage. This book examines the implications of the legal recognition and non-recognition of civil unions in particular and of same-sex relationships more generally.

Part of the reason that the legal recognition of same-sex relationships is so hotly contested is that it implicates so many legal and non-legal issues: What should be done when individuals within a society have sharply differing moral visions? Which rights are constitutionally protected and which are subject to popular vote? What protections should exist when a couple with a legally recognized relationship in one state travels through or moves to another? What implications are there for the ideal of equal treatment under the law if same-sex relationships are not given legal recognition or if they are recognized in some jurisdictions but not others? The answers to these questions are not at all obvious, and these issues will likely be the source of a great deal of litigation during the next several years.

One of the reasons that it is less clear how courts will resolve these issues is that society is gradually becoming more accepting of lesbians, gays, bisexuals, and transgendered people. Although there is still far to go, this growing acceptance has important legal implications. Courts have become less willing to reject claims by lesbians, gays, bisexuals, and transgendered people out of hand and have instead tried to show why applicable law protects or does not protect the interests at issue. This has led courts to recognize rights that would not have been recognized in the past but also has led courts to offer some at best surprising interpretations of existing law which, if followed in other contexts, would be of great concern to all Americans. Thus, in order to justify their denying the claims of lesbians, gays, bisexuals, and transgendered people, judges have sometimes been forced to offer extremely implausible accounts of the law that one suspects would never have been offered in any other context. Nonetheless, once these accounts have been offered as justifications, they acquire an air of acceptability and thus act to change the relevant jurisprudence. Unless corrected, these modifications will become part of the fabric of the law and will undermine the rights of all Americans.

While individuals have been seeking to marry their same-sex partners for decades, same-sex marriage did not seem likely to be recognized anywhere in the United States until 1993. That year, a plurality of the Hawaii Supreme Court held that statutes restricting marriage on the basis of sex triggered equal protection guarantees. The case was remanded so that a lower court could consider whether the state's implicated interests justified the state's reserving marriage for different-sex couples. By the time the Hawaii Supreme Court was ready to address the lower court's holding that the state had not been able to justify that exclusion, the Hawaii Constitution had been changed and the plurality and lower court holdings were made moot.

Once the Hawaii Constitution had been changed, the plurality decision no longer had the force of law, since it had been based on the former state constitution. The persuasiveness of the plurality's reasoning, however, was not at all undermined merely because the state constitution had been amended. The force of those arguments still has to be considered by all courts that want to deal with the issue fairly. Indeed, precisely because the state's claimed interests in reserving marriage for different-sex couples now requires examination and can no longer simply be taken for granted, it has become clear that the justifications offered are not nearly as plausible or coherent as had been assumed.

In *Baker v. State,* the Vermont Supreme Court held that the state constitution required that same-sex couples be afforded equal benefits and protections. That decision represents a milestone in the movement to secure equal rights for lesbians, gays, bisexuals, and transgendered people and will have great legal significance in the years to come. It, together with the *Baehr* plurality's reasoning, provides the basis upon which same-sex marriage bans can be challenged in other states and helps clarify why reserving marriage for different-sex couples involves an arbitrary distinction that violates state and federal constitutional guarantees. Nonetheless, the *Baker* court's federal equal protection analysis must be discussed and critically evaluated because it represents a departure from the established jurisprudence in this area, which, if followed, would seriously vitiate equal protection guarantees for all individuals.

Chapter 1 discusses the *Baker* equal protection analysis, which misrepresents the current doctrine and which cannot account for the decisions that the United States Supreme Court has reached in this area. The *Baker* court misunderstood the conditions under which courts should closely examine statutes to make sure that they meet constitutional requirements. Further, the court conflated discrimination against an individual with discrimination against a class and thus could not correctly apply the relevant test to determine whether Vermont's marital statute offended federal constitutional guarantees. Nonetheless, because the court held that the state constitution offered protections for same-sex couples, the Vermont legislature was required to do something to make sure that those guarantees were respected.

While the legislature could have amended the marriage statute to permit same-sex couples to marry, it decided instead to create a separate status for same-sex couples to afford them the equal benefits and protections guaranteed by the state constitution. An issue yet to be resolved is whether the creation of civil union status meets the state constitution's mandates. Chapter 2 discusses why civil unions, although more attractive for many same-sex couples than any status offered in any other state, nonetheless does not meet the state constitution's requirements. The solution offered by the Vermont Legislature has at least two distinct, fatal weaknesses. First, civil union couples and their children will likely receive less protection when traveling in other states than they would have received had the couple been allowed to marry. Thus, civil unions do not offer the same benefits and protections as marriages would. Second, the creation of a "separate and equal" status inevitably imposes a stigma, which the United States Supreme Court has already made clear is enough in some cases to violate federal constitutional guarantees.

In part because civil unions will likely not be treated like marriages in other states and in part because of the existence of the Federal Defense of Marriage Act and various state Defense of Marriage Acts, civil union members who travel with their children may not be afforded some of the protections that other couples take for granted. Chapter 3 discusses a particular issue that will be of vital concern to many such couples, namely, how to assure that the non-biological partner will be recognized as a legal parent of the child that both adults are raising. Although Vermont law affords the presumption of parenthood to a child born into a civil union just as it does for a child born into a marriage, that presumption will likely not be given weight in several states. Civil union members who plan on moving to or traveling through other states might consider making use of the second-parent adoption provision in Vermont law, notwithstanding the additional time and expense that would be involved in taking advantage of that provision. Second-parent adoptions are much more likely to be recognized in other states, at least in part, because a second-parent adoption can be granted even if the adults are not part of a legally recognized relationship and thus the parental rights acquired through such an adoption are not subject to the exception created by the Defense of Marriage Act.

That individuals would be forced to choose between traveling through their own country and keeping their parental rights secure is shocking in this day and age. A recent decision of the United States Supreme Court has reaffirmed that the right to travel through and move to other states is protected by the Federal Constitution and, further, that this right incorporates more than merely the right to physically enter or cross states in the Union. Chapter 4 discusses that decision and its implications for same-sex couples and their children, suggesting that the right to travel provides yet another basis upon which the unconstitutionality of the federal and state Defense of Marriage Acts can be established.

Hawaii was the first state where it was thought that same-sex marriages might actually be recognized. The 1998 referendum amending that state's constitution seems to have removed any realistic possibility that such marriages will be recognized in Hawaii any time soon. Yet, the referendum itself was constitutionally suspect, especially in light of its interpretation by the Hawaii Supreme Court in *Baehr v. Miike*. Chapter 5 discusses the retroactive effect given to the Hawaii constitutional amendment by the Hawaii Supreme Court and why that interpretation undermined the legitimacy of the amendment itself. The chapter also discusses some of the more welcome aspects of the *Miike* opinion and why ultimately these aspects of the opinion will have more lasting legal significance than the questionable finding of retroactive effect.

Same-sex marriage opponents sometimes point out that the law recognizes a distinction between toleration and endorsement and then suggest that the state should not legally recognize same-sex relationships because such relationships should not be endorsed but at most tolerated. Such an argument is unpersuasive because it wrongly assumes both that the state endorses all those marriages that it recognizes and that it is appropriate for the state to manifest a preference for some citizens over others. Chapter 6 discusses the toleration versus preference argument in light of how interracial marriages have been treated in various states over the past several decades and in light of Establishment Clause jurisprudence. Ironically, that jurisprudence supports the claim that the state should *not* endorse certain marriages over others and thus that the state should legally recognize same-sex relationships.

At least one reason that people object to the legal recognition of same-sex relationships is that religious sensibilities are thereby offended. Yet, it is a mistake to believe that all religions condemn same-sex unions; on the contrary, only some do. For the state to refuse to recognize same-sex marriages and, for example, only to permit "civil" unions because recognizing the former would be religiously offensive is, itself, a violation of the constitutional requirement of religious neutrality. Chapter 7 discusses that constitutional requirement and why the refusal to recognize same-sex relationships offends that constitutional guarantee.

In order for the state refusal to legally recognize same-sex relationships to pass constitutional muster, the understanding of past Supreme Court decisions must be radically reworked. Chapter 8 focuses on *Loving v. Virginia* and discusses some of the attempts by courts and commentators to recast the protections that have already been recognized by the Supreme Court in a way that would permit states to refuse to legally recognize same-sex relationships without offending the Constitution. A significant reworking of that jurisprudence is required, however, to reach that result. This chapter points out some of the undesirable implications that would have to be accepted were these analyses correct representations of the law.

It is not only equal protection jurisprudence that must be reworked if indeed the state refusal to recognize such relationships is to survive constitutional scrutiny. Chapter 9 discusses the substantial changes in the right to privacy that must be accepted if same-sex marriage bans are to pass muster and also discusses why the claimed parade of horribles that would result from such a recognition involves a misunderstanding of the relevant jurisprudence. Claims to the contrary notwithstanding, the right to marry a same-sex partner falls within most plausible understandings of the right to privacy rather than requires a significant extension of it.

The recognition of civil union status is a welcome development, which permits same-sex couples to enjoy benefits and protections that simply are not available anywhere else in the United States. Yet, that status nonetheless does not offer the benefits and protections that the recognition of same-sex marriage would and, further, is stigmatizing because it suggests that recognizing same-sex marriages would somehow sully the institution.

When the reasoning of the *Baker* court is understood, especially after the court's misunderstanding of federal constitutional protections has been corrected, that decision will provide a powerful basis upon which to challenge the refusal of other states to afford same-sex relationships legal recognition. When recent United States Supreme Court decisions are also taken into account, it will become even clearer why the various Defense of Marriage Acts are unconstitutional and why the Federal Constitution requires the recognition of such relationships. Any other holdings would significantly vitiate the force of existing constitutional guarantees.

Chapter One

Vermont's Creation of Civil Unions

Vermont made history when it passed the first civil union statute in the United States. That courageous decision may have important ramifications for other states, since it may provide the impetus for other state legislatures or courts to recognize similar or perhaps more robust protections for same-sex couples. As a separate matter, Vermont's having created this new status may force other states to decide under what conditions and in what respects civil unions will be recognized, for example, when Vermont couples travel through or move to other states.

An analysis of the civil union statute would be incomplete without a consideration of the context in which the legislature passed and the governor signed the bill creating this new status. In December of 1999, the Vermont Supreme Court issued *Baker v. State,* in which the court held that the Vermont Constitution required that same-sex couples have the opportunity to receive the kinds of benefits and protections that different-sex married couples can receive. While the *Baker* court declined to fashion a remedy and did not hold that the state constitution required the recognition of same-sex marriages, the court nonetheless made clear that the Vermont legislature's response had to take account of these state constitutional guarantees. After much debate, the Vermont legislature created a new status that accorded to same-sex couples the benefits but not the prestige of marriage.

STATE CONSTITUTIONAL GUARANTEES

The *Baker* decision illustrates various aspects of the constitutional system existing in the United States, for example, the relationship between federal and state constitutional guarantees, the conditions under which state supreme court decisions may be appealed to the United States Supreme Court, the effect that one state supreme court interpretation of its own constitution may have on other state supreme court interpretations of their respective constitutions, etcetera. It also illustrates how constitutional doctrine develops and, sometimes, why it will not be corrected even if it has been misunderstood and misapplied.

AN ILLUSTRATION OF THESE PRINCIPLES

There are at least two distinct reasons why it might be thought significant that the *Baker* decision was based on state rather than federal constitutional grounds. First, that decision was not reviewable by the United States Supreme Court because the decision was predicated upon a particular provision of the Vermont Constitution rather than of the United States Constitution. Second, precisely because the decision was based on a particular provision of the Vermont Constitution, the decision had no necessary implications for the interpretations that will be afforded by other state supreme courts when interpreting their own state constitutional provisions and thus, although controversial, the decision was much less controversial than it might otherwise have been.

Independent State Grounds

A state supreme court's interpretation of its own state's constitution will not be reviewed by the United States Supreme Court if that interpretation is not simply predicated on the interpretation of an analogous federal constitutional provision but instead is based on independent state constitutional grounds. Thus, if the state constitution is interpreted to offer protections that the Federal Constitution does not, the United States Supreme Court will not second-guess the state supreme court's interpretation of its own constitution. This qualification makes sense and reflects a policy of recognizing and deferring to the court that has specialized expertise in interpreting the constitutional provision that is determining the resolution of the matter at hand.

Suppose that a state supreme court were to hold that a law is unconstitutional on state constitutional grounds. Because the state supreme court, unlike the United States Supreme Court, is frequently put in the position of having to interpret the nuances of that very constitution, the state supreme court is considered the expert on the correct interpretation of that document. As a matter of institutional competence, it makes sense for the United States Supreme Court to defer to the state supreme court's interpretation of its own state constitution.

Suppose, however, that a state supreme court were to hold that the state constitutional provision at issue tracked an analogous federal constitutional provision; that is, the former provision offered no more and no less protection than did the latter either with respect to the kinds of cases that would trigger its protection or with respect to the degree of protection that would be afforded when the constitutional protections had been triggered. In that event, the presumption of the state supreme court's superior institutional competence would disappear. The state supreme court would be denying that any special understanding of state constitutional law would be necessary to offer the correct interpretation of the provision at issue, since that court basically would have admitted that the state constitutional provision was in lockstep with the federal one. Indeed, since the United States Supreme Court has specialized knowledge with respect to the proper interpretation of the federal provision with which the state provision was admitted to be in lockstep, the institutional competence theory rightly predicts that a decision by a state supreme court regarding a state constitutional provision that tracks a federal one would be reviewable by the United States Supreme Court. Basically, the United States Supreme Court may review a state supreme court decision if that decision were either (1) based on the United States Constitution rather than on the constitution of a particular state, or (2) based on a state constitutional provision that mirrors an analogous federal provision.

Two claims should not be conflated: (1) whether a particular state constitutional provision tracks an analogous federal constitutional provision, and (2) whether a provision of the United States Constitution requires, permits, or prohibits the particular practice that has been challenged. As a general matter, the United States Supreme Court will defer to the state supreme court with respect to (1), since specialized competence is required to decide whether a state constitutional decision tracks a federal one or, instead, offers special protections. However, the Court will not defer with respect to (2) when the state supreme court is interpreting the dictates of a *federal* provision, since the interpretation of the breadth and depth of the protections of the federal provision falls within the specialized expertise of the United State Supreme Court. Thus, if the state supreme court holds that the state constitutional provision tracks an analogous federal constitutional provision, the United States Supreme Court will not second-guess *that* decision, just as the Court would not have second-guessed a decision holding that the state constitutional provision did not track an analogous federal provision but instead offered greater protection. The United States Supreme Court may well second-guess an interpretation of the Federal Constitution that has been offered by a state court, however, and an interpretation of a state constitutional provision that has been admitted to track a federal one is in effect an interpretation of the Federal Constitution.

No Federal Guarantees Violated

While the United States Supreme Court will defer to the state supreme court on matters of state constitutional law, this deference does not entail that the state will be permitted to violate federal constitutional guarantees because of provisions in the state constitution. For example, suppose that a state constitution precludes interracial couples from marrying but that the Federal Constitution protects the right of individuals to marry someone of a different race. The United States Supreme Court would defer to the state supreme court with respect to whether or not the state constitution precluded interracial couples from marrying, but would not defer with respect to whether the Federal Constitution permitted states to enforce such a prohibition. Deference with respect to the former, but not the latter, would permit the institutional competence of the different courts to be respected. The United States Supreme Court would not disagree with the state supreme court about the proper interpretation of that state constitution. Rather, the Court would grant that this was the proper interpretation of the provision but would explain that the United States Constitution precluded enforcement of the provision so construed. Of course, if the United States Constitution did not bar such marital limitations, the state constitutional provision would have to be enforced until it had been amended or repealed.

Misinterpretations of Federal Law

Suppose that a state supreme court holds that a particular statute violates state constitutional guarantees but, in addition, incorrectly suggests that the statute does not violate federal guarantees. The United States Supreme Court would not hear such a case, notwithstanding the potential damage to the understanding of federal law that might take place. The particular individuals who challenged the law would have suffered no harm if their claim had been upheld on state rather than federal grounds, since their rights would in fact have been vindicated. Because it would be irrelevant *for these claimants* whether the federal constitutional provision in addition to the state constitutional provision protected the activity in question, the United States Supreme Court would wait for another occasion to review whether the Federal Constitution was violated by the law at issue.

THE LIMITED APPLICABILITY OF STATE CONSTITUTIONS

When a state supreme court issues an opinion which relies on an interpretation of a particular provision of that state's constitution, the court is not issuing an opinion about the protections that other state constitutions offer. Indeed, just as a theory of institutional competence would preclude the United States Supreme Court from offering a definitive interpretation of a state constitutional provision, that same theory precludes one state supreme court from issuing an opinion about another state's constitution which would be binding on that latter state. Each state supreme court will be the final arbiter of what its own state constitution means.

There are at least two distinct reasons why a state supreme court's interpretation of its own constitution would not bind other state supreme courts when interpreting their own constitutions. First, the provision of the former constitution may contain language that differs from the language contained in the latter constitution. An interpretation of one state constitutional provision would, of course, have no necessary implications for the interpretation of a provision in a different state constitution that did not incorporate that same language.

Suppose, however, that a provision in the constitution of State A and a provision in the constitution of State B are worded identically. Still, that would not mean that they would have to be interpreted in the same way. The conditions under which these provisions were adopted in the respective states might have differed and, further, the ways that the provisions had been interpreted by the respective state supreme courts over time might have differed as well. Thus, two identically worded provisions in different state constitutions might be interpreted differently by the respective state supreme courts, and one provision but not the other might be interpreted to offer protection in a particular set of circumstances.

When examining the *Baker* decision, the above discussion will be important to keep in mind. The *Baker* decision was based on independent state constitutional grounds, so (1) it has no necessary implications for other states, and (2) its analysis of both the federal and the state constitutional provisions implicated by Vermont's marriage law was not subject to review by the United States Supreme Court.

A LITTLE BACKGROUND ON *BAKER*

In 1997, three couples filed a lawsuit against the state of Vermont after having been denied marriage licenses by their respective town clerks. They lost at the trial level and appealed to the Vermont Supreme Court. The Vermont Supreme Court reversed the lower court but suspended its own judgment to give the legislature an opportunity to enact legislation that would meet the state constitution's requirements.

The *Baker* court distinguished between the rights and benefits of marriage and the ability to marry per se, holding that the Vermont Constitution required that same-sex couples be afforded the opportunity to receive the former. The *Baker* court did not address whether a separate system that accorded all of these benefits and protections might nonetheless be unconstitutional, for example, because of the stigma thereby imposed, deferring that issue for another day.

In *Baker,* the court held that the state is required by the Vermont Constitution to extend to same-sex couples the common benefits, protections, and security of the law. That might have been accomplished in a few ways. For example, the Vermont legislature might simply have amended the marriage statute to permit same-sex couples to marry or, instead, might have created a parallel system for same-sex partners that would afford the benefits but not the status of marriage. The Vermont legislature chose to do the latter, permitting same-sex couples who celebrated civil unions to "have all the same benefits, protections, and responsibilities under law, whether they derive from statute, administrative, or court rule, policy, common law, or any other source of civil law, as are granted to spouses in a marriage."[1]

The *Baker* court's decision was based on the Vermont Constitution's Common Benefits Clause. The court noted that although that clause was the counterpart of the Equal Protection Clause of the Fourteenth Amendment to the Federal Constitution, the former differed markedly from the latter in its origin, language, purpose, and development. The court concluded that the failure to offer the benefits and protections of marriage to same-sex couples violated the Common Benefits Clause of the Vermont Constitution but suggested that such a failure did not offend federal equal protection guarantees.

THE COMMON BENEFITS CLAUSE OF THE VERMONT CONSTITUTION

The Common Benefits Clause states that "government is, or ought to be, instituted for the common benefit, protection, and security of the people, nation, or community, and not for the particular emolument or advantage of any single person, family, or set of persons, who are a part only of that community. . . ."[2] The assumptions underlying the clause are that all Vermonters should be afforded all the benefits and protections bestowed by government and that the Common Benefits Clause requires "the elimination of artificial governmental preferments and advantages."[3] The court made clear that because the Common Benefits Clause is the primary safeguard of all Vermonters' rights and liberties and the Federal Equal Protection Clause merely supplements that safeguard, the Common Benefits Clause could require that lesbian, gay, and bisexual Vermonters be extended the benefits at issue even if federal equal protection guarantees did not.

The Vermont court was not suggesting that the Common Benefits Clause required that all Vermonters be offered the same benefits and protections if there were relevant factors that made the individuals dissimilar in a constitutionally significant way. The court recognized that its duty was to "ultimately ascertain whether the omission of a part of the community from the benefit, protection and security of the challenged law bears a reasonable and just relation to the governmental purpose."[4] If the exclusion were sufficiently closely related to the government's asserted end, then the exclusion would be upheld. If the exclusion undermined rather than supported the articulated purpose, however, then the statute and the articulated goal would not be sufficiently closely related, and the statute would not pass state constitutional muster.

An important state purpose in licensing civil marriages is to legitimize children and provide for their security. Yet, the statute reserving marriage for different-sex couples would expose the children of same-sex couples to the very risks that the marriage laws are designed to help children avoid. The court suggested that the statute could not pass constitutional muster because it was not rationally related to the legitimate goal (protecting children) articulated by the state. None of the other reasons offered by the state were thought any more persuasive.

"RATIONAL BASIS WITH BITE" SCRUTINY

The test to determine whether the guarantees of the Common Benefits Clause have been violated is deferential with respect to the government's choice of ends but is more exacting with respect to whether the means chosen bears a just and reasonable relation to the governmental objective. This test, the *Baker* court explained, is to be contrasted with the federal rational basis test under which nearly all economic and commercial legislation will be upheld if rationally related to a conceivable, legitimate governmental interest. The *Baker* court cited the United States Supreme Court decision of *City of Cleburne v. Cleburne Living Center, Inc.* as support for its claim that the federal rational basis test is extremely deferential, notwithstanding that the *Cleburne* Court had struck down a zoning ordinance excluding homes for the mentally handicapped on rational basis grounds.

The *Cleburne* decision merits closer examination, since zoning ordinances involve commercial legislation. If such legislation will be upheld when rationally related to any conceivable, legitimate governmental purpose and if there were legitimate governmental purposes that might have been served by the Cleburne zoning ordinance, then one would have expected that the ordinance would have been upheld. Nonetheless, the Court struck it down, even though the reasons offered normally would have sufficed under deferential rational basis review.

A more credible explanation of the *Cleburne* Court's analysis is that the kind of scrutiny actually used was a less deferential rational basis test. Had the *Baker* court employed the rational basis test that the *Cleburne* Court seemed in fact to have employed, the court would have struck down the Vermont marital statute as a violation of both state and federal constitutional guarantees.

Some commentators have suggested that the Court's rational basis test itself involves two tiers. Under the more forgiving rational basis test, the Court is extremely deferential and will uphold legislation that is rationally related to almost any legitimate government purpose. Under the less forgiving rational basis standard, however, the Court will more closely examine the statute at issue to ensure that it bears a reasonable relation to the asserted state goals. Employing this closer scrutiny, the Court struck down the zoning ordinance at issue in *Cleburne* and also the state constitutional amendment at issue in *Romer v. Evans*. That same less forgiving scrutiny would have exposed the fatal flaws of a statute reserving marriage for different-sex couples.

In both *Cleburne* and *Romer*, the Court did not object to the legitimacy of the states' asserted goals, but to the means chosen to effectuate those goals. By the same token, the *Baker* court accepted that the state's goals were legitimate but rejected the means chosen to effectuate those goals. For example, the *Baker* court found that the state has a legitimate interest in promoting a permanent commitment between couples for the sake of their children but rejected that the state's chosen means (making it much more difficult for same-sex couples to make such a commitment) was a reasonable way to promote that goal. Thus, the kind of scrutiny employed by the *Baker* court bore a strong resemblance to the kind of scrutiny that the Court had employed in both *Cleburne* and *Romer*, protestations to the contrary notwithstanding.

THE IMPLICATIONS FOR OTHER STATES

In *Baker*, the court suggested that Vermont's same-sex marriage ban implicated state but not federal constitutional protections. Because the state constitutional protections are allegedly more stringent than the analogous federal protections, the basis for the *Baker* decision might seem not to have much import for other states' laws unless, for example, those states have something comparable to the Common Benefits Clause in their own state constitutions.[5]

Yet, the *Baker* court's analysis of the *federal* equal protection guarantees might have important implications when other courts are interpreting federal (or perhaps their own state) constitutional guarantees. Consider a court in a sister state seeking guidance about how to apply the federal rational basis test in a particular case. A court consulting the *Baker* opinion might well be misled into believing that the rational basis test must always be applied in an extremely deferential manner.

The *Baker* opinion might cause additional misunderstandings of equal protection jurisprudence concerning when equal protection guarantees are triggered in cases involving race- or sex-based classifications. Further, because the *Baker* decision was based on independent state constitutional grounds, it was not reviewable in federal court, and so its incorrect analysis of federal protections could not be corrected. Other courts might view the *Baker* analysis of federal law as persuasive unless they can be shown why it involved a misrepresentation of that law. Thus, to clarify both why other courts would be mistaken to employ the Vermont court's federal equal protection analysis and why the correct analysis has national implications for laws banning same-sex marriages, the *Baker* court's analysis is critically examined below.

SEX-BASED CLASSIFICATIONS

The *Baker* court recognized that statutes reserving marriage for different-sex couples facially classify on the basis of sex. However, because males were not permitted to do something that females were prohibited from doing and females were not permitted to do something that males were prohibited from doing, the court suggested that equal protection scrutiny was not even *triggered* by the statute. Were this analysis in fact correct, both the purpose and the usefulness of equal protection scrutiny would be strongly undermined.

The *Baker* court's analysis was flawed because it was predicated upon a misunderstanding of what triggers heightened scrutiny. Ultimately, the United States Supreme Court will have to decide whether same-sex marriage bans implicate the equal protection guarantees imposed when sex-based classifications are at issue. As the *Baker* opinion illustrates, however, that Supreme Court decision will have important implications for equal protection jurisprudence generally, because the Court will have to make clearer both what triggers heightened scrutiny and, possibly, what counts as an exceedingly persuasive justification.

To understand what is at issue, it will be helpful to compare the analyses offered by the supreme courts of Hawaii and Vermont of their respective same-sex marriage prohibitions. Both states recognized that such bans employ a sex-based classification, although only the Hawaii court recognized that constitutional guarantees against sex-discrimination were thereby implicated.

A COMPARISON OF THE HAWAII AND VERMONT OPINIONS

In *Baehr v. Lewin,* a plurality of the Hawaii Supreme Court held that Hawaii's same-sex marriage ban implicated equal protection guarantees because the statute regulated access to marriage on the basis of sex. Because the statute involved a sex-based classification, the statute had to be examined with strict scrutiny (because of state constitutional guarantees). The case was remanded to give the state an opportunity to establish that the statute was narrowly tailored to promote compelling state interests. On remand, a Hawaii circuit court found that the state had not met its burden, although that decision was stayed pending state supreme court review. Before the state supreme court had completed review of that decision, the Hawaii electorate modified the state constitution to permit the legislature to reserve marriage for different-sex couples.

The plurality decision in *Baehr v. Lewin* discussed two different issues: (1) whether the state's marriage statute employed a sex-based classification, and (2) if so, whether strict rather than heightened scrutiny should be employed to determine whether the classification at issue was constitutionally offensive. The court accepted that a sex-based classification was at issue, since a man could marry a woman but not a man, and a woman could marry a man but not a woman.[6] That such a classification required examination with strict rather than heightened scrutiny required more explanation. The court spent several pages in the opinion explaining why the Hawaii Constitution included more robust protections against sex discrimination than did the Federal Constitution.[7]

STRICT VERSUS HEIGHTENED SCRUTINY

A statute will be found constitutional when examined with strict scrutiny only if the statute is narrowly tailored to promote a compelling state interest. In contrast, a statute examined with mere heightened scrutiny will be upheld if the statute is substantially related to an important state interest. Thus, the fact that sex is a suspect classification according to the Hawaii Constitution is not insignificant, since a statute might survive heightened but not strict scrutiny.

Nonetheless, statutes examined with "mere" heightened scrutiny are often struck down. As the Supreme Court made clear in *United States v. Virginia*, a statute employing a sex-based classification requires an exceedingly persuasive justification. Indeed, recent amendment to the Hawaii Constitution notwithstanding, the current Hawaii marriage statute is constitutionally vulnerable on federal grounds. As a sex-based classification, it should be examined with heightened scrutiny. Establishing that such a statute is substantially related to an important state interest will be no easy task, as the *Baker* decision illustrates.

The important point to understand here is the feature of the Hawaii Constitution that makes it unusual. The *Baehr* plurality did not suggest that the Hawaii Constitution included a broader category of sex-based classifications that would trigger closer scrutiny, that is, suggest that certain sex-based classifications would receive close scrutiny because of state but not federal guarantees. On the contrary, the *Baehr* plurality suggested that the Hawaii Constitution was similar to the Federal Constitution in that both would subject all sex-based classifications to close scrutiny. The real question for the court was just how close that scrutiny should be. Thus, while the *Baehr* plurality admitted that the equal protection clauses of the United States and Hawaii Constitutions are not identical, the plurality made clear that the differences between them were whether discrimination on the basis of sex was expressly or merely impliedly prohibited and whether such classifications should be examined with strict rather than heightened scrutiny. There was no suggestion in *Baehr* that a particular classification might be viewed as sex-based under the Hawaii but not the Federal Constitution.

The *Baehr* plurality pointed out that the plain language of the relevant statute restricts marriage to one man and one woman. The *Baker* court reached a similar conclusion, noting that the marriage statute expressly applied to different-sex couples and suggesting that the statute excluded anyone who wished to marry a same-sex partner. Thus, these two courts did not disagree about whether a statute reserving marriage for different-sex couples classifies on the basis of sex; rather, they disagreed about whether the statute's use of a sex-based classification was enough to trigger (at least) heightened scrutiny. Indeed, the *Baker* court cited *Baehr* for the proposition that the marriage statute involved a sex-based classification, but nonetheless refused to impose heightened scrutiny when examining that classification.

FACIAL NEUTRALITY

The *Baker* court rejected that equal protection guarantees were implicated by the sex-based classification in the statute because the court believed that law was "facially neutral." After all, the statute prohibited both men and women from marrying a person of the same sex and thus, allegedly, did not discriminate on its face. Because of this alleged facial neutrality, the court suggested that the statute did not even *trigger* heightened scrutiny and, at least as far as the Federal Constitution was concerned, only had to be subjected to the very deferential rational basis test.

The *Baker* court's analysis was predicated upon a particular interpretation of *Loving v. Virginia*, the case in which the United States Supreme Court struck down Virginia's statute barring interracial marriage. Yet, the *Baker* interpretation is a plausible account neither of the opinion itself nor of the relevant jurisprudence. The *Baker* court had misunderstood what constitutes "facial neutrality" within the context of equal protection jurisprudence and thus offered an overly narrow reading of the conditions under which closer scrutiny will be triggered.

There are two different senses in which a statute might be thought facially neutral with respect to a particular classification: (1) the statute does not even employ the classification at issue, so it is neutral in its wording (neutral$_w$), or (2) the statute employs the classification but does not treat the classes resulting from that classification unequally, so it is neutral in effect (neutral$_e$). Consider the statute at issue in *Loving*, which precluded blacks from marrying whites and whites from marrying blacks. The statute appeared neutral$_e$ in that it seemed to impose the same burdens on blacks and whites, but not neutral$_w$, since it explicitly relied on a racial classification. The question at hand was whether strict scrutiny was triggered by a statute that classified on the basis of race but seemed not to treat the races unequally, that is, whether a statute that was neutral$_e$ but not neutral$_w$ triggered close scrutiny.

The *Loving* Court answered that question in the affirmative. The Court rejected Virginia's claim that the appropriate standard was whether the state had a rational basis upon which to treat interracial marriages differently from other marriages, instead pointing out that "the fact of equal application does not immunize the statute from the very heavy burden of justification which the Fourteenth Amendment has traditionally required of state statutes drawn according to race."[8] Thus, the *Loving* Court rejected the idea that apparent facial neutrality with respect to the imposition of burdens or the according of benefits would require that the Court not employ close scrutiny but, instead, the deferential rational basis test.

Loving has important implications for the appropriate analysis in *Baker*. Just as the statute at issue in *Loving* had to be closely examined even though it allegedly prohibited members of all of the races from marrying persons outside of their race, the statute at issue in *Baker* should have been closely examined even though it prevented all persons from marrying someone of their own sex. The *Baker* court understood that its own analysis might seem undermined by *Loving*, but distinguished the latter decision by claiming that the *Loving* Court had had little difficulty in discerning that the purpose behind the Virginia statute was to maintain the pernicious doctrine of white supremacy.

It is important to establish the respects in which the *Baker* analysis of *Loving* was correct and the respects in which it was not. The *Baker* court was correct that the *Loving* Court struck down the Virginia antimiscegenation statute because it was "designed to maintain White Supremacy."[9] The *Loving* Court had noted that the Virginia statute had targeted interracial marriages involving whites and that "Negroes, Orientals, and any other racial class may inter-marry without statutory interference."[10] Thus, the races were not being treated equally, and the statute was not neutral$_e$.

Nonetheless, various implicated issues should not be conflated. A *sufficient* ground for striking down the Virginia statute was that it was designed to promote white supremacy. However, that hardly establishes that a finding of invidious purpose was *necessary* for striking down that statute. Thus, the *Loving* Court did not hold that statutes that classify on the basis of race are unconstitutional *only* if they attempt to promote white supremacist views or, for that matter, supremacist views about any particular race. Instead, the Court suggested that a race-based statute designed to promote white supremacy was unconstitutional, but also suggested that race-based statutes might be struck down even if there were no hint of a supremacist purpose.

The *Loving* Court noted that it was obvious that the Virginia interracial ban rested solely on a race-based distinction, that is, that the statutes *facially* classified on the basis of race and thus were not neutral$_w$. A separate question was whether that facial discrimination itself was invidious, and the Court answered that question in the affirmative. The Court had two distinct questions before it that had to be addressed: (1) Did Virginia's marriage statutes facially discriminate on the basis of race? and (2) Was that facial discrimination constitutionally permissible?

When a statute is described as facially discriminatory, the speaker might be suggesting that a statute on its face classifies or the speaker might instead be suggesting that the statute on its face invidiously classifies. The term "discriminatory" can, but need not, suggest that an impermissible classification has been effected. When determining whether the Virginia statute was discriminatory on its face, the *Loving* Court sought to determine whether the statute *classified* on the basis of race, not whether the statute invidiously classified or even whether the statute affected the races differently. Indeed, the *Loving* Court explicitly stated that the fact of equal application did not prevent the Court from closely scrutinizing the statute at issue, thereby making quite clear that unequal application was not the touchstone for close scrutiny.

As the *Baker* court pointed out, statutes that are not facially discriminatory may nonetheless offend constitutional guarantees. Nonetheless, it is by no means easy to establish the constitutional invalidity of such statutes, since substantial hurdles must be overcome to establish the unconstitutionality of a facially neutral statute.

In *Personnel Administrator of Massachusetts v. Feeney*, the United States Supreme Court rejected a sex-discrimination challenge to a Massachusetts veterans' preference law. In explaining its holding, the Court pointed out that "even if a neutral law has a disproportionately adverse effect upon a racial minority, it is unconstitutional under the Equal Protection Clause only if that impact can be traced to a discriminatory purpose."[11]

The *Baker* court interpreted *Feeney* to say that the "test to evaluate whether a facially gender-neutral statute discriminates on the basis of sex is whether the law 'can be traced to a discriminatory purpose.'"[12] Yet, the *Baker* court seemed not to understand when the *Feeney* test is to be applied, since the discriminatory purpose test is employed *only* where (1) the statute on its fact is gender-neutral, and (2) the law has disproportionate adverse effects. This means that if the *Feeney* approach were to be applied when examining a neutral law that treated the races equally, it would not matter that the purpose was discriminatory; the statute would not offend equal protection guarantees.

Suppose that the *Loving* Court had adopted the *Baker* approach with respect both to what constitutes race-neutrality and to when statutes with a discriminatory purpose would be struck down. The Court would then have said that anti-miscegenation statutes that are "facially neutral" (i.e., according to the *Baker* court, "treat the races equally") are unconstitutional only if they are adopted to promote white supremacy. However, the Court would have said, such statutes pass constitutional muster if they are not designed to promote white supremacy but instead have the even-handed purpose of preserving the integrity of all of the races. Yet, the *Loving* Court explicitly found that racial classifications in marriage statutes violate constitutional guarantees, even assuming "the fact of equal application"[13] and "even assuming an even-handed state purpose to protect the 'integrity' of all races,"[14] and thus the *Baker* court was mistaken in believing that its decision was in accord with the lessons of *Loving*.

The *Baker* court's analysis flies in the face of the established jurisprudence when suggesting that express racial classifications do not trigger strict scrutiny as long as the races are being treated equally. In *Shaw v. Reno*, in which the Court examined North Carolina's reapportionment plan creating a second, majority-black district, the Court explicitly rejected the kind of analysis offered in *Baker*. The *Shaw* Court made clear that "racial classifications receive close scrutiny even when they may be said to burden or benefit the races equally."[15] Thus, the *Baker* claim that a facially discriminatory statute should not receive close scrutiny if it treats the different classes equally is a misreading of equal protection jurisprudence.

It was precisely because the *Loving* Court held that equal application did not preclude the imposition of close scrutiny that the Court was able to uncover the invidious discrimination contained in the statutes. Had the "fact" of equal application required deferential review, the statutes at issue in *Loving* would have been upheld.

There is yet another reason that the *Baker* court's reliance on *Feeney* was misplaced: the court misunderstood why the statute at issue in that case was gender-neutral. The *Baker* court failed to notice that, unlike the Vermont statutory scheme making marriage a union between a man and a woman, the statute at issue in *Feeney* did not facially discriminate on the basis of sex and instead used the term "veteran." The *Feeney* Court found that the statute under examination was neutral because (1) the definition of "veterans" in the statute had always been gender-neutral, (2) Massachusetts had consistently defined veteran status in a way that has been inclusive of women who have served in the military, and (3) the statute as applied did not preclude all women from receiving the relevant benefit.

Certainly, the *Feeney* Court recognized that the class benefited by the statute was overwhelmingly male. However, the Court pointed out that disproportionate impact is not dispositive, since a *neutral* law having a disproportionate impact violates equal protection guarantees only if a discriminatory purpose can be established.

In *Feeney*, the Court determined that the statute at issue was facially neutral because its wording did not classify on the basis of sex (it was neutral$_w$), although the statute was not neutral$_e$, since it clearly had a disproportionate adverse impact on females. In contrast, the statute at issue in *Baker* was thought to be neutral$_e$, but clearly was not neutral$_w$.

The *Feeney* Court explained that when a statute that is facially neutral with respect to gender is challenged, a twofold inquiry should be made. The first question is whether the statutory classification is indeed neutral, that is, whether the classification is overtly or covertly based on gender. If that question is answered in the negative, then the Court examines whether the neutral statute has nonetheless been motivated by invidious discrimination. However, the statute at issue in *Baker* did not meet the first prong of *Feeney*. Because the statute used the terms "man" and "woman," it was not gender-neutral. An examination of the second prong would not be necessary, and *Feeney* suggests that heightened scrutiny would be triggered because of the failure to meet the first prong of the test.

The *Baker* court's analysis of the equal protection claim was reminiscent of the analysis that courts had used in the past when upholding interracial marriage bans. For example, in *Green v. State*, the Supreme Court of Alabama considered the state's anti-miscegenation law and pointed out, "What the law declares to be a punishable offense, is, marriage between a white person and a negro. And it no more tolerates it in one of the parties than the other—in a white person than in a negro or mulatto; and each of them is punishable for the offense prohibited, in precisely the same manner and to the same extent."[16] The court concluded that there was no equal protection violation because the races were being treated equally.

By the same token, in *Ex parte Kinney*, the court suggested that Virginia's law banning interracial marriage did not treat the races unequally. The court explained that there is no "discrimination against either race in a provision of law forbidding any white or colored person from marrying another of the opposite color of skin. If it forbids a colored person from marrying a white, it equally forbids a white person from marrying a colored. . . . [T]he law is a prohibition put upon both races alike and equally."[17]

The kind of analysis offered in *Kinney* was accepted by the United States Supreme Court in *Pace v. Alabama*. In *Pace*, the Court examined the constitutionality of a statute that punished interracial fornication and adultery more severely than intra-racial fornication and adultery. When upholding the statute, the Court pointed out that the "punishment of each offending person, whether white or black, is the same,"[18] suggesting that the races were not being treated unequally. Yet, according to the *Baker* court, if there is equal treatment of the races, then the statute is race-neutral. Further, since *Feeney* suggests that race-neutral statutes are unconstitutional *only* if (1) they have a disparate impact, *and* (2) that impact can be traced to a discriminatory purpose, the *Baker* analysis would suggest that *Pace* should still be good law, because the statute at issue was not shown to have had a disparate impact. Yet, in *McLaughlin v. Florida*, in which the Court struck down a Florida statute punishing interracial fornication and adultery more severely than intra-racial fornication and adultery, the United States Supreme Court made clear that "*Pace* represents a limited view of the Equal Protection Clause which has not withstood analysis in the subsequent decisions of this Court."[19] Indeed, such a "narrow view of the Equal Protection Clause" has been "swept away"[20] by the subsequent jurisprudence.

In *McLaughlin*, the Court struck down Florida's statute because the law "treat[ed] the interracial *couple* made up of a white person and a Negro differently than it . . . [did] any other couple."[21] This differential treatment violated the Constitution, notwithstanding that the Court accepted the state's contention that each member of the interracial couple was being treated the same. Just as the statute at issue in *McLaughlin* treated the interracial couple differently than it treated other couples, regardless of whether it treated the races differently, the statute at issue in *Baker* treats same-sex couples differently than it treats other couples, regardless of whether it treats the sexes differently.

ON DIFFERENTIAL TREATMENT OF INDIVIDUALS AND CLASSES OF INDIVIDUALS

One potentially confusing aspect of equal protection analysis is that the criterion for differential treatment is open to misinterpretation. Consider a statute mandating that all public schools in a state be single-sex institutions. Girls would not be allowed to attend schools that boys attended, and vice versa. Such a statute might not be thought to be treating the sexes differently (bracketing for a moment a comparison of the schools' facilities), although it is clear that but for a particular child's sex he or she would be attending a different school. This example suggests that it is important to establish whether the focus for the relevant analysis is on the class or on the individual, since differential treatment might be established if the focus is on the individual even if it could not be established when focusing on the class.

The *Baker* court explained the relevant test to determine whether close scrutiny was triggered in cases involving sex-based classifications but then misapplied it, because the court failed to differentiate between discriminating against classes and discriminating against individuals. The court suggested that "to trigger equal protection analysis at all . . . a defendant must show that he was treated differently as a member of one class from treatment of members of another class similarly situated."[22] Yet, insofar as that is the relevant test, the plaintiffs should not have had much difficulty in meeting their burden. A woman who wished to marry another woman would show that she was treated differently as a member of one class (females) from treatment of members of another class (males) similarly situated (since both she and the postulated male competitor would have wished to marry the same individual). When Justice Johnson in her concurring and dissenting opinion in *Baker* offered the example of two doctors (one male and one female) who each wished to marry a particular X-ray technician,[23] she was pointing out a way in which the standard for triggering equal protection analysis had been met.

When attempting to determine whether heightened scrutiny had been triggered, the *Baker* court offered its own example, pointing out that both men and women were denied the right to marry someone of the same sex and thus neither was being treated unequally. Yet, the court's example focuses on whether the class as a whole had been disadvantaged rather than on whether a member of one class has been disadvantaged.

In *Orr v. Orr*, the United States Supreme Court examined whether Alabama's statute providing spousal support for females but not for males was unconstitutional. The Court noted that there was no question but that Mr. Orr bore a burden he would not have borne were he a woman, thus focusing on how the *individual* was affected. The point here is not that there would have been a different result in *Orr* had the effects on the class rather than on the individual been examined (since the classes were being treated differently as well), but merely that the focus was on whether the individual was being treated differently because of his sex. By the same token, when the Court examined whether the refusal of the Mississippi University for Women School of Nursing to allow men to take courses for credit violated constitutional guarantees, the Court noted that were Hogan a woman, he would not have been forced to choose between foregoing credit and having to drive a considerable distance to get credit for nursing courses. Again, the focus was on the individual. Further, as Justice Scalia has pointed out, *Mississippi University for Women v. Hogan* would presumably have been decided the same way even had Mississippi created an all-male nursing school in a different part of the state.[24] Thus, there would have been a constitutional violation even if the sexes had been treated equally (in that women would have been barred from attending the all-male nursing school and men would have been barred from attending the all-female nursing school), because individuals would have been denied an opportunity on the basis of sex.

Had the *Baker* court's focus on the class rather than on the individual been used in *McLaughlin,* the case presumably would have been decided differently. The *McLaughlin* Court recognized that "all whites and Negroes who engage in the forbidden conduct (non-marital intercourse) are covered by the section and each member of the interracial couple is subject to the same penalty."[25] According to the *Baker* analysis, the statute would not be treating the different races unequally and therefore equal protection guarantees would not even be *triggered*. Further, because there was no suggestion in *McLaughlin* that the statute was designed to promote white supremacy, it would have been much more difficult to establish an invidious purpose and, indeed, the *McLaughlin* Court did not impugn the state's purposes. Thus, according to its own analysis, the *Baker* court would have to have upheld the statute at issue in *McLaughlin*.

The same mistaken analysis and result might have been offered in the context of gender discrimination had the *Baker* court been forced to decide *United States v. Virginia*. At issue in that case was whether the refusal of Virginia Military Institute (VMI) to admit women violated the Equal Protection Clause of the Fourteenth Amendment.

Virginia had proposed that it would maintain its male-only admissions policy at VMI and would create a parallel program for women that would be located at Mary Baldwin College. Thus, it might be argued that while women were being kept out of the VMI program, men were being kept out of the Virginia Women's Institute for Leadership (VWIL). Because each was precluded from entering the other program, the *Baker* court would presumably have held that equal protection analysis was not even triggered. Yet, the Supreme Court's focus was not on whether the classes were being treated differently, but on the particular women who had the will and capacity to attend VMI and on the loss of VMI's unique training and opportunities that these women would have suffered had VMI's exclusion of women not been struck down. Had the VMI program been examined with deferential review, it would have been upheld.

The *Baker* court would presumably have said that the policy at issue in *Virginia* treated the sexes equally and thus was gender-neutral. While the court might have agreed that women were not receiving the same benefits that men were, that fact would not have been dispositive. As the *Feeney* Court explained, even if a gender-neutral statute has a disproportionate, adverse effect upon one sex, that statute violates equal protection guarantees only if motivated by a discriminatory purpose. Thus, according to the *Baker* court's analysis, VMI's exclusionary policy would be struck down only if it could be established, for example, that VMI had adopted or maintained its admissions policy for some misogynistic reason. Mere disparate effects would not have sufficed. However, Virginia's impermissible purposes were not established at trial; rather, at most, the state's asserted legitimate purposes were undercut as unpersuasive. Again, the *Baker* analysis would have yielded a result contrary to what the Supreme Court has in fact already decided.

The *Virginia* Court did not have to address whether the state's purposes were impermissible because the statute involved an explicit sex-based classification. "Classifications by gender must serve important governmental objectives and must be substantially related to achievement of those objectives."[26] That requirement is not waived merely because the state's impermissible purposes cannot be established. While the Supreme Court has made clear that the heightened review standard used to examine sex-based classifications will not always result in that classification being struck down, the state will have to do more when seeking to justify such a statute than merely show that its purposes were not invidious.

The Supreme Court has explained that it will closely examine statutes containing sex-based classifications because of the inherent risk that they contain to reinforce stereotypical notions about women and their abilities. If the state can achieve its legitimate purposes just as effectively without employing a sex-based classification, the Court will strike down the statute. This strong preference for statutes that do not employ sex-based classification is not limited to those statutes with impermissible purposes or even to those statutes that treat the sexes unequally. A statute that treats the sexes equally may nonetheless carry with it the baggage of sexual stereotypes and thus must also be examined closely to make sure that the same ends cannot be achieved with a gender-neutral statute.

CONCLUSION

The *Baker* court held that the Vermont Constitution requires the state to afford same-sex couples the opportunity to receive the kinds of benefits and protections that married couples have. The opinion was courageous and should be applauded. It pointed out why and how a variety of the state's arguments in favor of the state's same-sex marriage ban were specious; thus, the opinion may be of invaluable persuasive power when other courts examine the constitutionality of their own marital statutes.

Nonetheless, the *Baker* opinion inaccurately reflects certain aspects of equal protection jurisprudence; for example, the opinion suggests that close scrutiny will not be triggered unless a race- or sex-based statute allocates benefits or burdens unequally. The *Baker* court committed at least two errors in its equal protection analysis: (1) it offered an analysis of when close scrutiny is triggered that cannot account for the Court's jurisprudence with respect to either race- or sex-based classifications, and (2) it misapplied its own test when wrongly concluding that marriage statutes classifying on the basis of sex do not implicate equal protection guarantees. Had the court not made these errors, it would have indicated even more clearly why same-sex marriage bans as a general matter are constitutionally vulnerable.

Currently, all of the marriage laws in the United States classify on the basis of sex. Further, with respect to the application of any of these statutes, most defendants could easily show that they had been treated differently than they would have been treated had they been of the other sex. For example, a woman, Doreen, could show that had she been a man she would not have been prevented from marrying her life partner, Pamela.

When a statute explicitly classifies on the basis of race or sex, courts must closely examine the statute to make sure that it neither causes members of particular classes to be treated unfairly nor promotes outdated stereotypes regarding individuals' abilities. Were the Supreme Court to have held that it would only closely examine those statutes explicitly employing those classifications that in addition clearly involved unequal treatment, the Court would have undermined the whole purpose of close scrutiny, namely, uncovering non-obviously invidious discrimination. A number of foundational cases would have been decided differently if the *Baker* court's analysis of equal protection were correct. The Court would then not have considered the statutes at issue closely enough to uncover their invidious purposes or effects. Thus, the *Baker* court's analysis must be corrected both because of its implications for same-sex marriage in particular and for equal protection jurisprudence more generally.

To determine whether a statute discriminates on the basis of sex, the court should examine whether the person adversely affected would have been treated differently but for her sex. A separate question not focused upon here is whether same-sex marriage bans would survive heightened scrutiny, although there is reason to doubt that they would. In *Baker*, "the State made every conceivable argument in support of the marriage laws, including what it perceived to be its best arguments,"[27] and those arguments nonetheless failed to satisfy the rational-basis test as articulated under the Common Benefits Clause. If the state's best arguments could not meet even second-order rational basis scrutiny, then it should be clear that any higher form of scrutiny would also uncover the flaws of such arguments and the impermissible bases of such a statute.

The current statute entitles same-sex couples in civil unions to all of the benefits that different-sex married couples receive from the state. The Vermont Supreme Court may still have to decide whether the state's "separate but equal" status for same-sex couples nonetheless offends constitutional guarantees, perhaps because these civil unions would not be as likely to be recognized in other states as same-sex marriages would have been or because this specially created separate status is itself stigmatizing. Were the court to recognize that equal protection guarantees were implicated by the state's marriage law and by the separate status created for same-sex couples, the court would impose heightened rather than "rational basis with bite" scrutiny and would be even more likely to find that the statute offended state and federal constitutional guarantees.

NOTES

1. See 15 Vermont Statutes Annotated 1204(a).
2. Vermont Constitution ch.1, art. 7.
3. *Baker*, 744 A.2d at 876.
4. *Id*. at 878-879.
5. See *Baker*, 744 A.2d at 877 n.9 (discussing Common Benefits provisions in other state constitutions).
6. For a discussion of why the classification was appropriately recognized as sex-based rather than orientation-based, see chapter 8. Of course, it is true that as a general matter those with a same-sex orientation are much more severely impacted by such a sex-based classification than are those with a different-sex orientation, but that is a different point.
7. See *Baehr*, 852 P.2d at 63–67.
8. *Loving v. Virginia*, 388 U.S. 1, 9 (1967).
9. *Id*. at 11.
10. *Id*. at 11 n.11.
11. *Personnel Administrator of Massachusetts v. Feeney*, 442 U.S. 256, 272 (1979).
12. See *Baker*, 744 A.2d at 880 n.13 (quoting *Feeney*, 442 U.S. at 272).
13. *Loving*, 388 U.S. at 9.
14. *Id*. at 11 n.11.
15. *Shaw v. Reno*, 509 U.S. 630, 651 (1993).
16. *Green v. State*, 1877 WL 1291, *2 (Ala. 1877).
17. *Ex parte Kinney*, 14 F. Cas. 602, 605 (E.D. Va. 1879).
18. *Pace v. Alabama*, 106 U.S. 583, 585 (1883).
19. *McLaughlin v. Florida*, 379 U.S. 184, 188 (1964).
20. *Id*. at 190.
21. *Id*. at 188 (emphasis added).
22. See *Baker*, 744 A.2d at 880 n.13.
23. *Id*. at 906 (Johnson, J., concurring in part and dissenting in part).
24. See *United States v. Virginia*, 518 U.S. 515, 590 (Scalia, J., dissenting).
25. *McLaughlin*, 379 U.S. at 188.
26. See *Craig v. Boren*, 429 U.S. 190, 197 (1976).
27. *Baker*, 744 A.2d at 905 n.9 (Johnson, J., concurring in part and dissenting in part).

Chapter Two

When Are Benefits Equal?

The *Baker* court held that the Common Benefits Clause of the Vermont Constitution requires same-sex couples to be afforded the opportunity to receive the same benefits and protections that married couples receive. The Vermont legislature responded by creating a separate status for same-sex couples, entitling them to the benefits if not the name of marriage. There is good reason to believe, however, that the civil union status created by the Vermont legislature does not meet the state constitution's requirements. A civil union alternative for same-sex couples, while better than what any other state has offered thus far, cannot offer equal benefits, protections, and security, precisely because civil unions are less likely than marriages to be recognized in other jurisdictions. If that is so, however, and if there are particular benefits and protections that same-sex married couples would be able to enjoy in other jurisdictions that same-sex civil union partners would not, then the Vermont legislature has failed to meet the state constitutional mandate by failing to permit same-sex couples to marry.

That same-sex marriages would likely offer greater benefits and protections in some of the other states is not dependent on whether the constitutionality of the Defense of Marriage Act (DOMA) will be upheld, since DOMA does not preclude states from according recognition to same-sex marriages but merely gives them the choice of whether to do so. Yet, it should not be assumed that DOMA will pass constitutional muster when it is finally challenged, and its constitutional vulnerability itself has implications.

Suppose that DOMA is struck down as an unconstitutional exercise of congressional power or even that only the DOMA section reserving federal benefits for different-sex couples is struck down. Civil union partners would presumably be treated like domestic partners who, whether or not they are of the same sex, are not entitled to the federal benefits that married partners receive. If that is so, then the civil union system set up by Vermont would not entitle Vermont same-sex couples to the federal benefits to which they would have been entitled had they been allowed to marry. Thus, the invalidation of the federal benefits provision of DOMA would even more clearly establish that the civil union system in Vermont does not meet the state's constitutional requirements.

Even if one sets aside the fact that same-sex civil union partners will not receive the benefits that they might have received had they been married, the stigmatization that occurs by setting up a separate civil union system for same-sex couples alone suffices to establish that the separate system does not pass constitutional muster. Indeed, it is hard to imagine a parallel system according identical benefits that would not have overtones of stigma. Thus, if the Vermont Constitution requires that all Vermonters receive equal benefits, it is difficult to imagine how that could be interpreted to require anything less than the state's recognition of same-sex marriages.

BENEFITS AND PROTECTIONS

Suppose that the Vermont Supreme Court had to decide whether the civil union status accorded to same-sex couples satisfied the constitutional requirement of equal treatment. One of the complicating issues in the analysis would be that certain benefits cannot be afforded to individuals without the cooperation of other states or of the federal government. Thus, at least one issue that the Supreme Court of Vermont will have to address is whether the state constitutional requirements have been met when, by recognizing civil unions instead of same-sex marriages, the Vermont legislature offered Vermont same-sex couples fewer benefits and protections than it might have vis-à-vis other states and, perhaps, the federal government.

INTERSTATE RECOGNITION

When it seemed that Hawaii might recognize same-sex marriages, some commentators suggested that other states would be required to recognize those same-sex marriages validly celebrated in Hawaii. This prompted Congress to pass the Defense of Marriage Act, one part of which dealt with the conditions under which states would have to recognize marriages validly celebrated in other states. The Act reads in relevant part:

No State, territory, or possession of the United States, or Indian tribe, shall be required to give effect to any public act, record, or judicial proceeding of any other

State, territory, possession, or tribe respecting a relationship between persons of the same sex that is treated as a marriage under the laws of such other State, territory, possession, or tribe, or a right or claim arising from such relationship.[1]

There is some confusion about how this section of the Act should be interpreted. When it was discussed in Congress, proponents suggested that this section was necessary to prevent a same-sex couple domiciled in one state from going to another state where such marriages were recognized, marrying, and then returning to their home state demanding that the marriage be recognized. Yet, if that were the purpose, then this section of the Act was unnecessary, because domiciles already had the power not to recognize marriages validly celebrated in other jurisdictions. Indeed, a brief examination of either the *Restatement (First)* or the *Restatement (Second) of the Conflict of Laws* reveals that domiciles have long had the power to refuse to recognize marriages that are legally void in the domicile even if validly celebrated elsewhere.

Some commentators suggest that this DOMA section was merely intended to reaffirm that the domicile at the time of the marriage has the right to refuse to recognize a marriage validly celebrated elsewhere and that the courts should not hold otherwise. Yet, the language of the section is much broader than that and, in fact, does not even include the term "domicile." A literal reading of the section allows any state to refuse to recognize a same-sex marriage, regardless of when or where it was contracted.

This broad, literal interpretation would permit a significant change in the interstate recognition practices that had existed up to the time of the Act's passage. Though both *Restatements* suggest that the domicile at the time a marriage is celebrated need not recognize a marital union if that union violates an important public policy of the state, they both also suggest that a marriage valid in the domicile at the time of the marriage will be recognized as valid by all of the states.

Two different points may be made about the emphasis in each of the *Restatements* on the law of the domicile at the time of the marriage. First, insofar as either *Restatement* is persuasive in a particular jurisdiction, a court in that jurisdiction would tend to follow it and hold that the domicile at the time of the marriage could refuse to recognize a marriage validly celebrated elsewhere, but that a state having no connection to the marriage at the time of its celebration should recognize it as long as it was valid in the domicile at that time. Congress's having passed DOMA and having (allegedly) accorded each state the power to refuse to recognize a same-sex marriage validly celebrated elsewhere does not speak to whether such a marriage *should* be recognized. Thus, absent local legislation to the contrary, courts should recognize same-sex marriages validly celebrated in another domiciliary state because of the important interests in protecting the predictability of marriage, strengthening and preserving the integrity of marriage, and safeguarding family relationships.

Second, a separate point is that the interpretation of DOMA should itself be affected by the positions offered in the *Restatements*. DOMA proponents suggested that the Act was merely intended to affirm existing practices, and the *Restatements* offer influential characterizations of what those existing practices were and are. Thus, because both *Restatements* suggest that the law of the domicile at the time of the marriage will determine the validity of the union, congressional intent in passing DOMA should be interpreted to permit domiciles at the time of the marriage to refuse to recognize a same-sex marriage validly celebrated elsewhere, but as not permitting a state having no connection to the marriage at the time of its celebration in a sister domicile to refuse to recognize that union.

Suppose that the DOMA section under examination here is given a broad interpretation, notwithstanding its proponents' claimed goal to reflect current law. A separate question is just what that broad interpretation would permit. Perhaps it would "merely" entitle future domiciles to refuse to recognize same-sex unions. On the other hand, a broad interpretation might do much more than that, for example, permit any state to refuse to recognize a same-sex marriage, notwithstanding the current recognition of the union by the couple's domicile.

A very broad interpretation of this section would be of doubtful constitutional validity, however, as the alleged reason for its passage was quite narrow: preventing the domicile at the time of the marriage from being forced to recognize a marriage validly celebrated elsewhere. The Supreme Court struck down Colorado's Amendment 2 in *Romer v. Evans* because "its sheer breadth [was] so discontinuous with the reasons offered for it that the amendment seem[ed] inexplicable by anything but animus toward the class that it affect[ed]."[2] The Court would have reason to make a similar finding with respect to DOMA, especially since there is good reason to think that its passage was motivated by animus.

The resolution of how broadly this DOMA section should be read is especially important in the context discussed here. The *Baker* holding suggests that Vermont same-sex couples must be afforded equal benefits; it does not suggest that domiciliaries of other states are entitled to such benefits. Even were it possible for a Vermont same-sex couple to marry in that state, a same-sex couple domiciled in a state declaring such marriages void would find that their marriage "celebrated" in Vermont would not even be recognized by Vermont. Vermont law prevents a domiciliary of another state from coming to Vermont and marrying if such a marriage would be void in that individual's domicile . Thus, if this section of DOMA merely was meant to assure that domiciliaries would be unable to go back to their domicile and demand recognition of their same-sex union validly celebrated elsewhere, the section would be doubly unnecessary in the context under discussion here, because (1) states already had that power any-way, and (2) according to Vermont law, such marriages would not be valid.

Consider a different scenario. Suppose that Vermont were to recognize same-sex marriages and that a Vermonter were to marry her female part-ner. Suppose further that this same-sex couple traveled to another state to honeymoon. If that second state subscribed to the recognition position articulated in either the *First* or *Second Restatement,* that second state would recognize the marriage, because the couple's domicile (Vermont) recog-nized the union. If there were an accident in that latter state during the honeymoon, then the privileges enjoyed by a spouse, for example, those associated with visiting a patient in the hospital or having a say in the patient's medical treatment if she were unable to express her own prefer-ences, would presumably be accorded to the patient's partner. Further, even if the right to sue for wrongful death or loss of consortium were lim-ited to family members, the marital partner might nonetheless be able to bring such a cause of action.

Suppose the above scenario is modified slightly and the Vermont couple had instead contracted a civil union. The second state where they were honeymooning would be much less likely to recognize their civil union status and, instead, probably would view the civil union benefits accorded by Vermont as purely local and not requiring recognition. Were there an accident, the domestic partner might be treated as a legal stranger to the patient.

There are at least two different reasons that a state might be unwilling to recognize another state's civil union benefits. First, the state might have its own domestic partnership system that accords less robust benefits than does Vermont, for example, not recognizing the right to sue for wrongful death or loss of consortium. The state might well be unwilling to accord a benefit to Vermont civil union partners that it did not accord to local domestic partners. Second, the state might consciously have decided not to recognize domestic partnership or civil unions and thus might refuse to recognize Vermont's "novel" system. In such a case, the claim would not be merely that the states differed with respect to which individuals would be entitled to become domestic partners but rather that the states differed with respect to whether to recognize such an institution at all.

It might be claimed that the analysis above ignores the argument that by passing DOMA Congress has authorized the states to refuse to recog-nize same-sex marriages. Yet, this is beside the point for two different rea-sons. First, DOMA is vulnerable on a number of constitutional grounds. If the only reason that states can refuse to recognize same-sex marriages validly celebrated in other domiciliary states is that Congress has autho-rized them to do so and if this authorization is void and of no legal effect because Congress did not have the power to so authorize them, then all states would have to recognize a marriage validly celebrated in another domiciliary state. Second, even if DOMA is constitutional, it authorized rather than required the non-recognition of same-sex marriages. As long as *some* states would choose to recognize the Vermont same-sex marriage, for example, because of the strong public policy promoted by upholding the validity of a marriage wherever possible, there would be important implications for the Vermont legislation.

One of the reasons that theorists were tempted to think that states might recognize same-sex marriages celebrated in Hawaii was the growing trend for states to recognize marriages validly celebrated elsewhere, even if these marriages could not be validly celebrated in the domicile. This trend is important to consider because it indicates the unique status of marriage and the very strong tendency of states to recognize marriages that have been validly celebrated in another jurisdiction. It is important to consider for another reason as well. The developing trend that theorists recognized was for the domicile *at the time of the marriage* to recognize a marriage validly celebrated elsewhere, notwithstanding that (1) the marriage could not have been celebrated in the domicile, and (2) the long-established jurisprudence recognizing that the law of the domicile at the time of the marriage's celebration determines the validity of the marriage. Here, what is being discussed is something far less "radical" than subverting the law of the domicile at the time of the marriage and, indeed, is in accord with the articulated positions in both the *First* and the *Second Restatement,* namely, that states should recognize the validity of a marriage that is considered valid in a sister domiciliary state. If the emerging trend suggests that domiciles at the time of the marriage should recognize marriages validly celebrated elsewhere, it certainly suggests that marriages valid in the domicile at the time of the marriage should be recognized throughout the country and, *a fortiori,* that a marriage valid in the domicile at the time of the marriage *and* in the couple's current domicile should be recognized by all of the states.

Given the strong presumption regarding the validity of marriages validly celebrated in sister domiciles and the perceived differences between marriage and domestic partnerships that will likely cause such partnerships to be viewed as purely domestic creations, it would seem extremely likely that some jurisdiction (let us call it State X) would recognize a same-sex marriage but not a civil union. That the former would be recognized and some benefits accorded while the latter would not suggests that civil unions are an inferior alternative to marriage that cannot offer equal protections and security.

The point here should not be misunderstood. Assuming that Vermont recognized same-sex marriages, it would not matter for purposes here that State X (a) would not allow its own domiciliaries to marry a same-sex partner or even (b) would not recognize a same-sex marriage of current domiciliaries who had validly contracted the marriage while living in

Vermont. As long as State X would recognize a same-sex marriage of individuals traveling through the state, for example, those who were still domiciled in Vermont and were vacationing in the state, but would not recognize the civil union status of such a couple, and as long as affording the former recognition would translate into some benefits and protections, then the Vermont constitutional requirement that same-sex couples be afforded equal benefits could not be met by offering the civil union option instead of marriage.

The claim here is not that Vermont is required by its own constitution to regulate how other states treat the marriages of Vermonters, but merely that the State is required by its own constitution to extend to same-sex couples the benefits and protections that flow from marriage and that setting up a separate civil union system does not meet this mandate. To see why this is so, it will be helpful to consider first-cousin marriages.

First-cousin marriages are permitted in Vermont, although numerous states prohibit such marriages. A different state might have a law declaring that first-cousin marriages will not be recognized no matter where or when celebrated, which would bar recognition of such marriages even if validly celebrated in Vermont by Vermont domiciliaries.[3] Assuming that the latter state has the power to enforce such a law, there would be nothing that Vermont could do to assure that a Vermonter's first-cousin marriage would be recognized in the other state. By the same token, were DOMA amended to permit every state to refuse to recognize the marriage of first cousins and were that amendment held constitutional, there would be nothing that Vermont could do to assure that Vermonters who marry their first cousins would have those marriages recognized in other states.

The fact that Vermont could not assure that other states would recognize the marriages of Vermont domiciliaries who had married their first cousins would not justify setting up a separate classification of first-cousin civil unions so that the relationship would be recognized in even fewer other states. Those who wished to marry their first cousins rather than establish civil unions with them would rightly complain if Vermont claimed to be treating them equally but merely gave them the latter option, even if in fact the benefits within the state were equal in all respects, because the state would thereby have diminished the partners' protections and security when they traveled in other states.

The issue that interested many commentators who discussed whether other domiciles would be forced to recognize a same-sex marriage validly celebrated in Hawaii is not the issue of interest here. The Vermont Constitution offers protections to Vermonters, not to Georgians who wish to evade the marriage laws of that state, and thus the question of interest is whether civil union status affords Vermonters sufficient benefits and protections.

Precisely because the issue of interest involves *Vermonters'* benefits, an examination is required of the benefits and protections accorded current Vermont domiciliaries who, for example, might travel elsewhere. The very reason that protecting Vermonters is important to Vermont is the reason that other states would be most likely to defer to Vermont and recognize the same-sex marriages of Vermont domiciliaries, namely, that the ties to Vermont would be substantial and long-lasting whereas the ties to another state would be slight and temporary. Indeed, in the nineteenth century when states were thought to have even more power with respect to whether they would recognize a marriage within the state, a Virginia court in *Ex parte Kinney* noted that the state would have to recognize an interracial marriage if the couple had merely been traveling through the state, even if Virginia could refuse to allow its own domiciliaries to enter into such marriages.[4]

The admission that travelers' interracial marriages would have to be recognized is significant, given that interracial marriages were considered strongly offensive to local policy at the time. In fact, in the year preceding the *Kinney* opinion, the Virginia Supreme Court offered its view of the importance of prohibiting interracial marriage. "The purity of public morals, the moral and physical development of both races, and the highest advancement of our cherished southern civilization, . . . all require that . . . [the races] should be kept distinct and separate, and that connections and alliances so unnatural that God and nature seem to forbid them, should be prohibited by positive law."[5]

Earlier in that decade, the Tennessee Supreme Court offered its own view concerning the degree of offensiveness of such marriages. That court suggested that if interracial marriages were recognized, then polygamous and incestuous marriages would also have to be recognized,[6] implying that no marriages were more contrary to public policy than interracial marriages.

If states were constitutionally required to recognize the interracial marriages of individuals traveling through the state even though (1) interracial marriages were thought at least as offensive to local policy as any other kind of marriage, and (2) states were viewed as having the same power to establish marital restrictions for their own domiciliaries as they would have had were they separate countries, then states are currently constitutionally required to recognize the same-sex marriages of Vermont domiciliaries who are merely traveling outside the state, since states are now understood to have less sovereignty than they once were thought to have. Thus, because other states, out of comity or constitutional obligation, would likely recognize the same-sex marriages of vacationing Vermonters and (temporarily) afford them increased protections accompanying that recognition, the Vermont legislature must recognize same-sex marriage if it is to accord Vermonters equal protection.

MARRIAGES FOR FEDERAL PURPOSES

The DOMA section discussed above authorizes states to refuse to recognize same-sex marriages if they so desire. A different DOMA section prevents same-sex couples from being accorded the federal benefits of marriage, notwithstanding the recognition of their union by the couple's domicile. That DOMA section reads:

In determining the meaning of any Act of Congress, or of any ruling, regulation, or interpretation of the various administrative bureaus and agencies of the United States, the word "marriage" means only a legal union between one man and one woman as husband and wife, and the word "spouse" refers only to a person of the opposite sex who is a husband or a wife.[7]

It might be thought that because this DOMA section "merely" concerns the federal benefits that married couples enjoy, Congress can do as it chooses and, probably, has often exercised its prerogative to decide which couples are married for federal purposes. Both assumptions would be mistaken. Indeed, Congress deferred to the states' definitions of marriage even when many, but not all, states refused to allow interracial couples to marry.

Congress's previous practice of deferring to the state definition of marriage was likely due to the fact that family law is a "peculiarly state province."[8] As then-Justice Rehnquist explained, family law is a matter "of peculiarly local concern and therefore governed by state and not federal law."[9] Indeed, in *United States v. Lopez,* the Court struck down Congress's power to criminalize the possession of a firearm within a school zone, at least in part, because the federal government's rationale would imply that "Congress could regulate any activity that it found was related to the economic productivity of individual citizens: family law (including marriage, divorce, and child custody), for example."[10]

The claim here is not that Congress is always prohibited from passing regulations affecting family law. For example, Congress has passed the Parental Kidnapping and Prevention Act and the Full Faith and Credit for Child Support Orders Act, and those have not been held by the Court to violate constitutional guarantees. Nonetheless, Congress bears a heavy burden if it is to justify the displacement of state law. As the Supreme Court has explained, "Before a state law governing domestic relations will be overridden, it must do major damage to clear and substantial federal interests."[11]

Perhaps it would seem that Congress is not displacing state law in this DOMA provision because it is only defining marriage for federal purposes. Yet, this would misrepresent the relevant jurisprudence. The Court explained that the "scope of a federal right is, of course, a federal question, but that does not mean that its content is not to be determined by state, rather than federal law."[12] Indeed, it is especially appropriate to apply state law where a family relationship is at issue, since there is no federal law of domestic relations.

Congress might be able to justify displacing state law if, for example, national defense were at issue. The Court has made clear, however, that a mere assertion that an important federal interest is at issue will not suffice. Rather, it must be clear that "substantial interests of the National Government, which cannot be served consistently with respect for such state interests, will suffer major damage if the state law is applied."[13]

When this DOMA section is finally challenged, the Court will have to decide whether the provision is preventing major damage to clear and substantial federal interests. Although it is unclear what the Court will decide, there are at least two reasons to believe that this Act will be held unconstitutional: (1) the claim involving no major damage to clear and substantial federal interests has been successful in the past in limiting federal displacement of state family law, and (2) the current Court has become increasingly willing to limit Congress's power over the states.

Those arguing for the constitutionality of this DOMA section will have some difficulty establishing what clear and substantial federal interests it serves. The section's proponents might claim that the federal government has a legitimate interest in saving money and that same-sex marriages would involve the extension of benefits that would not otherwise have to be extended. The Court has already indicated, however, that the mere saving of money, while legitimate, is not a sufficiently important interest to justify displacement of state law.

Were the Court to hold that saving money met the relevant standard, then Congress would seem permitted to deny recognition to any sort of marriage that it chose (e.g., Republican, Democratic, etc.) in the interest of protecting the Federal Treasury. Further, Congress would seem entitled to pass a variety of measures regulating the family as long as federal funds might thereby be saved.

The federal benefits provision of DOMA is at the very least constitutionally vulnerable. Were it in fact found unconstitutional, there would be yet another reason that Vermont's civil union status would not pass state constitutional muster. Because same-sex civil union partners still would not be entitled to federal marital benefits, but same-sex marital partners would be, the Vermont civil union system would not be according Vermonters the common benefits, protections, and security of the law in yet another respect: the Vermont civil union partners would have been denied the federal benefits that would flow from marriage under Vermont law.

Regardless of whether DOMA is constitutional, the civil union option will not be according same-sex couples equal benefits. Thus, it would be unnecessary to wait for DOMA to be declared unconstitutional to establish this inequality, although a declaration of the Act's unconstitutionality would make the inequality between marital and civil union status even clearer.

WHEN ARE EQUAL BENEFITS BEING ACCORDED?

Suppose that the issue of equal benefits was somehow resolved so that marriages and civil unions were held to accord the same benefits. One issue would be whether some of the relevant benefits had not been included within the comparison. A separate issue would be whether setting up a separate civil union system that accords equal benefits nonetheless imposes a stigma and, for that reason, is unconstitutional. It is difficult to see how the Vermont Supreme Court could examine the civil union legislation and fail to find both that some benefits had not been included in the comparison and that, in any event, the separate system was stigmatizing and hence unconstitutional.

The Vermont Supreme Court made clear that the possible parallel system to be set up by the Vermont legislature would have to accord same-sex couples equal benefits. The court did not make clear, however, which *kinds* of benefits had to be offered.

The issue of concern here can be made clearer when one considers the attempts that have been made to create separate but equal institutions in other contexts. For example, the United States Supreme Court struck down Texas's attempt to set up a segregated law school to avoid integrating the University of Texas. The Court noted some of the differences between the schools' students, faculty, and library and also noted a difference in "those qualities which are incapable of objective measurement but which make for greatness in a law school."[14] By the same token, when striking down Virginia Military Institute's single-sex admissions policy, the Court suggested that intangible differences are sometimes even more important than the tangible ones. Thus, the Court has made clear that intangible qualities, or qualities incapable of measurement, can have constitutional significance when a determination must be made regarding whether equal protection requirements have been met or whether equal benefits have been accorded.

When the Court rejected Virginia's proposal to set up a separate program for women at Mary Baldwin College so that the Virginia Military Institute would not have to accept female applicants, the Court pointed out that the Mary Baldwin program would not qualify as VMI's equal because, among other things, the two were not equal in prestige. One question for the Vermont Supreme Court will be whether the prestige of the option is itself a constitutionally significant consideration, for it is difficult to understand how the civil union alternative plausibly could be considered equal to marriage in prestige.

The claim, of course, is not that no one would choose civil union status over marriage. Even those who have the option of marrying sometimes choose to register as domestic partners instead. The point here is merely that the benefits accorded are not equal if the prestige or other intangible or difficult-to-measure qualities are unequal, even if particular individuals might nonetheless choose for their own reasons the option that accorded fewer benefits.

ON ACCORDING EQUAL BENEFITS TO INFERIORS

The *Baker* court understood that the symbolic or spiritual significance of the marital relation would not be included within the benefits accorded by domestic partnership status but suggested that the case before the court merely involved the secular benefits and protections of marriage. As suggested above, however, because qualities are intangible or difficult to measure does not make them of merely symbolic or spiritual significance. The benefits afforded by the more prestigious alternative can be quite real.

The above point notwithstanding, the importance of the symbolic should not be minimized. Indeed, the Vermont court seemed to appreciate the importance of symbolism when it explained that the plaintiffs were asking to have their relationships included in the family of state-sanctioned human relations.[15] The court seemed not to notice that equality guarantees require not only that same-sex relationships be included within the "family" of human relations, but also that they not be included within the family merely as a poor relation. While it may be preferable to be considered a poor relation rather than a complete stranger, it should never be thought that according better treatment necessarily meets the requirement to accord equal treatment. Commentators are correct when they complain that lesbians and gays seek more than mere tolerance but are incorrect when falsely implying that seeking equality somehow involves seeking preferential treatment.

In *Plessy v. Ferguson,* the Supreme Court rejected the claim that "the enforced separation of the two races [in railway cars] stamps the colored race with a badge of inferiority," instead claiming that were a badge of inferiority thereby imposed, it would not be "by reason of anything found in the act, but solely because the colored race chooses to put that construction upon it."[16] Ultimately, the Court repudiated the claim that the stamp of inferiority imposed by requiring racial separation in railway cars had been "chosen." It should be noted that both proponents and opponents of same-sex marriage recognize the symbolic importance of whether such unions are legally recognized, and neither denies that the failure to recognize such marriages has implications for equality.

A brief examination of the *Congressional Record* reveals what some members of Congress believe is at stake if same-sex marriages are recognized.

Some members apparently believe that the survival of the country hangs in the balance, which sounds strikingly familiar to the claims made by the Virginia Supreme Court with respect to what would happen were interracial marriages recognized. Others suggest that legal recognition of same-sex unions would somehow trivialize and demean marriage, notwithstanding that same-sex couples who contracted marriages would have the same rights and responsibilities that different-sex couples have and, notwithstanding the claim of these same opponents that such marriages, even if recognized, would not be "real" anyway. What is manifestly clear is that many opponents of same-sex marriage want to assure that same-sex relationships are not viewed as "equal" to different-sex marriages and that lesbians, gays, bisexuals, and transgendered people are not viewed as the equals of others. These commentators seem to have forgotten that part of the rationale in *Loving v. Virginia* for striking down Virginia's anti-miscegenation statute was that Virginia had been attempting via its marriage statute to promote the view that one group was superior to another.

In his *Plessy* dissent, Justice Harlan asked rhetorically, "What can more certainly arouse race hate, what more certainly create and perpetuate a feeling of distrust between these races, than state enactments which, in fact, proceed on the ground that colored citizens are so inferior and degraded that they cannot be allowed to sit in public coaches occupied by white citizens?"[17] An analogous question might be asked with respect to the refusal to permit same-sex marriages, since the state is implying that lesbian and gay citizens "are so inferior and degraded" that they cannot be allowed to marry their life-partners.

Many same-sex marriage opponents seem to have the implicit, if not explicit, attitude that lesbians, gays, and bisexuals are, at best, second-class citizens who are not equal to everyone else. Yet, the Court struck down the VMI policy, at least in part, because the state's policy denied women "full citizenship stature."[18] As the Court has explained, by perpetuating "archaic and stereotypic notions" or by stigmatizing members of the disfavored group as "innately inferior" and therefore as less worthy participants in the political community, discrimination itself can cause serious non-economic injuries to those persons who are personally denied equal treatment solely because of their membership in a disfavored group.[19] Denying same-sex couples the right to marry will continue to cause them both economic and non-economic injuries, and the issue in Vermont and elsewhere will be whether it is constitutionally permissible to continue to cause these harms.

The Court has already made clear how important it is to be "exempt[] from legal discriminations, implying inferiority in civil society."[20] Yet, the states' singling out those who would marry a same-sex partner and denying them the right to marry "is practically a brand upon them, affixed by the law, [that is] an assertion of their inferiority."[21] It is precisely this kind of stigmatization that is an affront to our constitutional system.

The *Romer* Court suggested that laws are unconstitutional if they "raise the inevitable inference that the disadvantage imposed is born of animosity toward the class of persons affected."[22] It is difficult to see how laws preventing same-sex marriage that are supported by claims to "protect" marriage and to prevent it from being "demeaned" and "trivialized" can fail to raise an inference of impermissible hostility.

CONCLUSION

In *Baker v. State,* the Vermont Supreme Court held that the state constitution requires that same-sex couples be afforded the opportunity to receive the same benefits, protections, and security that married couples receive. Yet, the Vermont legislature has not fulfilled that constitutional mandate by setting up a parallel civil union system, at least in part, because of the differing treatment that same-sex marriages and civil union would receive in other states. Because marriage has a unique status and accords benefits that simply could not be duplicated by a "parallel" civil union, the latter simply cannot be viewed as affording all of the benefits that flow from the recognition of the former.

Even if marital and civil union status could offer the same benefits, it is difficult to understand why a state would go to the trouble of setting up a parallel system if the state did not somehow feel that marriage would be "tainted" by allowing same-sex couples to enjoy that status. Yet, sincere worries about taint notwithstanding, states would be prohibited from setting up a parallel system for interracial or interfaith marriages that afforded equal benefits, because it would be stigmatizing for the states to do so. The taint justification is no more persuasive in the context of same-sex marriage than it would be in the context of interfaith or interracial marriages.

Even if Vermont could accord equal benefits by recognizing civil union status, the state is nonetheless constitutionally prohibited from setting up a parallel system precisely because of the stigma that will be associated with that status. Although the civil union status discussed here is better for those who would marry a same-sex partner than what any other state has thus far offered, equality guarantees require more than a lessening of inequality so that those who would marry a same-sex partner will be treated as poor relations rather than as complete strangers. Those guarantees require the according of full citizenship and equal stature. That is something that a "separate but equal" status simply cannot achieve.

NOTES

1. U.S.C. § 1738C.
2. U.S. 620, 632 (1996).
3. See, for example, Delaware Code Annotated Tit. 13 § 101(a), (d) (1999); Arizona Revised Statutes Annotated §§ 25–101(A), 25–112(A) (2000). Although these statutes have not yet been construed by the courts with respect to this issue in particular, the language suggests that this would be the position that the state would take.
4. See *Ex parte Kinney*, 14 F. Cas. 602, 606 (E.D. Va. 1879).
5. *Kinney v. Commonwealth*, 71 Va. (30 Gratt.) 858, 869 (1878).
6. See *State v. Bell*, 66 Tenn. (7 Heisk.) 9, 11 (1872).
7. U.S.C. § 7 (1994).
8. *United States v. Yazell*, 382 U.S. 341, 353 (1966).
9. *McCarty v. McCarty*, 453 U.S. 210, 237 (1981) (Rehnquist, J., dissenting).
10. *United States v. Lopez*, 514 U.S. 549, 564 (1995).
11. *Rose v. Rose*, 481 U.S. 619, 625 (1987) (quoting Hisquierdo v. Hisquierdo, 439 U.S. 572, 581 (1979)).
12. *DeSylva v. Ballentine*, 351 U.S. 570, 580 (1956).
13. *Yazell*, 382 U.S. at 352.
14. *Sweatt v. Painter*, 339 U.S. 629, 634 (1950).
15. *Baker*, 744 A.2d at 889.
16. *Plessy v. Ferguson*, 163 U.S. 537, 551 (1896).
17. *Id.* at 560 (Harlan, J., dissenting).
18. *Virginia*, 518 U.S. at 532.
19. *Heckler v. Mathews*, 465 U.S. 728, 739–40 (1984).
20. *Strauder v. West Virginia*, 100 U.S. 303, 308 (1879).
21. *Id.*
22. *Romer v. Evans*, 517 U.S. 620, 634 (1996).

Chapter Three

Civil Unions and Parental Status

The advantages of civil unions status should not be taken lightly. Civil union members are accorded a variety of rights and benefits, including the right to be considered the legal parent of a child born into the relationship. Just as a husband is rebuttably presumed to be the father of a child born into the marriage, a civil union partner is rebuttably presumed to be a parent of a child born into a civil union.

For many families, this presumption will prove quite helpful, since the couple will not have to spend time, money, and energy in establishing the partner's parental rights. Yet, there is a potential risk for these families that should at least be acknowledged, namely, that a different state will refuse to recognize the presumptive or declared parental rights of the partner who is not biologically related to the child. If, for example, a state through which the family is traveling or to which the family moves has passed a Defense of Marriage Act, then that state may refuse to recognize the rebuttable presumption of parenthood that has been established by virtue of the existence of the civil union established in Vermont. Indeed, even a judicial declaration of the civil union partner's parental status may not suffice to ensure recognition of that status in other states.

One might suggest to such parents that they simply not move to or even travel through those states. Yet, couples have a different option, which will not severely limit them in their travels within their own country and which will nonetheless afford them increased protection: they can take advantage of Vermont's second-parent adoption provision. Because the parental relationship would then have been established without having relied on the legal recognition of a same-sex marriage or marriage-like relationship, it would not be open to a DOMA-based challenge. Although a second-parent adoption would require an investment of resources that doubtless could otherwise be spent in a variety of worthwhile ways, such an investment might nonetheless be a wise expenditure, preventing or reducing the loss of many hours and dollars in possible future litigation, and significantly reducing if not completely eliminating the likelihood of a different state's refusing to recognize the partner's parental status sometime in the future.

FEDERAL AND STATE ACTS IN DEFENSE OF MARRIAGE

Two separate kinds of Acts must be considered when discussing the possible reactions of states to the rebuttable presumption created by the Vermont civil union statutes. First, there is the Federal Defense of Marriage Act, which both defines "marriage" for federal purposes and which permits states to refuse to recognize same-sex marriages validly celebrated in other states. Second, there are the Defense of Marriage Acts passed by numerous states in response to the Federal Act, which make clear that the states will not recognize same-sex marriages validly celebrated in other jurisdictions. These acts create the potential that a state might refuse to recognize a parental status arising out of a legally recognized marriage-like relationship between same-sex partners, even if the state would have recognized the parental rights of the partner if that status had been established in a different way.

THE FEDERAL DEFENSE OF MARRIAGE ACT

As suggested in the previous chapter, the Defense of Marriage Act passed by Congress is open to a variety of interpretations, which run the gamut from Congress's merely permitting domiciles at the time of the marriage to refuse to recognize same-sex marriage-like relationships validly celebrated in other states to Congress's permitting any state to refuse to recognize such a relationship, regardless of when or where it had been validly celebrated. Thus, according to one reading of the Act, a couple that had contracted a same-sex marriage or marriage-like relationship in one state and had lived there for twenty years might have a subsequent domicile, for example, where they had moved for their retirement years, refuse to recognize their marriage. According to an even more expansive reading of the Act, a *non-domicile* might refuse to recognize such a relationship contracted twenty years earlier.

Suppose that a same-sex couple had been married for twenty years. After retiring from their jobs, they decided to take an extended cross-country trip. The validity of the marriage became an issue in one of the states in which the couple was traveling, for example, because they had been in an accident and one wanted to authorize needed medical treatment for his or her partner. Were the state to refuse to recognize the relationship, the partner, who might then be viewed as a legal stranger to the victim, might not be permitted to authorize the necessary procedure. The broadest reading of DOMA would permit this kind of scenario to take place.

The language of DOMA has implications beyond whether a particular marriage is recognized, since the Federal Act permits states to refuse to give effect to any right or claim arising from a relationship between persons of the same sex that is treated as a marriage under the laws of some other state. This means, for example, that a support award or property settlement granted in a dissolution of a same-sex relationship would not have to be enforced in a state refusing to recognize such relationships, Full Faith and Credit Clause notwithstanding.

Of course, the ambiguity discussed above, namely, whether the Act is meant to apply *only* to same-sex marriages that are celebrated contrary to the law of the domicile at the time of the marriage or to other marriages as well, also has import for which benefits and rights need not be enforced. If the Act is only meant to preserve the right of the domicile at the time of the marriage to determine the marital status of its own domiciliaries, then the Act is merely suggesting that those who seek to marry in another jurisdiction when their own jurisdiction declares the union void will be unable to claim as a matter of right the privileges or benefits that might otherwise have followed from having celebrated a marriage. If the Act is interpreted more broadly, however, then the Act might authorize other states to refuse to enforce a judgment issued in the marital domicile that orders spousal support or a property division, notwithstanding that the court in the domicile clearly had jurisdiction to decide the matter at hand.

Precisely because it is doubtful that Congress has the power to undermine the Full Faith and Credit Clause that way, the Court might well construe DOMA narrowly so as to avoid having to decide whether Congress has the power to negate the clause's function. The Supreme Court has explained that "if a serious doubt of constitutionality is raised, it is a cardinal principle that this Court will first ascertain whether a construction of the statute is fairly possible by which the question may be avoided."[1]

STATE DEFENSE OF MARRIAGE ACTS

The language of the Federal Defense of Marriage Act is permissive—states can recognize same-sex marriages validly celebrated in other jurisdictions, although they need not do so. In response to the Federal Act, states passed their own versions of the Defense of Marriage Act, sometimes called "mini-DOMAs." These range in type from (1) those that refuse to recognize a same-sex marriage validly celebrated elsewhere to (2) those that refuse not only to recognize such marriages but also any rights arising out of such marriages to (3) those that refuse to recognize any relationships treated like same-sex marriages and any rights arising out of such relationships. Although it is not clear how these statutes will be interpreted by the courts, for example, whether the difference between (2) and (3) will have any legal significance, it is clear that Vermonters who travel elsewhere will be on firmer legal ground with respect to their parental rights if they do not rely on the parental presumption built into the Vermont civil unions law.

Some of the state mini-DOMAs mirror the Federal DOMA with respect to the ambiguity regarding *which* marriages will not be recognized. Thus, on one interpretation of several of these acts, the statute will only apply to domiciliaries of the state who attempt to evade local law by celebrating a same-sex marriage-like relationship in a different state where such unions are recognized. At least some states have made clear, however, *both* that the same-sex marriage-like relationships of their domiciliaries that are celebrated elsewhere in accord with local law will not be recognized and, *in addition,* that such relationships validly celebrated elsewhere will not be recognized should the couple *later* become domiciled in the state. These states would seem not to be limiting their refusal to recognize same-sex marriage-like relationships to those celebrated by their own domiciliaries at the time of the union but instead to be refusing to recognize such relationships more generally.

A few points might be made about these state laws. First, they *may* not be authorized by Congress, since that depends upon whether (1) the federal statute is construed narrowly or broadly, and (2) if construed broadly, whether the congressional statute passes constitutional muster. Thus, if the Federal Defense of Marriage Act is only intended to support the traditional power of the domicile at the time of the marriage to determine the marital status of its own domiciliaries, then those states claiming the power to refuse to recognize a marriage valid in a sister domiciliary state at the time of the marriage are going beyond what Congress has authorized. Or, if the Federal Defense of Marriage Act is construed broadly but is held unconstitutional because Congress has exceeded its constitutional powers in passing such an Act, the states will be without valid congressional authorization to refuse to recognize those marriage-like relationships validly celebrated in the domicile at the time of the union.

CAN STATES REFUSE TO RECOGNIZE MARRIAGES VALIDLY CELEBRATED IN OTHER DOMICILES?

Two different questions must not be conflated: (1) Can a state refuse to recognize a marriage validly celebrated in a foreign country in which the parties are domiciled at the time of the marriage? and (2) Can a state refuse to recognize a marriage validly celebrated in another state in which the parties are domiciled at the time of the marriage? The answers to these questions may but need not be the same. It may be, for example, that particular protections built into the United States Constitution require that a marriage valid in a sister domiciliary state be recognized by all of the states. However, these constitutional guarantees might not be applicable to a marriage celebrated in another country by individuals who are domiciled in that country. Thus, the United States Constitution might not require states to recognize a same-sex marriage celebrated in the Netherlands by Dutch citizens, even if it would require one state to recognize a same-sex marriage validly celebrated in a sister domiciliary state.

The United States Supreme Court has not yet addressed whether states (with or without congressional approval) have the *power* to refuse to recognize marriages validly celebrated in a sister domiciliary state, although states apparently believe that they have that power. For example, the Federal Defense of Marriage Act, even if construed very broadly, only permits states to refuse to recognize *same-sex* marriage-like relationships validly celebrated elsewhere; it does not permit states to refuse to recognize other kinds of marriages that have been validly celebrated in other domiciliary states, even if those marriages nonetheless violate an important local public policy. Nonetheless, lack of congressional authorization to do so notwithstanding, states *seem* to be stating that they will refuse to recognize certain different-sex marriages, even if those marriages have been validly celebrated in other domiciliary states. For example, both Delaware and Arizona have statutes that seem to preclude the recognition of first-cousin marriages validly celebrated in other domiciliary states,[2] even though the traditional exception that allows states not to recognize incestuous marriages validly celebrated in other domiciles does not include first-cousin marriages, and thus these states could not rely on that exception to justify their refusal to recognize such unions. Ultimately, the United States Supreme Court will have to decide under what conditions, if any, a state will be permitted to refuse to recognize a marriage validly celebrated in a sister domiciliary state.

CIVIL UNIONS AND ESTABLISHING PARENTAL STATUS

It would be quite significant were the Supreme Court to rule that states do not have the power to refuse to recognize marriages validly celebrated in other domiciliary states. Even were the Court to so hold, however, that would not establish that states do not have the right to refuse to recognize civil unions validly celebrated elsewhere, since civil unions would likely not be accorded the same constitutional deference as would marriages. It is thus important to understand more about civil unions and more about the possible options that Vermont same-sex couples might have if they wish to establish and protect the parental rights of a partner not (yet) legally related to the child that both individuals are raising.

Although Vermont has made clear that a civil union is not a marriage, the state will nonetheless afford members of civil unions numerous rights including the right to be the presumed parent of a child born into the union. For example, if a particular couple has been recognized by the state as having a civil union and then, a year later, one of the members of the couple delivers a child after having been artificially inseminated, the partner who has not delivered the child will be presumed by law to be a parent of that child. The non-biological parent will not need in addition to adopt the child in order for Vermont to recognize the partner's (presumptive) parental status.

Though this presumption is rebuttable, it should not be thought a hurdle that is easily overcome. The Vermont Supreme Court has noted that the "presumption of paternity has been described as one of the strongest and most persuasive known to the law."[3] Historically, the way to rebut the presumption of paternity was either by establishing that the husband had been away at the time of conception or by establishing that the husband was impotent.

In the kinds of cases of concern here, the question will not be whether the civil union partner was in the geographical area at the time of conception or even whether the partner was sterile but, instead, whether the partners had agreed that a child would be born into the civil union. If one of the partners had been away on a job assignment for a few months, that would hardly establish that she had not consented to or even actively encouraged her partner's being artificially inseminated during that time and thus would hardly serve to rebut the presumption that the couple had jointly agreed to have and raise a child.

The civil union presumption will presumably mirror the kind of presumption employed when a child is born into a marriage as a result of artificial insemination because the husband is unable to father a child. Just as a sterile husband who agreed to have his wife inseminated would not be able to overcome the presumption of paternity by claiming that he had not been in the geographical vicinity at the time of conception or by claiming that he had no biological connection to the child, the same would be true for same-sex partners.

DECLARATORY JUDGMENTS

The civil union partner will be *presumed* by the law to be the legal parent of a child born into a civil union. If the couple is worried that another state will not recognize that parental presumption, the couple might try to get a declaratory judgment that the partner is indeed the legal parent of the child. However, it is unclear both whether such a judgment would be issued and, were it issued, how the judgment would be treated in the other jurisdiction.

Vermont law suggests that "courts within their respective jurisdictions shall have power to declare rights, status, and other legal relations."[4] The Vermont Supreme Court has explained that the purpose of a declaratory judgment is to make clear the rights of the parties and that the Declaratory Judgments Act is to be liberally construed so that it can serve that purpose. Precisely because of the importance of the rights, status, and legal relation at issue when a parent seeks to establish her parental status and because the Vermont legislature has made clear that a liberal construction of the Declaratory Judgments Act is appropriate, it is at least arguable that couples should be able to get a declaratory judgment establishing that a partner is indeed a legal parent of the child that they are raising together.

At least as a general matter, declaratory judgments *are* appropriately issued to make clear who has parental rights and responsibilities with respect to a particular child. For example, were two same-sex partners to disagree about whether the adult not biologically related to the child had parental rights and obligations, a declaratory judgment could appropriately be issued. The parties would clearly have adverse legal interests and the matter would be important to resolve. As the Supreme Court of Colorado has made clear, much is at stake when parties disagree about which party has parental rights:

The determination of parenthood includes the right to parenting time; the right to direct the child's activities; the right to make decisions regarding the control, education, and health of the child; and the right to the child's services and earnings. Legal [parent]hood imposes significant obligations as well, including the obligation of support and the obligation to teach moral standards, religious beliefs, and good citizenship.[5]

The potential difficulty in getting a court to issue a declaratory judgment establishing the civil union partner's parental rights and responsibilities is neither that this is the kind of issue that courts are not allowed to hear nor even that the issuance of the judgment would fail to terminate the uncertainty. The difficulty is that it is unclear whether a court can issue a declaratory judgment when neither party really contests the nonbiological partner's parental relationship with the child.

Declaratory relief is available when there is a threat of actual injury to a protected legal interest. The focus of concern here, however, is not the kind of injury that might arise were the biological parent to deny visitation privileges to a former partner; rather, at issue here is whether a partner could get a declaratory judgment to establish her parental rights so as to prevent the *possibility* that those rights would not be recognized in a different state. A mere possibility of non-recognition might not be thought a threat of actual injury to a protected legal interest and might instead be viewed as too speculative to permit the court to issue a declaratory judgment.

Arguably, civil union partners who anticipated traveling with their child in certain other states would face a situation "beset with uncertainty and insecurity,"[6] and a declaration of rights and responsibilities might "stabilize and quiet the relations between these parties."[7] Perhaps, then, a court would issue a declaratory judgment on these matters, especially considering that otherwise the partners might be forced to avail themselves of other legal options if in fact a declaratory judgment recognizing the partner's parental status could not be obtained. On the other hand, the court might deny that it could issue a declaratory judgment when neither adult contested the partner's parental status and the judgment was sought as a kind of travel insurance, believing that because the consequences are based merely upon the fear of what might occur and are not reasonably to be expected, a declaratory judgment could not appropriately be issued.

SECOND-PARENT ADOPTIONS

Suppose that a declaratory judgment could not be issued to establish the parental rights of the parent not biologically related to the child when the partners themselves agreed that the partner had that status. Vermont law offers the couple a different option, namely, the partner can adopt the child via a second-parent adoption, that is, an adoption of the child by the parent's non-marital partner.[8] Further, there is no requirement that the individual be a member of a marriage or civil union in order to acquire parental status via a second-parent adoption. As long as the adoption would promote the best interests of the child, second-parent adoption laws permit an individual's domestic partner to adopt that individual's child even if the two adults do not have a legally recognized relationship.[9]

Consider a parent and child who live together with the parent's partner. The couple might have met long after the parent had given birth to the child. If the partner wants to adopt the parent's child, the parent agrees, and the adoption would promote the best interest of the child, the state will permit the adoption. Further, where the child has not been born into a marriage or civil union, the parent's partner may well *not* be considered the legal parent of the child unless that partner formally adopts that child.[10] Thus, an individual who enters into a marriage or civil union *after* the birth of the partner's child will not enjoy the presumption of parenthood that the individual might have enjoyed had the legal relationship been established before the birth of the child.

An individual who establishes a legally recognized parental relationship with his or her partner's child via a second-parent adoption will have a relationship that is less vulnerable to nonrecognition in other states. It is precisely because there need not be a same-sex marriage or marriage-like relationship in order for a same-sex partner to establish a parental relation with his or her partner's child via a second-parent adoption that such an adoption would not come under the DOMA exception referred to above and would be subject to the full faith and credit guarantees that adoptions are afforded generally.

PARENTAL RELATIONS AND FULL FAITH AND CREDIT

At least three different issues should be distinguished. One is whether a state could refuse to recognize an adoption that has been finalized in a sister jurisdiction. Another is whether a state could ignore a declaratory judgment establishing parenthood that has been issued in another jurisdiction, and still another is whether a state could refuse to recognize a presumption of parenthood that has been afforded in a sister jurisdiction. All of these must be analyzed in terms of full faith and credit guarantees. The Defense of Marriage Act adds another layer of complexity to what may already be considered a difficult and confusing area.

The Full Faith and Credit Clause of the Federal Constitution reads, "Full Faith and Credit shall be given in each State to the public Acts, Records and Judicial Proceedings in every other State. And the Congress may by general Laws prescribe the Manner in which such Acts, Records and Proceedings shall be proved, and the Effect thereof."[11]

Although one might infer that the *same* amount of credit would be given to judicial proceedings on the one hand and public Acts and Records on the other, the Supreme Court has made clear that such an inference would be incorrect.[12] Assuming no fraud or lack of jurisdiction, final judgments issued by a court in one state are entitled to full faith and credit in every state.[13] The same exacting rule regarding full faith and credit is not imposed with respect to other states' acts (laws), however, since the forum state's public policy is a permissible consideration in deciding whether another state's law should be applied in a particular case.[14] Thus, as a general matter, another state's law that strongly offends local policy need not be applied if the case is being heard for the first time in a particular forum state. If the case were heard and a judgment were entered in another state, however, that judgment would be subject to full faith and credit guarantees even if it were based on a law that the forum state finds strongly offensive to public policy. For example, a gambling debt might not be enforceable if initially brought in a forum state in which gambling and the enforcement of such debts are thought to violate an important public policy. However, if that debt had already been reduced to judgment in a different state, that judgment would have to be enforced, public policy of the forum state notwithstanding.

The exacting rule with respect to other states' judgments needs further exposition. As a general matter, a judgment that is modifiable in the issuing state is modifiable in the forum state as well. Thus, because "the Full Faith and Credit Clause obliges States only to accord the same force to judgments as would be accorded by the courts of the State in which the judgment was entered,"[15] a judgment that is not final in the issuing state need not be treated as final in the forum state unless, for example, Congress has passed legislation to the contrary.[16] However, when a final judgment has been issued in one state, other states are not at liberty to modify it.

APPLYING FULL FAITH AND CREDIT TO PRESUMPTIONS AND JUDGMENTS

Suppose that Congress had never passed the Defense of Marriage Act. States would still have to decide how to treat (1) the presumption in Vermont law that a civil union partner is the parent of a child born into the civil union, and (2) a declaratory judgment that a same-sex partner is the legal parent of a particular child.

Certainly, a state might decide to credit the presumption that a particular individual is the parent of a child, given that the state itself will presume that an individual is a child's parent under certain circumstances. States have made clear in a variety of ways that they believe that the child's best interests are served by not disturbing parent-child relations absent important justification for doing so. Nonetheless, were a state court to find that the Vermont statutory presumption violated an important public policy of the state, the Full Faith and Credit Clause would not bar the state from refusing to credit Vermont's statutory presumption of parenthood. Basically, the public policy exception to giving full faith and credit to other states' laws would permit the forum state to refuse to recognize the Vermont parenthood presumption.

As the United States Supreme Court has made clear, however, where a final judgment has been issued by a court in a sister state, that judgment must be enforced even if it violates the forum state's public policy. States may have to submit "even to hostile policies reflected in the judgment of another state."[17] Indeed, it is "when a clash of policies between two states emerges that the need of the Clause is greatest."[18]

Vermont law makes clear that a declaratory judgment has the same force and effect as a final judgment.[19] While Vermont's rebuttable presumption of parenthood might well be subject to a public policy exception analysis in a different state, a declaratory judgment regarding parenthood would not be, assuming that such a declaratory judgment could be issued in the context under discussion here and that such a judgment would not fall under the exception that has perhaps been created by the Federal Defense of Marriage Act.

Suppose that a Vermont court issued a declaratory judgment that a parent's same-sex partner was indeed a co-parent of that parent's child. A court in a different state refused to accord that judgment full faith and credit, arguing that because Vermont had declared the judgment "final" for state purposes did not make it "final" for federal constitutional purposes.

At least a few points might be made about this hypothesized scenario. First, the question would not even be whether the judgment would be final for federal constitutional purposes generally but, rather, whether the judgment would be final for full faith and credit purposes. Were the courts to find that such a judgment was not final for these federal constitutional purposes in particular, a whole host of "final" judgments would potentially be challenged as not final for full faith and credit purposes. The federal courts might be inundated with claims until the jurisprudence had been sorted out. Second, some principle would have to be offered to establish which final judgments were really final. If, for example, the importance of the implicated interests and the importance of respecting reasonable and settled expectations were to play essential roles in the analysis, it is hard to imagine which kinds of cases would meet the relevant standard if this kind of case would not. Third, the Court has made clear that the Constitution includes no roving public policy exception that permits states to refuse to enforce valid, final judgments issued in other states.[20] Yet, that means that the Court must be on guard to prevent public policy considerations from getting into the analysis via the back door, which would likely occur if the finality of judgments for full faith and credit purposes were permitted to be undermined. For all of these reasons, it is unlikely that the Supreme Court would permit such a judgment not to be enforced. Nonetheless, it is of course true that the Court could adopt such a tack, which is yet another respect in which issues surrounding same-sex partners and their children put constitutional interpretation at a crossroads.

DOMA AND DECLARATORY JUDGMENTS

The Federal Defense of Marriage Act has yet to be construed by the United States Supreme Court, and so it is somewhat difficult to say what the Act permits states to do. If the Act merely permits the domicile at the time of the celebration of the same-sex marriage or marriage-like relationship to refuse to (1) recognize that relationship, notwithstanding its having been validly celebrated in another state, and (2) give effect to any rights or benefits arising from such a relationship, then DOMA would *not* permit a state to refuse to enforce a declaratory judgment recognizing the parental rights of a civil union partner domiciled in Vermont, even if the recognition of such parental status violated a strong public policy of the forum state.

Suppose that DOMA is given the broadest interpretation possible and that the Act's constitutionality is upheld. In that event, the Full Faith and

Credit Clause would not require other states to enforce a declaratory judgment recognizing the parental rights of a same-sex partner if those rights arose by virtue of the existence of a civil union. However, even if DOMA is given a very broad interpretation, DOMA does not permit states to ignore the judgments issued in other state courts where the rights thereby recognized do not arise from the legal recognition of a same-sex relationship. Thus, DOMA does not say that *any* rights afforded to same-sex couples need not be recognized in other jurisdictions but merely that any rights afforded to same-sex couples by virtue of their having contracted a same-sex marriage or marriage-like relationship need not be enforced.

The difference pointed to here is important because rights acquired by virtue of a second-parent adoption do not fall within the exception created by DOMA. Since same-sex couples who have not entered into a civil union can nonetheless take advantage of the second-parent adoption provision and become the legal parents of the same child, such a judgment would be subject to full faith and credit guarantees, assuming that the Court does not radically rework the full faith and credit framework.

It might be suggested that any state that permits second-parent adoptions would recognize the parental status of a civil union partner. That issue will not be addressed here, since it would be beside the point even were it true. Here, the point is that second-parent adoptions can be granted to individuals who are not part of a civil union or same-sex marriage. The DOMA exception to the Full Faith and Credit Clause, namely, that rights or claims *arising out of* the legal recognition of same-sex marriage or marriage-like relationships are not subject to full faith and credit guarantees, will not have been triggered by a second-parent adoption, and such adoptions would still have to be accorded full faith and credit.

Consider a recent statute passed in Mississippi that precludes the recognition of adoptions by same-sex couples.[21] Mississippi did not limit its statutory exclusion to those adoptions that might arise by virtue of a same-sex marriage or marriage-like relationship but instead has declared that it simply will not recognize such adoptions. The Full Faith and Credit Clause does not permit states to treat the final judgments of sister states in such a cavalier fashion, and a judgment establishing that two same-sex partners were parents of the same child would be subject to full faith and credit guarantees, Mississippi public policy notwithstanding.

CONCLUSION

Vermont's creation of civil union status offers same-sex couples a variety of benefits including the right to be presumed the parent of a child born into the relationship. Such a presumption helps establish the parental rights of civil union partners without forcing them to have those parental rights recognized by a court.

This presumption has other implications as well. An individual who seeks to establish his or her parental status will be able to employ that presumption to his or her advantage when, for example, the biological parent contests those rights. Such a presumption might also be helpful if both members of the couple wished to establish the partner's parental rights, although it is not clear that Vermont rules regarding the issuance of declaratory judgments would permit such a judgment to be issued in that kind of case.

The Federal Defense of Marriage Act requires explication. If it merely permits the domicile at the time of the same-sex marriage or marriage-like relationship to refuse to recognize that union and in addition to refuse to recognize any rights or benefits arising from that relationship, then states that had not been the parties' domicile at the time of the marriage will not be able to make use of DOMA to refuse to recognize such relationships or any rights arising out of such relationships, as long as the domicile at the time of the marriage recognized the union.

A separate question is whether states (with or without DOMA) have the right to refuse to recognize marriages validly celebrated in sister domiciliary states or rights arising from such marriages. This ultimately will have to be decided by the United States Supreme Court, although there are reasons to think that the United States Constitution imposes limits on the ability of states to refuse to recognize such relationships. Even were the Court to make clear that a marriage recognized by a domiciliary state at the time of the marriage must be recognized by all of the states, however, that would not establish that civil unions would have to be recognized by all of the states, since Vermont law makes quite clear that civil unions are not marriages.

The Supreme Court has made clear that the Full Faith and Credit Clause does not include a public policy exception when the final judgments of other state courts are at issue, as long as those courts had jurisdiction to issue the judgment in question. It is unclear whether DOMA intended to modify that constitutional guarantee and, if so, whether the Constitution permits Congress to make such a modification.

If DOMA did create an exception to the general rules regarding full faith and credit to judgments and if that exception passes constitutional muster, then same-sex couples whose rights are predicated on the legal recognition of their relationship are at risk when they travel in other states if those latter states have manifested their intention to take full advantage of the exception afforded by DOMA. DOMA does not permit states to refuse to recognize all rights of same-sex couples, however, and thus couples can protect themselves and their children by having their parental rights established in a way that does not require the existence of a marriage-like relationship.

That couples may be forced to expend time, energy, and resources by availing themselves of the second-parent adoption option just to protect their own interests and the interests of their children helps illustrate the invidiousness of DOMA and of state mini-DOMA statutes. For most people, the legal recognition of a marriage-like relationship offers protection to their families. For same-sex couples, such recognition can have the opposite effect and make their families more vulnerable.

Perhaps the counter-intuitive result that legal recognition of a marriage-like relationship may make the families more rather than less vulnerable will help convince the Court that it "is not within our constitutional tradition to enact [or permit] laws of this sort."[22] Until that time, however, Vermont same-sex couples who are members of civil unions should at least consider some of the risks entailed in moving to or traveling though other states. They may find that their availing themselves of the second-parent adoption option before venturing out would be a wise investment for their own sakes and, even more importantly, for the sake of their children, notwithstanding that a country or state really committed to "family values" would never force families to expend possibly scarce resources to protect something so basic as the right to remain a family.

NOTES

1. *U.S. v. Rumely*, 345 U.S. 41, 45 (1953).
2. See Arizona Revised Statutes § 25–101 (a) ("Marriage between parents and children, including grandparents and grandchildren of every degree, between brothers and sisters of the one-half as well as the whole blood, and between uncles and nieces, aunts and nephews and between first cousins, is prohibited and void.") and Arizona Revised Statutes § 25–112 (A) ("Marriages valid by the laws of the place where contracted are valid in this state, except marriages that are void and prohibited by S 25–101."); 13 Delaware Code § 101 (a) ("A marriage is prohibited and void between a person and his or her ancestor, descendant, brother, sister, uncle, aunt, niece, nephew, first cousin or between persons of the same gender.") & 13 Delaware Code § 101 (d) ("A marriage obtained or recognized outside the State between persons prohibited by subsection (a) of this section shall not constitute a legal or valid marriage within the State.")
3. See *Godin v. Godin*, 725 A.2d 904, 909 (Vt. 1998).
4. Vermont Statutes Annotated § 4711.
5. *N.A.H. v. S.L.S.*, 9 P.3d 354, 359 (Col. 2000).
6. *Price v. Rowell*, 159 A.2d 622, 626 (Vt. 1960).
7. *Id.*
8. A Vermont Statutes Annotated § 1–102 (b) ("If a family unit consists of a parent and the parent's partner, and adoption is in the best interest of the child, the partner of a parent may adopt a child of the parent. Termination of the parent's parental rights is unnecessary in an adoption under this subsection.")
9. See *id.*
10. See *Titchenal v. Dexter*, 693 A.2d 682 (Vt. 1997) (same-sex partner who had

not adopted her partner's child did not have the status of legal parent of that child).

11. United States Constitution art. IV, § 1.

12. See *Baker v. General Motors Corp.*, 522 U.S. 222, 232 (1998) ("Our precedent differentiates the credit owed to laws (legislative measures and common law) and to judgments.")

13. *Id.* at 223 ("As to judgments, the full faith and credit obligation is exacting. A final judgment in one State, if rendered by a court with adjudicatory authority over the subject matter and persons governed by the judgment, qualifies for recognition throughout the land.")

14. See *id.* at 233 ("A court may be guided by the forum State's public policy in determining the *law* applicable to a controversy.")

15. See *Thompson v. Thompson*, 484 U.S. 174, 180 (1988).

16. The Parental Kidnapping Prevention Act (PKPA), Public Laws 96–611, was passed precisely because states otherwise could modify the custody decisions issued in other states.

17. *Estin v. Estin*, 334 U.S. 541, 546 (1948).

18. *Union National Bank v. Lamb*, 337 U.S. 38, 43 (1949).

19. See 12 Vermont Statutes Annotated § 4711.

20. See *Baker*, 522 U.S. at 233.

21. See Mississippi Code 1972 93–17–3 §1 (2) ("Any adoption by couples of the same gender that is valid in another jurisdiction does not constitute a legal or valid adoption in Mississippi.")

22. See *Romer v. Evans*, 517 U.S. 620, 633 (1996).

Chapter Four

The Right to Travel

A theme running through the past two chapters is that any analysis of the legal recognition of same-sex relationships must include a consideration of how those relationships and the rights and obligations arising therefrom will be treated in other states. Ours is an increasingly mobile society, and individuals must consider what may happen when they move to or travel through another state.

Another reason that it is important to consider interstate travel is that the United States Constitution protects the right to migrate to and travel through other states. This protection places limitations on both Congress and the states with respect to the kinds of burdens that they can impose on United States citizens and may be especially important in the context under discussion here.

The Constitution expressly protects citizens' privileges and immunities. Some courts and commentators suggest that privileges and immunities protections are best understood as prohibiting discrimination against nonresidents, whereas others claim that much more is involved. Courts and commentators agree, however, that the privileges and immunities protections include, at the very least, the right to travel.

In *Saenz v. Roe*, the United States Supreme Court recently affirmed the right of individuals to migrate to new states without fear that they will be discriminated against for doing so. The Court so held, notwithstanding Congress's having authorized the discriminatory treatment at issue. *Saenz* not only suggests that the Constitution still offers robust protections for the right to travel but also that the Constitution prohibits Congress from authorizing states to impose undue burdens on that right. The Court's recent holding is likely to have important implications, not the least of which are that it provides (1) yet another basis upon which the Defense of Marriage Act should and will be held unconstitutional, and (2) a basis upon which the Court should strike down state statutes precluding recognition of same-sex marriages that were valid in the states of celebration and domicile at the time of the marriage.

PRIVILEGES AND IMMUNITIES

The United States Constitution has two separate clauses that protect the privileges and immunities of United States citizens, one contained in Article IV and the other contained in the Fourteenth Amendment. Many courts and commentators have suggested that the latter protects more than the former, although much debate exists about how much protection each offers and about whether these clauses should merely be understood to provide protection from nondiscrimination or, in addition, protection of substantive rights. Though the Supreme Court has interpreted privileges and immunities protections to provide relatively few substantive guarantees, the articulated jurisprudence nonetheless suggests that those guarantees may be more robust than is commonly appreciated.

THE TWO CLAUSES

Section 2 of Article IV of the United States Constitution reads in relevant part: "The Citizens of each State shall be entitled to all Privileges and Immunities of Citizens in the several States." Section 1 of the Fourteenth Amendment of the United States Constitution reads in relevant part: "No State shall make or enforce any law which shall abridge the privileges or immunities of citizens of the United States." Some commentators distinguish between the two clauses by calling the former the "Privileges and Immunities Clause" and the latter the "Privileges or Immunities Clause," whereas others distinguish between them by calling the former the "Comity Clause" and the latter the "Privileges or Immunities Clause."

On first reading, one might infer that the two clauses protect the same rights, the former making a positive assertion—citizens are entitled to certain privileges and immunities—and the latter making a negative assertion—no state shall make a law abridging privileges or immunities. The latter clause would be using "or" rather than "and" to prevent a state from abridging privileges but not immunities, or vice versa. Thus, had the latter clause used "or," a state would not have violated the clause by passing a law that abridged privileges but not immunities, since the law would not then have abridged the privileges and immunities of United States citizens.

If the only difference between the two clauses is a matter of form (one making a positive assertion about the content of an entitlement and the other making a negative assertion concerning what states are prohibited from doing) and if the clauses basically are describing the same guarantees of citizenship, then it would seem that one of the clauses is superfluous. One of the canons of constitutional interpretation, however, is that, if possible, all of the words in the Constitution will be given effect. Presumably, then, the two clauses differ in an important substantive way, and the Fourteenth Amendment Privileges or Immunities Clause does not simply and solely protect that which is already protected by the Article IV Privileges and Immunities Clause.

One possible way to differentiate between the two clauses involves distinguishing between the entities whose powers are being limited. Consider Sections 9 and 10 of Article I of the United States Constitution. Section 9 reads, "No bill of Attainder or ex post facto Law shall be passed," whereas Section 10 reads, "No State shall . . . pass any Bill of Attainder [or] ex post facto Law." Section 9 has been interpreted to limit congressional power, whereas Section 10 has been interpreted to limit state power. It might be thought that the difference between the Comity Clause and the Privileges or Immunities Clause involves the identity of the entity whose powers are being limited. On this view, Section 2 of Article IV would be read to limit the power of Congress, whereas Section 1 of the Fourteenth Amendment would be read as a limitation on the power of the states. An interpretation of the Comity Clause as limiting federal power, however, has been rejected by the Court; indeed, the Court has described Article IV as the "States' Relations Article"[1] and thus this way of differentiating between the two clauses does not seem plausible.

WHAT DOES THE COMITY CLAUSE PROTECT?

The proper interpretation of the Comity Clause is controversial in at least two respects. Courts and commentators disagree both about whether that clause protects any substantive rights and about how much equality protection it offers, for example, under what conditions, if any, are states constitutionally permitted to favor their own citizens? Courts and commentators also disagree about when the clause is implicated: whether it applies when individuals who are citizens in one state wish to become citizens of a different state or only when a citizen of one state temporarily visits another state.

In *Corfield v. Coryell*, Justice Washington suggested that "the privileges and immunities of citizens in the several states . . . [are] those privileges and immunities which are, in their nature, fundamental; which belong, of right, to the citizens of all free governments."[2] Believing them somewhat tedious to enumerate, he suggested that they included the "right of a citizen of one state to pass through, or to reside in any other state, for purposes of trade, agriculture, professional pursuits, or otherwise."[3]

Justice Washington thereby suggested that the Comity Clause protected, among other things, the right to travel, which includes both the right to pass through a state and the right to establish residence in any state.

Not all justices agree with that interpretation of the Comity Clause's travel protections, however, since some claim that the Comity Clause precludes states from discriminating against out-of-state visitors but does not preclude states from discriminating against individuals who plan on remaining within the state. For example, Chief Justice Rehnquist recently suggested in his *Saenz v. Roe* dissent that the Privileges and Immunities Clause only applies to individuals who plan on returning to their home states, not those who are attempting to migrate to a new state.[4]

Two issues must be distinguished: whether there is a fundamental right to establish residence in a new state and whether that right is protected by the Comity Clause. Justice O'Connor has suggested that it is difficult to imagine a right more essential to the Nation as a whole than the right of individuals to establish residence in a new State.[5] Because the primary purpose of the Comity Clause was to make a collection of independent, sovereign states into one nation, it would make sense to locate the right to establish a new residence in the Comity Clause. Nonetheless, different courts have located the source of that right in different parts of the Constitution. Thus, it may be that the Fourteenth Amendment precludes certain kinds of discrimination that the Comity Clause does not and that the right to move to a new state is based upon Fourteenth Amendment protections.

The Supreme Court has suggested that the purpose of the Comity Clause is "to require each state to accord equality of treatment to the citizens of other states in respect of the privileges and immunities of state citizenship."[6] If equality of treatment of nonresidents is the sole purpose of the clause, then the Court's indication that the Comity Clause "was designed to insure to a citizen of State A who ventures into State B the same privileges which the citizens of State B enjoy"[7] should only be understood to mean that a citizen of State A visiting State B will be entitled to the privileges that State B citizens have. It would not mean, for example, that new citizens of B (who perhaps were former citizens of A) would be entitled to all of the privileges that the long-time citizens of B enjoyed. Nor would it mean that the Comity Clause would preclude B from trying to deter citizens of other states from becoming citizens of B. Rather, because the Comity Clause would merely be viewed as an antidiscrimination clause precluding B from discriminating against nonresidents by according its own citizens certain rights without also according those rights to citizens of other states, B could deny a particular right to citizens of other states as long as that right was also denied to its own citizens.

For purposes here, it is unnecessary to decide whether it is the Comity Clause, the Fourteenth Amendment, or some other clause of the Constitution that offers protections for new citizens. Even if one assumes that some other part of the Constitution rather than the Comity Clause protects those rights and thus that Comity Clause jurisprudence does not require a discussion of which, if any, distinctions between new and old citizens are constitutionally permissible, that jurisprudence still needs further explication, since the Comity Clause protections for the citizen of one state who visits another state need clarification.

It is generally agreed that the Comity Clause protects equality rights so that states will be precluded from giving certain advantages to their own citizens. It would be an exaggeration, however, to claim that the Comity Clause precludes states from making any distinctions between citizens and non-citizens. For example, a state may accord certain hunting privileges to its citizens that it does not also accord to noncitizens. The Court has denied that states are prohibited from considering citizenship or residency when making distinctions, recognizing that the United States is composed of individual states and that distinctions based on residency are at least sometimes permissible.

If some distinctions on the basis of citizenship are permissible and some are not, it is important to establish which are which. The Court has suggested that "[o]nly with respect to those 'privileges' and 'immunities' bearing upon the vitality of the Nation as a single entity must the State treat all citizens, resident and nonresident, equally."[8] The Court thereby suggested that privileges and immunities protections are triggered only when certain interests are implicated. To determine whether in fact those protections are implicated, the Court will examine the privilege at issue, for example, whether hunting is merely recreational or instead involves the person's livelihood. Assuming that the privilege is sufficiently important, the Court will decide whether the distinction offends constitutional guarantees in light of the state's reasons for sanctioning the discrimination.

The relevant question for privileges and immunities purposes is not whether the activity itself involves a fundamental right but whether the activity at issue is sufficiently basic to the livelihood of the nation to be one of the fundamental privileges of citizenship and thus to implicate the clause. If the activity does not meet that standard, then the state may make distinctions between its own citizens and other citizens with respect to that activity without offending the Constitution, assuming that no other constitutional guarantees are violated.

Suppose, however, that the activity is sufficiently fundamental to the promotion of interstate harmony as to implicate the Privileges and Immunities Clause. In that event, the Court will closely scrutinize the statute at issue and will invalidate the restriction on noncitizens unless it is closely related to the advancement of a substantial state interest. For example, in *Memorial Hospital v. Maricopa County*, the Court struck down Arizona's durational residence requirement for free, nonemergency medical care, notwithstanding the appellant's not having a fundamental constitutional right to that care. In *Supreme Court v. Piper*, the Court noted that discrimination against nonresidents may be permissible if "there is a substantial reason for the difference in treatment [and] the discrimination . . . bears a substantial relationship to [that] objective."[9] Thus, two distinct issues emerge if a right is deemed fundamental to national citizenship: (1) whether a legitimate and substantial objective is offered to justify the discrimination, and (2) whether discriminating between residents and nonresidents is substantially related to the articulated objective.

The "legitimate" objective allegedly justifying discrimination against nonresidents cannot simply be the state's preference to benefit its own citizens. Something more must be offered. Further, some interests that are legitimate and independent of the discrimination itself may nonetheless not suffice to justify discrimination against nonresidents. For example, the *Memorial Hospital* Court noted that neither the claim that discriminating against out-of-staters would save tax dollars nor the claim that such discrimination would make a program more politically viable would suffice as a justification for severely burdening the right to migrate to a new state.[10] Thus, discrimination against nonresidents cannot be justified merely by claiming (even quite plausibly) that the electorate approves of the discrimination or that the electorate would strongly prefer not to accord nonresidents a particular important benefit because, for example, lower taxes would result.

Even if the state offers a sufficiently important state interest to justify its discrimination against nonresidents, the statute still might not survive privileges and immunities scrutiny. The means chosen will also be examined in light of those guarantees. Because the purpose of the clause is to preclude classifications based on the fact of noncitizenship unless "noncitizens constitute a peculiar source of the evil at which the statute is aimed,"[11] the Court requires that the discriminatory legislation bear a close relation to the interests articulated by the state.

To determine whether the connection between the discrimination and the state objectives is sufficiently close, the Court will consider whether there were other ways of achieving those state objectives without discriminating against nonresidents. If indeed the state might have achieved its asserted objectives relatively easily without discriminating against nonresidents at the same time, the Court will likely strike down the statute as offending privileges and immunities guarantees.

When deciding whether Arizona's durational residence requirement violated privileges and immunities protections, the *Memorial Hospital* Court not only examined the asserted state interest but also the nature of the connection between the law at issue and the promotion of that interest. While admitting that the prevention of fraud was a worthy state goal, the Court nonetheless concluded that the statute at issue was ill suited to promote that goal. Because the discriminatory statute did not bear a sufficiently close relation to the asserted state objective, the Court struck down the state's exclusionary policy.

THE FOURTEENTH AMENDMENT'S PRIVILEGES OR IMMUNITIES CLAUSE

Many of those interpreting the Comity Clause as guaranteeing only equality rights have nonetheless interpreted the Fourteenth Amendment's Privileges or Immunities Clause as protecting substantive rights, although which substantive rights the Fourteenth Amendment is supposed to protect remains contested. Some who advocate a more expansive reading have suggested that the clause was meant to protect some of the rights protected by the Bill of Rights, whereas others have been even more expansive when describing the rights that the clause was meant to protect.

In *The Slaughter-House Cases*, the Court offered a very short list of rights covered by the Privileges or Immunities Clause. Some commentators have suggested that the *Slaughter-House* Court was unduly restrictive, whereas others have cautioned that an expansive reading of the privileges and immunities protected by national citizenship would be difficult to contain. Yet, even if the Court refuses to expand privileges and immunities protections beyond those that have already been recognized, the current guarantees are sufficiently robust to invalidate some recently enacted statutes.

Even the *Slaughter-House* Court recognized that one of the privileges protected by the Fourteenth Amendment was that a citizen of the United States could become a citizen of any state and thereby acquire the same rights as other citizens of that State had.[12] In *Ward v. Maryland*, the Court explained that privileges and immunities include:

the right of a citizen of one State to pass into any other State of the Union for the purpose of engaging in lawful commerce, trade, or business without molestation; to acquire personal property; to take and hold real estate; to maintain actions in the courts of the State; and to be exempt from any higher taxes or excises than are imposed by the State upon its own citizens.[13]

When the *Colgate* Court did not attempt to define or enumerate the privileges and immunities protected by the Fourteenth Amendment, the Court made clear that the right to pass freely from one State to another was clearly among those privileges.[14] The Court was not thereby suggesting, however, that the right to travel was expressly mentioned in the amendment. Indeed, as the Court pointed out in *United States v. Guest*, notwithstanding that the right to travel from one State to another is a right that has been firmly established and repeatedly recognized, it nonetheless is not explicitly mentioned anywhere in the Constitution.[15]

Though the right to travel is fundamental, the Court has not suggested that anything that might impinge on the right to travel, no matter how minor, will somehow violate privileges and immunities protections. An element of the Court's privileges and immunities analysis involves an examination of how severely the statute at issue will curtail that right. For example, states are allowed to make some distinctions between residents and nonresidents in the provision of tax benefits,[16] notwithstanding that this distinction might be viewed as discrimination against nonresidents and thus as affecting the right to travel.

WHY PROTECT THE RIGHT TO TRAVEL?

The Court has discussed in numerous decisions why protecting the right to travel is important. In *Attorney General v. Soto-Lopez*, the Court discussed "the unquestioned historic acceptance of the principle of free interstate migration, and of the important role that principle has played in transforming many States into a single Nation."[17] Describing the Comity Clause, the Court in *Paul v. Virginia* stated that "no provision in the Constitution has tended so strongly to constitute the citizens of the United States one people as this."[18] The Court further suggested that absent a constitutional provision that afforded equality between citizens of different states, "the Republic would have constituted little more than a league of States; it would not have constituted the Union which now exists."[19] The *Colgate* Court explained that as "citizens of the United States we are members of a single great community consisting of all the states united and not of distinct communities consisting of the states severally."[20] As Justice Harlan noted, "the right to unimpeded interstate travel, regarded as a privilege and immunity of national citizenship, was historically seen as a method of breaking down state provincialism, and facilitating the creation of a true federal union."[21]

Precisely because great benefits can accrue from having a single nation rather than a mere collection of separate, autonomous sovereignties, states may be precluded from effecting particular classifications in the interests of interstate harmony. To become part of a country rather than remain a member of a federation of separate nations, each state had to surrender some of its sovereignty for the sake of the whole. As the Court has explained, "local policy must at times be required to give way ... [as] 'part of the price of our federal system.'"[22] Precluding states from discriminating against citizens of other states contributes to making the citizens of the United States one people.

A statute may implicate the right to travel when it actually deters travel, when deterring travel is its primary goal, or when it serves to penalize the exercise of the right to travel. In *Crandall v. Nevada*, the Court held that a state that levies a tax upon residents who wish to leave or on individuals who wish to travel through the state, unduly burdens the right of travel and is unconstitutional, even if the tax is only one dollar. Further, as Justice Douglas explained, "[i]f a state tax on that movement, as in the *Crandall* case, is invalid, a fortiori a state statute which obstructs or in substance prevents that movement must fall."[23] Thus, the Court has been willing to strike down seemingly permissible legislation (e.g., a one-dollar tax) if that legislation could potentially impose a significant burden on interstate travel.

In *Saenz v. Roe,* the Court struck down a California statute limiting the maximum welfare benefits that would be payable to a family residing in the state for less than twelve months to the amount that they would have received in the state where they had previously resided.[24] The statute was declared unconstitutional because it would have a chilling effect on interstate migration and because privileges and immunities protections include the right to equal treatment in a citizen's new state of residence. In effect, the statute penalized the exercise of an individual's right to migrate to a new state. The *Saenz* holding was important not only because it reaffirmed that the right to travel includes the right to migrate but also because the Court struck down the statute, notwithstanding its prior congressional authorization. The Court noted that although congressional decisions and classifications will be given some deference, "neither Congress nor a State can validate a law that denies the rights guaranteed by the Fourteenth Amendment."[25]

The right at issue in *Saenz* was not whether everyone in the country had a right to have his or her own state accord the level of benefits that California affords its citizens. Rather, the right was simply the right to be treated equally—the right not to be discriminated against with respect to an interest that was sufficiently important that its denial might significantly chill the exercise of the right to travel.

Welfare and medical benefits are not the only benefits sufficiently important to trigger privileges and immunities guarantees, since the denial of other benefits will also significantly chill the exercise of the right to travel. Consider the interests that a couple has in the continued recognition of their marriage, which had been validly celebrated in their previous domicile. This interest would seem sufficiently important to trigger the relevant protections. Indeed, were the discussion here about different-sex marriages valid in the states of celebration and domicile at the time of the marriage, there would be no question for most people that such marriages should be recognized in all of the states. Yet, it is not at all clear what principled reason could be offered to establish why it would be tolerable for same-sex couples to have their valid marriages treated as void by other states but intolerable for different-sex couples to be accorded that same treatment. Indeed, precisely because there seems to be no principled basis for such differential treatment, states will either be (1) prohibited from refusing to recognize marriages valid in the previous domiciliary state, or (2) allowed to refuse to recognize both different and same-sex unions valid in the previous domicile.

MARRIAGE AND THE RIGHT TO TRAVEL

Over the past several years, various states have passed legislation making marriages between same-sex partners void and have passed legislation making clear that the state will not recognize such marriages even if they are validly celebrated in a different state. The Court's recent decision in *Saenz v. Roe* suggests that several of these statutes may violate the constitutionally protected right to travel.

The argument here is not predicated on a recognition that the Due Process or Equal Protection Clauses protect the right of same-sex couples to marry. In other words, the argument is not that because all states must recognize the right of their own citizens to marry a same-sex partner, states must recognize the right of citizens of other states to marry. Rather, the argument is that even if states are constitutionally permitted to prohibit their own domiciliaries from celebrating a same-sex marriage, they are precluded from refusing to recognize such a union if it was valid in the states of domicile and celebration at the time of the marriage. Because permitting states to refuse to recognize such unions would significantly chill the right to travel, the privileges and immunities guarantees of the Federal Constitution preclude the states from passing or enforcing legislation to that effect.

CHOICE OF LAW IN THE CONTEXT OF MARRIAGE

Traditionally, a marriage that is recognized in the states of celebration and domicile at the time of the marriage will be recognized in all of the states. It does not matter that other states might prohibit the marriage; the validity of the marriage turns on the law of the state where the couple is domiciled and on the law of the state where the ceremony is performed. If the marriage violates an important public policy of the domiciliary state at the time the marriage is contracted, then the union will be invalid even if it is permitted by the state of celebration. If the marriage does not violate an important public policy of the domicile at the time the ceremony takes place, then the marriage will be valid in all of the states if it was valid in the state where it was celebrated.

Suppose that Lynn and Kim, who reside in State A, wish to marry. Because State A permits their marrying, it does not matter that State B does not. Lynn and Kim will have a valid marriage when they marry in A. Suppose further that a few years after Lynn and Kim have married, they move to B to take advantage of some business opportunity. It does not matter that B prohibits its domiciliaries from contracting such marriages. Because the marriage of Lynn and Kim was valid in the state of celebration and domicile at the time of the marriage, B (if subscribing to either the *First* or the *Second Restatement of the Conflict of Laws*) will recognize the marriage of Lynn and Kim as valid.

Consider a different example. Robin and Leslie, who live in B, wish to marry. B, however, prohibits their marrying. Although the couple might go to A to marry (assuming that A permits them to marry), B (the domicile) might nonetheless refuse to recognize the marriage validly celebrated in A if that marriage violates an important public policy of B. Thus, the marriage of A's (former) domiciliaries might be recognized in B whereas the marriage of B's domiciliaries would not be, even though both couples had married in A in accord with local law and now live in B.

It might seem unfair that the marriage of Lynn and Kim would have to be recognized by B but that the marriage of Robin and Leslie would not. There is an important difference between the two couples, however. Lynn and Kim had every reason to believe that their marriage was valid, since it was recognized by the state of celebration and domicile at the time of their marriage. (In this example, A was both the state of celebration and the state of domicile at the time of the marriage.) The couple could make plans based on the good faith belief and reasonable expectation that their marriage was and would be considered valid. After all, they were planning on remaining in their domicile, which had recognized the marriage. In contrast, Leslie and Robin knew that their domicile (B) refused to recognize their marriage, which was why they attempted to evade local law by going to A in the first place. Because they were on notice at the time of their marriage that their domicile prohibited such unions, they would not have similar good faith beliefs and reasonable expectations concerning the validity of their marriage. Because the two couples are dissimilar in this important respect, it might be quite fair to recognize the one marriage while not recognizing the other. Of course, it may well be that both marriages should be recognized, either as a matter of individual rights or as a matter of good public policy, but that is a separate point. The couple marrying in accord with the laws of the states of celebration and domicile at the time of the marriage would have justifiable and reasonable beliefs about the validity of their marriage, whereas the couple evading the domicile's law would be on notice that their domicile at the time of the marriage might not recognize the union even if it was validly celebrated elsewhere.

PAST ANALYSES OF PRIVILEGES AND IMMUNITIES MARRIAGE PROTECTIONS

Several courts have addressed whether the privileges and immunities guarantees affect the right of a state to refuse to recognize a marriage of one of its current domiciliaries. When courts have examined whether privileges and immunities guarantees affected which marriages had to be recognized by the states, the courts did not consider whether states had to recognize same-sex marriages but instead considered whether states had to recognize interracial marriages. Many of these courts believed that the United States Constitution simply did not address state regulations of marriage. For example, in *Ex parte Kinney,* the court suggested that the United States Constitution placed no constraints on the state's power to determine the marital status of her own citizens[26] and that the state had the same power to determine the marital status of her citizens as she would have had were she a separate country.[27]

Other courts have also claimed that the Fourteenth Amendment did not limit the right of states to create the marriage statutes that they deemed appropriate as long as those regulations did not deny to citizens the equal protection of the laws.[28] These courts denied that interracial bans violated the Fourteenth Amendment,[29] a position that was not repudiated by the United States Supreme Court until 1967.

Two issues, however, should not be conflated: (1) whether a state can set the marriage laws for its own domiciliaries, and (2) whether marriages validly celebrated in other domiciles must be recognized. Most of the courts that addressed whether privileges and immunities guarantees limited the right of a state to establish its own marital laws discussed whether those protections affected the state's right to determine the conditions under which its own domiciliaries might marry. Yet, privileges and immunities protections might well be construed as affecting the second issue. Even the *Kinney* court recognized that allowing a state to determine the marital status of its own domiciliaries would not entitle it to refuse to recognize a marriage validly celebrated in another domiciliary state.

Although recognizing that a state's power to determine the conditions under which its own domiciliaries would marry did not entail a power to refuse to recognize marriages validly celebrated in other states, the *Kinney* court nonetheless concluded that states had the latter power as well. The *Kinney* court reasoned that privileges and immunities protections would not apply to a couple validly married elsewhere who had moved to Virginia, because the state's powers to control the marital status extended to all citizens of the state. Thus, the court explained, "[E]ven if this petitioner had been a citizen of another state, lawfully married there, and had come here bringing his wife, intending to live here in a condition of matrimony forbidden by our laws, he could not claim the protection of the national constitution, or of any law of Congress in thus violating our laws."[30] After all, the *Kinney* court believed that the state's power over the marital relation of its own citizens was no more limited than the power of any sovereign nation over the marital status of its own citizens. The court suggested that each state was only subject to its own laws regarding which of its domiciliaries' marriages had to be recognized and that marriages validly celebrated in other domiciliary states could be recognized by Virginia as a matter of comity but would not have to be recognized as a matter of federal constitutional obligation.

Ironically, the *Kinney* court did recognize that the privileges and immunities guarantees would preclude a state's refusal to recognize a marriage contravening local policy if an individual was still a citizen of a different state and was not seeking to change his or her state citizenship. Thus, because the privileges and immunities protections did not extend to those who were attempting to become citizens of a new state, the new state would be free to refuse to recognize the marriages of those citizens. Where privileges and immunities guarantees were applicable, however, for example, when a citizen of another state was merely visiting, the state had to recognize the marriage that was valid in the other state.

The *Saenz* Court reaffirmed that privileges and immunities protections are implicated when a citizen seeks to establish residence in a new state in addition to when that citizen merely visits a new state. Given the *Kinney* court's recognition that privileges and immunities protections preclude a state from refusing to recognize a marriage validly celebrated in another domiciliary state and the *Saenz* Court's recognition that privileges and immunities protections also apply to those attempting to migrate to a new state, it seems that even the *Kinney* court would have to admit that states are required by privileges and immunities guarantees to recognize a marriage validly celebrated in another domiciliary state.

MARRIAGE AND THE RIGHT TO TRAVEL

A number of different arguments might be made with respect to the implications of the right to travel for the right to marry. Consider how John Harrison analyzed privileges and immunities protections for the right to marry someone of a different race:

Under a ban on interracial marriage, the rights of individuals of different races are not the same under all descriptions, because blacks can marry blacks and whites cannot, even though all are prevented from marrying members of the other race. But if the rights are different under any description, they are not the same. No rule that requires reference to a citizen's race in order to know that citizen's rights, therefore, will give citizens of all colors the same rights.[31]

Professor Harrison essentially suggests that privileges and immunities protections preclude states from passing or enforcing interracial marriage bans, protestations of some of those voting on the amendment to the contrary notwithstanding, because individuals would then be precluded from marrying other individuals on the basis of a forbidden classification. He thus suggests that the right to marry a partner of another race is a privilege of national citizenship.

Harrison also suggests that a plausible reading of the privileges and immunities protections precludes states from constructing marriage laws that discriminate on the basis of sex.[32] Yet, if that is so, then it would seem that a ban on same-sex marriage would be similarly unacceptable. The current rights of individuals of different sexes are not the same under all descriptions, because women can marry men and men cannot (and men can marry women and women cannot), even though all are prevented from marrying members of the same sex. Thus, by parity of reasoning, it seems that privileges and immunities protections preclude any state from banning marriages on the basis of the forbidden classification of sex, and the Privileges or Immunities Clause precludes *all* states from banning same-sex marriages.

Perhaps it would seem that the right to travel does not prohibit a state from refusing to recognize one's marriage, since such a refusal does not preclude one from moving to that state but merely forces one to pay a price for one's new citizenship. Yet, this interpretation is a misreading of the Court's privileges and immunities jurisprudence. The Court has already explicitly rejected the contention that the "Privileges and Immunities Clause does not reach a State's discrimination against nonresidents when such discrimination does not result in their total exclusion from the State."[33]

In *Shapiro v. Thompson*, the Court invalidated a welfare scheme that would have prevented new residents from receiving welfare aid. Such a scheme would not have prevented individuals from migrating to the state, although these individuals might have been forced to pay a heavy price for migrating there. The Court recognized that a one-year waiting period was well suited to discouraging the influx of families needing assistance but held that such a purpose was constitutionally impermissible.[34] The Court thus invalidated a law that did not preclude individuals from moving to the state, but only discouraged that migration. Further, that legislative classification was unconstitutional, notwithstanding the Court's recognition that the legislation was motivated by the state's valid interest in preserving the fiscal integrity of its programs.[35]

The *Saenz* Court invalidated a scheme that would not have precluded migration to the state and would not have cut off benefits entirely for new residents but would have merely limited those benefits to those that the individuals might have received in the previous state. The Court rejected the claim that because California did not entirely deprive new arrivals of benefits, the case was distinguishable from *Shapiro* and invalidated the measure as an unconstitutional violation of the fundamental right to travel.

In *Dunn v. Blumstein,* the Court struck down a Tennessee statute which precluded individuals from voting until they had resided in the state for one year. Although the statute did not entirely preclude migration to Tennessee, the Court noted, "Travel is permitted, but only at a price; voting is prohibited. The right to travel is merely penalized, while the right to vote is absolutely denied."[36] That voting requirement (one-year residence) meant that one's right to vote would have been absolutely denied until one had been a resident for one year.

The Court has made clear that a temporary deprivation of very important benefits and rights can penalize migration and offend privileges and immunities guarantees.[37] Yet, if temporary deprivations implicate the privileges and immunities protections, permanent ones should do so as well. Thus, if the one-year waiting requirement were unconstitutional, it also would have been unconstitutional for Tennessee to declare that new residents could never vote in the state.

Suppose that a state passed a law mandating that same-sex couples with marriages valid in their domiciles at the time of celebration would have to wait a year before their marriages would be recognized. This temporary deprivation would *seem* to violate privileges and immunities guarantees, although that is not clear because of a different Supreme Court case.

In *Sosna v. Iowa,* the Supreme Court rejected a privileges and immunities challenge to Iowa's one-year residency requirement for divorce.[38] By permitting the state to impose such a restriction on divorce, the Court was thereby permitting the state to delay the exercise of the fundamental right to marry, and thus it might seem that a state could delay recognition of a marriage validly celebrated in another domicile.

Yet, there are several reasons to believe that *Sosna* does not permit states to pass such laws. First, the state would have to offer a reason to justify its policy of delaying recognition, and it is difficult to imagine what rationale would be offered to justify delaying recognition of that particular subset of validly celebrated marriages. One of the factors considered important by the *Sosna* Court was the protection of the interests of the marital partner, which was a reason to uphold the statute at issue there[39] but would be a reason to strike a statute delaying recognition of a marriage that had already been validly celebrated.

Second, *Sosna* imposed a waiting period on when parties would be *eligible* to marry; it did not suspend recognition of a marriage that had already been celebrated. Thus, *Sosna might* permit a state's imposing a one-year waiting requirement on the exercise of the right to marry but would not justify a one-year suspension of recognition of a marriage already celebrated.

Ironically, both the *Dunn* and *Shapiro* Courts struck down waiting periods that had been imposed on the exercise of a right, so one might have assumed that the *Sosna* Court would have done the same. However, the *Sosna* Court recharacterized those cases, suggesting that they involved an appellant's being "irretrevably foreclosed from obtaining some part of what she sought," whereas the appellant in *Sosna* allegedly would receive all of what she sought after some delay.[40] Yet, there is reason to question that analysis, since the appellant in *Dunn* would have received all of what he sought (the right to vote) after some delay.

Nonetheless, suppose that one accepts the *Sosna* Court's characterization of *Dunn* and *Shapiro*. Suppose further that one ignores the difference between (1) imposing a waiting period before a right can be exercised, and (2) delaying the recognition of a marriage that has already been celebrated. Finally, suppose that one could somehow imagine that a state could offer a colorable justification for delaying recognition of a marriage for a year. Even so, that would not justify what states currently seek. The price exacted that is at issue here does not merely involve a temporary deprivation; instead, same-sex couples are forever denied the right to have their same-sex unions recognized. If indeed the telling difference between *Sosna* and the other cases is that the former involved a mere delay but the latter entirely precluded the exercise of a right, then statutes precluding rather than merely delaying recognition of valid same-sex marriages would also be unconstitutional violations of the right to travel.

The point of focus here—whether marriages validly celebrated in a sister domicile will be recognized when that couple moves to or travels through a new state—is selected because it has played an important role in the interstate recognition of marriage jurisprudence. It has long been established that marriages validly celebrated in a sister domiciliary state may be recognized in a particular state even if the state's own domiciliaries could not enter into such a marriage. Because individuals who validly celebrate a marriage in their domicile have a just and reasonable belief in the validity of their marriage, they are relevantly dissimilar to individuals who go through a marriage ceremony while knowing that their domicile will not recognize the marriage. It should thus be no surprise that the law has traditionally treated these two types of couples quite differently.

Residents and nonresidents are treated differently under mini-DOMA statutes, since state residents' reasonable expectations concerning the validity of their marriages are not undermined by these statutes. Residents of states banning same-sex marriages are on notice prospectively that their same-sex marriages will not be recognized in the domicile, even if valid in the state of celebration. Only nonresidents might have their marriages valid in their domicile at the time of celebration nonetheless not recognized and, further, only certain nonresidents would be subjected to such treatment.

DOMA AS PROMOTING FEDERALISM

Many states will recognize a marriage, even if local law considers it void, as long as it was valid in the states of celebration and domicile at the time of the marriage. One of the issues here is whether states have the power not to recognize such a marriage. If they do not, then the question is whether Congress can grant them that power.

Some commentators claim that the Defense of Marriage Act is basically a federalism statute that returns power to the states. Yet, DOMA and most mini-DOMAs do not establish the right of a state to refuse to recognize any marriage void according to local law, notwithstanding the marriage's validity in the states of celebration and domicile at the time of the marriage. Rather, they subject only one type of marriage to that treatment. Thus, most states with mini-DOMAs distinguish among nonresidents and subject only one subclass of nonresidents to the choice of staying away or surrendering one's marriage. This is strikingly similar to the constitutionally offensive classification at issue in *Saenz*, which both discriminated between residents and nonresidents and also among the different nonresidents.

Saenz undermines the claim that even if states did not previously have the power to refuse to recognize marriages validly celebrated in sister domiciliary states, Congress's having passed DOMA authorized states to refuse to recognize same-sex marriages validly celebrated in other domiciles. As the *Saenz* Court noted, "Congress has no affirmative power to authorize the States to violate the Fourteenth Amendment and is implicitly prohibited from passing legislation that purports to validate any such violation."[41] Neither the state mini-DOMAs nor Congress's DOMA can withstand privileges and immunities scrutiny, and thus all of those statutes should be struck down as violating the rights of national citizenship.

DOMA AS CREATING A SPECIAL CHOICE OF LAW RULE

It might be argued that states with mini-DOMAs are merely creating a special choice-of-law rule that allows local law to be applied to determine the validity of a marriage validly celebrated years ago. Yet, there are a few reasons to find this argument unpersuasive. First, the *Saenz* Court struck down California's welfare scheme, notwithstanding the claim that the state was merely offering "a sort of specialized choice-of-law rule."[42] Second, the Court has already suggested that a choice-of-law rule that grossly upsets justified expectations may violate due process guarantees. As Justice Stevens has explained, a "choice-of-law decision that frustrates the justifiable expectations of the parties can be fundamentally unfair," and the "desire to prevent unfair surprise to a litigant has been the central concern in this Court's review of choice-of-law decisions under the Due Process Clause."[43]

The Supreme Court of Pennsylvania explained why marriages valid in one state should be treated as valid in other states: "In an age of widespread travel and ease of mobility, it would create inordinate confusion and defy the reasonable expectations of citizens whose marriage is valid in one state to hold that marriage invalid elsewhere."[44] There, the court discussed why a marriage valid in the state of celebration should be recognized, even if it were prohibited in the domicile at the time the marriage was contracted. Yet, here, the issue does not involve the domicile at the time of the marriage, but, instead, future domiciles and nondomiciles. Thus, the Pennsylvania court's rationales are even more forceful in the context of the present discussion. Public policy and the reasonable and justified expectations of the parties would seem to require that states recognize those marriages valid in the domicile at the time of celebration. The fact that this would be a heavy price to pay for those who wished to migrate to or travel though a new state provides yet another reason that such laws are unconstitutional.

CONCLUSION

The Comity Clause and the Privileges or Immunities Clause have been subject to much debate. Although it is not clear which substantive rights are appropriately categorized as falling within the privileges and immunities of national citizenship, it is clear that the right to travel through and migrate to different states is among them. Further, although it is false to claim that any differential treatment (no matter how minor) between residents and nonresidents of a state will trigger privileges and immunities guarantees, it is clear that differential treatment of very important interests will trigger that scrutiny.

The right to marry is fundamental and the right to marry a same-sex partner should be recognized as constitutionally protected. Arguably, the right to marry a same-sex partner should be recognized as one of the rights of national citizenship. Here, however, it is merely argued that being forced to give up one's marriage as a price of admission to a new state involves a cost of sufficient magnitude that privileges and immunities protections must thereby be triggered. Being forced to surrender one's reasonable expectations and good faith beliefs concerning something so fundamentally important as the existence of one's marriage in order to travel from one state to another simply cannot be countenanced if the states in fact compose a single nation. If the privileges of national citizenship do not include something as fundamental as the right to have one's marriage (valid in the domicile at the time of celebration) recognized in each state through which one might travel or to which one might migrate, then it is not clear what interests could possibly meet the relevant standard. Certainly, those state-imposed prices of admission that have already been held to trigger the relevant protections would be viewed by many as much less dear than the cost involved in having one's valid marriage no longer recognized, wishes of both members of the couple notwithstanding.

It might be thought that even if privileges and immunities protections were triggered by a refusal to recognize a previously valid marriage, the state could still show that a substantial interest was served by refusing to recognize same-sex marriages. Such a claim, however, is not plausible. Recognizing same-sex marriages valid in the domicile at the time of celebration will not destroy different-sex marriages. On the contrary, the recognition of the importance of the right to marry for same-sex as well as different-sex couples would only serve to bolster the institution of marriage. Just as it would be intolerable for different-sex couples to have to leave their marriages at the border, it would be intolerable for same-sex couples to be subjected to such treatment. For the Court to hold either that the interest in (a same-sex) marriage is not sufficient to trigger privileges and immunities protections or that the asserted state interests could possibly justify refusing to recognize marriages that had been validly celebrated in another domiciliary state years earlier would do more to desanctify marriage and undermine the unity of this nation than striking down such laws ever could. The Court must declare DOMA and the mini-DOMAs violations of privileges and immunities guarantees. Any other holding would contribute to this country's becoming a mere league of separate sovereign states rather than "a single great community consisting of all the states united."[45] Even a states' rights-oriented Court could hardly want that.

NOTES

1. *Baldwin v. Fish & Game Commission*, 436 U.S. 371, 378–79 (1978).
2. *Corfield v. Coryell*, 6 F. Cas. 546, 551 (E.D. Pa. 1823).
3. *Id.* at 552.
4. *Saenz v. Roe*, 526 U.S. 489, 512–13 (1999) (Rehnquist, J. dissenting).
5. *Zobel v. Williams*, 457 U.S. 55, 76-77 (O'Connor, J., concurring in the judgment).
6. *Colgate v. Harvey*, 296 U.S. 404, 431 (1935).
7. *Toomer v. Witsell*, 334 U.S. 385, 395 (1948).
8. *Baldwin*, 436 U.S. at 388.
9. *Supreme Court v. Piper*, 470 U.S. 274, 284 (1985).
10. See *Memorial Hospital*, 415 U.S. at 263, 266.
11. *Toomer*, 334 U.S. at 398.
12. *The Slaughter-House Cases*, 83 U.S. (1Wall) 36, 80 (1872).
13. *Ward v. Maryland*, 79 U.S. 418, 430 (1870).
14. *Colgate*, 296 U.S. at 429.
15. *United States v. Guest*, 383 U.S. 745, 757–58 (1966).
16. *Lunding v. New York Tax Appeals Tribunal*, 522 U.S. 287, 311 (1998).

17. *Attorney General v. Soto-Lopez* , 476 U.S. 898, 902 (1986).

18. *Paul v. Virginia*, 75 U.S. 168, 180 (1868).

19. *Id.*

20. *Colgate,* 296 U.S. at 426.

21. *Guest,* 383 U.S. at 767 (Harlan, J., concurring in part and dissenting in part).

22. *Sherrer v. Sherrer*, 334 U.S. 343, 355 (1948).

23. *Edwards v. California*, 314 U.S. 160, 181 (1941) (Douglas, J., concurring).

24. *Saenz,* 526 U.S. at 492.

25. *Id.* at 508.

26. *Ex parte Kinney*, 14 F. Cas. 602, 603 (E. D. Va. 1879).

27. *Id.* at 605.

28. See *In re* Hobbs, 12 F. Cas. 262, 264 (N. D. Ga. 1871).

29. *Id.* See also *Frasher v. State*, 30 Am. Rep. 131 (Tex. Ct. App. 1877) and *Doc Lonas v. State*, 50 Tenn. (3 Heisk) 287 (1871).

30. *Kinney,* 14 F. Cas. at 607.

31. John Harrison, "Reconstructing the Privileges or Immunities Clause," 101 *Yale Law Journal* 1385, 1451 (1992).

32. *Id.* at 1460–61.

33. *Supreme Court v. Friedman*, 487 U.S. 59, 66 (1988).

34. *Shapiro v. Thompson*, 394 U.S. 618, 629 (1969).

35. *Id.* at 633.

36. *Dunn v. Blumstein*, 405 U.S. 330, 341 (1972).

37. See *Attorney General*, 476 U.S. at 907.

38. U.S. 393 (1975).

39. See *id.* at 406–7.

40. *Id.* at 561.

41. *Saenz,* 526 U.S. at 508.

42. See *Saenz,* 526 U.S. at 509.

43. *Allstate Insurance Company v. Hague*, 449 U.S. 302, 327 (1981) (Stevens, J., concurring in the judgment).

44. *In re Estate of Lenherr*, 314 A.2d 255, 258 (Pa. 1974).

45. *Colgate v. Harvey*, 296 U.S. 404, 426 (1935).

Chapter Five

Retroactivity and the Hawaii Referendum

Although same-sex couples have been trying to have their relationships accorded legal recognition for decades, the attempts were not taken particularly seriously by many people until it looked like Hawaii might actually recognize same-sex unions. In *Baehr v. Lewin*, a plurality of the Hawaii Supreme Court held that the state statute reserving marriage for different-sex couples implicated equal protection guarantees and then remanded the case to give the state an opportunity to defend the statute's constitutionality. On remand, the lower court found that the state had failed to meet its constitutional burden, although that court stayed its own decision pending state supreme court review. In the meantime, the Hawaii electorate amended the state constitution via referendum to permit the legislature to reserve marriage for different-sex couples.

At one point, many hoped that Hawaii would be the first state to recognize same-sex marriages, and so the adoption of that amendment, coupled with the state supreme court's analysis of it, was extremely disappointing. At least part of that disappointment was due to the court's having issued an opinion that addressed the wrong issues and implicitly endorsed a position contrary to existing law. Nonetheless, there were also some positive aspects of the opinion, which may well be used to advantage in subsequent litigation in Hawaii in particular or in other states more generally. Not only did the Hawaii court provide the basis upon which the referendum might be challenged under *state* law but, in addition, provided arguments that will be of use when challenging same-sex marriage bans on federal grounds.

The Hawaii referendum raised a variety of constitutional issues. For example, if indeed the pre-amended state constitution guaranteed the right to marry a same-sex partner, then arguably there was a violation of federal constitutional guarantees when state constitutional protections were withdrawn and the marriage rights of a disfavored group were made subject to the will of the state legislature. When examining the referendum in *Baehr v. Miike*, however, the Hawaii Supreme Court ostensibly addressed a very narrow issue, namely, whether the amendment retroactively validated a law reserving marriage for different-sex couples, and actually addressed a different narrow issue, namely, how the court might reconcile potentially conflicting constitutional provisions.

The court implicitly held that the amendment retroactively validated a portion of the Hawaii marriage statute, although the opinion was remarkably terse, making its exposition and analysis somewhat difficult. Nonetheless, it is possible to reconstruct some of the possible positions of the court and some of the difficulties inherent therein. Had the court in fact considered retroactivity jurisprudence generally or Hawaii retroactivity jurisprudence in particular, it would have held at most that the constitutional amendment permitted the legislature to reserve marriage for different-sex couples. Had the court also considered federal equal protection guarantees, it would have held the referendum unconstitutional.

THE HAWAII REFERENDUM

In response to two court decisions suggesting that the state constitution might protect the right to marry a same-sex partner, the Hawaii electorate voted to amend their state constitution to empower the state legislature to reserve marriage for different-sex couples. By doing so, the electorate made it possible for the legislature to pass such a statute without having to worry that the courts might invalidate it on state constitutional grounds. Assuming that the referendum itself violated no constitutional guarantees and that states as a general matter have the power to reserve marriage for different-sex couples, the amendment clearly empowered the Hawaii legislature to enact a statute precluding same-sex couples from marrying. A separate issue is whether the amendment retroactively validated a portion of the marriage statute, thereby limiting marriage to different-sex couples or whether, instead, the amendment merely empowered the legislature to enact a new statute incorporating that restriction.

RETROACTIVITY DOCTRINE

Whenever a court or legislature modifies existing law, those potentially affected by the change need to know when it will go into effect. The general rule is that statutes apply prospectively and judicial decisions apply retroactively, although this general rule, like many others, has exceptions. Retroactive application of statutes is not favored in the law because it can undermine the parties' legitimate expectations based on the law existing at the time the rights were acquired and obligations incurred. Of course, the concern that a retroactive application of the law might undermine legitimate expectations would also support only applying judicial decisions prospectively, since individuals' reasonable expectations might be based on existing case law rather than on existing statutory law. Nonetheless, judicial decisions are often applied retroactively, and thus the desire to prevent unfairness cannot alone explain the different presumptions concerning the retroactivity of judicial and legislative acts.

In *Great Northern Railway Company v. Sunburst Oil & Refining Company*, the Court discussed the "ancient dogma that the law declared by its courts had a Platonic or ideal existence before the act of declaration, in which even the discredited declaration will be viewed as if it had never been, and the reconsidered declaration as law from the beginning."[1] For example, if the Court declared a statute unconstitutional but then subsequently overruled itself, the Court's initial ruling of unconstitutionality might be viewed as if it had never occurred, and the statute might be viewed as if it had been good law from the beginning. According to this theory, judges report what the law is rather than create the law, and a "misstatement" by a court about the law would not change the character of the law itself but, instead, would only be an inaccurate reporting of that law. Once the court corrects its inaccurate reporting, the law (which had always existed even if it had been mis-described) could even be applied to events that had occurred before the mis-description had been corrected.

Certainly, it might be suggested that the above theory inappropriately reifies the law and, further, imposes unfair burdens on individuals who might be acting in light of the court's past misstatement of the relevant law. States have the option of saying that individuals will be bound by the misstated law until the court has corrected its own misstatement, although states do not have to do so as long as no other constitutional provisions would thereby be violated.

The analysis above, distinguishing between the law on the one hand and how it is reported on the other, is not helpful in a situation in which a legislature has modified an existing law. In that situation, the modified law came into being in its current form when the legislature changed the former law. Because the law is new (insofar as it has been modified), it cannot be claimed that the law has always existed in its current form and thus would appropriately be applied retrospectively.

To make clear how the above theory treats legislative modifications on the one hand and judicial modifications on the other, consider a legislature that has passed a statute, repealed it, and then reenacted it. Each legislative enactment would be prospective, because the existing law would have changed after each enactment. Thus, absent specific language to the contrary, only events occurring after the enactment would be subject to the newly adopted rule.

Consider a different scenario: the legislature passes a law and opponents challenge it. The state supreme court holds that it is unconstitutional but then subsequently overrules the opinion striking down that law. According to the theory described here, the law would have existed the entire time, even though the court had mistakenly held that the law was unconstitutional. Further, the law could be applied to events that had occurred even before the court had overruled itself, because the law would have existed then even if the court had not recognized that fact.

The above theory regarding which changes to statutes should be applied retroactively does not entirely reflect current retroactivity practices. Considerations of fairness or public policy might militate against applying a law to particular parties when the court had once declared the law unconstitutional and subsequently declared it constitutional, notwithstanding that, at least in theory, the law had always existed and the court had simply been mistaken about the law's constitutionality.

There is another respect in which the above theory of retroactivity does not account for current practices. Statutes can be applied retroactively as long as two conditions are met: (1) the legislature clearly intended the statute to be retroactive, and (2) no constitutional guarantees would be violated by applying the statute retroactively.

The United States Supreme Court has made clear that the first rule of construction is that legislation will be presumed to be prospective. Especially where the statute regulates conduct or interferes with previously existing rights, statutes will not be interpreted to have a retrospective effect unless the legislature has made very clear that the statute should be so interpreted. Further, courts will decline to give a statute retroactive effect if doing so would result in manifest injustice.

A legislature that clearly expresses its intention to make a statute retroactive will not thereby guarantee the constitutionality of that statute. The retrospective aspect of legislation must itself meet the test of due process, and a statute might pass constitutional muster when applied prospectively but not when applied retroactively.

Retroactive legislation may be struck down if it abridges a vested right. Some courts and commentators reject the vested rights analysis in favor of a consideration of such factors as the significance of the state interest served by the law, the importance of the retroactive application of the law to the effectuation of that interest, the extent of reliance upon the former law, the legitimacy of that reliance, the extent to which actions were taken on the basis of that reliance, and the extent to which the retroactive application of the new law would disrupt those actions. Regardless of the preferred mode of analysis, however, it is clear that some retroactive statutes will be struck down even if they would have been upheld had they been prospective only.

The general rule is that modifications to the law made by legislatures are prospective only and that modifications made by judges are retrospective. Though legislative changes to the law can be retroactive, they are still disfavored, both in that the retroactive application must be clearly expressed and in that the retroactive application itself must survive constitutional analysis.

ON AMENDMENTS AND RETROACTIVE VALIDATION

Courts have taken a number of approaches with respect to whether a state constitutional amendment can retroactively validate a statute enacted prior to the amendment's adoption. Some courts have suggested that if a legislature is prohibited from passing a particular law and nonetheless does so, the enactment is void and the law cannot be made valid even if the legislature subsequently acquires the power to pass such a law. Basically, these courts suggest that an unconstitutional act should be treated as if it had never been passed. No subsequent amendment to the constitution would validate the act, since in the eyes of the law the act had never been passed in the first place. According to this view, if in fact the Hawaii legislature had been precluded from reserving marriage for different-sex couples before the adoption of the recent amendment, then any such marital exclusion would have been void and would have required re-enactment after the amendment's adoption in order for it to have the force of law.

The position above suggests that statutes cannot be retroactively validated by constitutional amendment, since at the time of their passage they were void and of no legal effect and thus there would have been nothing in existence to have been validated by the amendment. Yet, some courts have rejected the approach that amendments *cannot* validate an invalid statute and, instead, have merely insisted that certain steps must be taken if the amendment is to have that validating effect. The supreme courts of New Jersey and Alabama have explained that a constitutional amendment can validate and confirm a legislative act that had been unconstitutional at the time of its enactment as long as that intention was very clear when that amendment was adopted.[2]

According to this latter view, a constitutional amendment can validate a previously void law as long as that desired effect is clearly and expressly stated. The requirement of a clear and express statement is not taken lightly, however. An amendment that grants a legislature new powers but does not also expressly validate and confirm a previously existing law will not be interpreted to have resurrected that law. As the California Supreme

Court explained, to interpret an amendment that grants the legislature the *power* to pass a law as instead validating a previously invalid law would misconstrue the amendment, since the amendment would then have the effect of enacting a law instead of merely permitting the legislature to do so if it so chose.[3] There is a strong presumption against construing a power-granting amendment as validating a previously invalid statute, and such interpretations will not be offered unless that validating effect was clearly and expressly stated within the amendment at the time of its passage. Thus, while it is possible to validate laws via constitutional amendment, there is a strong presumption against retroactive validation that, at least as a general matter, can only be overcome by express language to that effect.

THE HAWAII CONSTITUTIONAL AMENDMENT

To determine whether the Hawaii amendment incorporated language that was sufficiently clear to justify overcoming the presumption against retroactive application, it is necessary to examine the text of the amendment itself, which reads, "The legislature shall have the power to reserve marriage to opposite-sex couples."[4] It should be clear that no language in the amendment expressly and unambiguously validates any statute that had been enacted prior to the amendment's passage. Indeed, no language in the amendment even addresses a prior statute. A plain reading of the amendment suggests that it is power-conferring rather than statute-validating and that it should not have been construed as doing the latter.

H.L.A. Hart distinguishes between two types of rules: those that impose duties and those that confer powers.[5] He explains, "Under rules of the one type, which may well be considered the basic or primary type, human beings are required to do or abstain from certain actions, whether they wish to or not."[6] In contrast, rules of the other type "provide that human beings may by doing or saying certain things introduce new rules of the primary type, extinguish or modify old ones, or in various ways determine their incidence or control their operation."[7] Rules of the former type impose duties, whereas rules of the latter type confer powers, public or private.

The power-conferring rules are divided into those that "confer[] legal powers to adjudicate or legislate (public powers)" and those that "create or vary legal relations (private powers)."[8] Consider a state statute that regulates who may marry whom. The statute would have been passed pursuant to the legislature's (public) power to enact marital regulations and would affect the (private) power of private citizens to enter into the marriage relation.

The Hawaii amendment on its face is power-conferring: the legislature has been given the power to reserve marriage for different-sex couples.

Were the legislature to choose to exercise its power acquired by virtue of that amendment, it would thereby restrict the power of private citizens to create a particular legal relation (marriage) with a same-sex partner. Precisely because power-conferring laws are of a different type than substantive laws, however, granting a legislature a power would not even speak to whether that power would be exercised.

It might be thought that it would not make any difference whether the Hawaii constitutional amendment is power-conferring or, in addition, retroactively validating, since the legislature would simply reenact the relevant legislation should the court have held that the reenactment was necessary. One should note, however, that subsequent to the passage of the amendment but prior to its having been interpreted as having a retroactive effect, the Hawaii legislature *failed* to pass legislation reserving marriage for different-sex couples, notwithstanding the introduction of bills to that effect in the appropriate committees.

As a general matter, there is good reason, both theoretically and practically, to require the reenactment of statutes once the legislature has been given the power to pass particular legislation. For example, the political alliances might have shifted since the passage of the previous statute, and the statute might not be reenacted. Or, even if it were, other concessions might have been made to secure passage of the legislation. Thus, as a matter of the settled law and of general public policy, amendments will not retroactively validate statutes passed prior to the amendment's passage unless there is explicit language to that effect.

THE SPECIAL HAWAII CONSTITUTIONAL PROVISION

Though the general jurisprudence regarding retroactive validation of statutes is clear, it might be argued that there is something special about the Hawaii Constitution that makes the general jurisprudence inapplicable to how this amendment in particular should have been interpreted. The Hawaii Constitution reads, "All laws in force at the time amendments to this constitution take effect that are not inconsistent with the constitution as amended shall remain in force, *mutatis mutandis*, until they expire by their own limitation or are amended or repealed by the legislature."[9] This section might be thought to alter the standard retroactivity presumptions in Hawaii.

TWO DIFFERENT PROVISION INTERPRETATIONS

The Hawaii constitutional provision is not clear on its face and so must be construed. One interpretation is that the provision simply says that whichever statutes are consistent with the amended constitution will be enforceable until they either expire or are repealed. If that were the intention, however, the section could easily have read, "All laws that are not inconsistent with the constitution as amended shall be in force until they expire by their own limitation or are amended or repealed by the legislature." Were the section meant to be a retroactive validation provision, there would have been no need to have limited the laws to which the section would be applied to those that were "in force at the time amendments to the constitution take effect." Indeed, by suggesting that those already in effect shall remain in force, the provision is saying that those laws that were valid would remain valid rather than that even those that had been invalid would now become valid.

An interpretation that better accounts for all of the provision's language is the following: a statute will remain good law if it was constitutional before the adoption of the amendment (i.e., was in force prior to the amendment's adoption) and, in addition, is consistent with the constitution even after the amendment's adoption. The reference to those laws in force at the time of the amendment's adoption limits the laws that will be viewed as affected by this section. Basically, this section suggests that the laws that will be valid after an amendment's adoption must have been valid before the amendment's adoption and must be consistent with the constitution as newly amended.

The provision of the current Hawaii Constitution was based on section 15 of the Admission Act, which read, "All Territorial laws in force in the Territory of Hawaii at the time of its admission into the Union shall continue in force in the State of Hawaii, except as modified or changed by this Act or by the constitution of the State, and shall be subject to repeal or amendment by the Legislature of the State of Hawaii."[10]

The latter act was passed to secure the continuity of laws. The difficulty that the Admission Act was intended to solve was that "upon admission of a State, all of the Territorial laws are abrogated except as continued in force by competent authority."[11] The Admission Act guaranteed consistency and continuity: those laws in effect before Hawaii became a state would continue after Hawaii became a state as long as those laws did not violate constitutional guarantees.

The provision of the current Hawaii Constitution is also intended to preserve consistency; its title is "Continuity of Laws." Consistency and continuity are double-edged, however; they include the laws that would continue to exist and also exclude those that might otherwise have been thought to spring into existence. Thus, on the interpretation offered here, the section was not intended to retroactively validate those statutes in accord with new constitutional amendments; rather, it was merely intended to make clear that statutes valid prior to the amendment that were not invalidated by that amendment would remain good law.

Case law supports the interpretation offered here. In 1960 in *G.E.M. Sundries Company, Incorporated v. Johnson and Johnson, Incorporated*, the

Ninth Circuit Court of Appeals had to interpret whether a Hawaii statute precluded by an act of Congress could be construed as "in force" at the time Hawaii became a state in 1959 and, thus, should be included among those laws covered by the Admissions Act. The court made clear that the statute was not "in effect" as a result of its initial passage, because the enactment at that time was in violation of federal law.[12]

The court's analysis is important to consider. The Hawaii statute was held not to be in effect because it had violated federal law, not because it had already been declared invalid by a court. Thus, an act that cannot be enacted because of federal or perhaps state constitutional guarantees should not be considered "in effect," even if it has not yet been struck down by a court. The only reason that the statute at issue in *G.E.M. Sundries* was considered good law was that it had been *reenacted* after the bar to its passage had been lifted.[13]

It might be thought that this Ninth Circuit decision was an obscure case that might have escaped the notice of those writing the current provision of the Hawaii Constitution. Yet, this is not a plausible claim, since the current provision lists section 15 of the Admissions Act as a cross-reference, and the case notes in the discussion of that section list *G E.M. Sundries*. Indeed, precisely because the notes refer to this Ninth Circuit case, it is plausible to believe that the intention of the drafters was that the "in effect" language be construed as it was there. As that case illustrates, however, a statute should not be described as "in force" if it is unconstitutional and void, even if a court has not yet recognized that it is void. Thus, the portion of the statute restricting marriage to different-sex couples could not be described as in force if it violated constitutional guarantees and would not be protected by the provision at issue in the Hawaii Constitution.

Suppose the legislature had not reenacted the statute at issue in *G.E.M. Sundries*. The appellate court made clear that the statute would then not have been in effect, that is, would not have been in force. By the same token, a statute that is unconstitutional when passed should be viewed as not in effect or in force, unless the legislature enacted that statute after the bar to its passage had been lifted.

The Hawaiian constitutional provision was designed to preserve continuity rather than to cause laws that had been void and of no legal effect to suddenly spring into being. Although the section under discussion here is open to different interpretations, the explanation that best accounts for its language and the relevant case law suggests that this provision does not make the Hawaii retroactivity jurisprudence any different from the generally accepted retroactivity jurisprudence. In Hawaii as elsewhere, a void statute or portion thereof should not be held retroactively validated absent an express declaration to that effect.

CONSTRUING INTENT

Hawaii jurisprudence follows the general retroactivity jurisprudence both in that retroactive legislation is permissible under some circumstances and that retrospective laws are disfavored; all laws will be construed as prospective unless the language clearly and expressly requires a different interpretation. Indeed, there is reason to think that Hawaii has an especially strong public policy disfavoring retroactive application, since Hawaii law provides, "No law has any retrospective operation, unless otherwise expressed or obviously intended."[14] Although that law is only a rule of statutory construction and may be overcome if the legislative intent to do so is clear, the existence of the statute nonetheless indicates that there is a strong policy against a construction of retrospective operation and that a substantial burden must be overcome when seeking to establish that a statute should be retroactively applied.

The Hawaii Supreme Court has made clear that where its task "is to ascertain whether there is an expression or obvious intendment that the [legislative] amendment was to have any retrospective operation," the court must begin "by examining the language."[15] It was established long ago in Hawaii that "no law will be construed to act retrospectively unless its language imperatively requires such a construction."[16] Yet, the language of the amendment—"The legislature shall have the power to reserve marriage to opposite-sex couples"—does not even mention retroactive application much less require that the amendment be given that construction.

At issue here is the construction of an amendment to the state constitution rather than a statute passed by the legislature. Yet, at least two points must be made. First, the same kinds of tools used in construing statutes may be used in construing amendments. Second, it is especially important in this kind of case to use the language of the amendment itself to determine its meaning, precisely because different interpretations of what it says will have been offered, and it will be impossible to tell which interpretations were heard or accepted by the voters.

To determine what the voters had in mind when they voted for the amendment, it simply will not do to consult the legislative history to see what the legislators believed they were doing when they passed a bill proposing that a bill be placed on the ballot. In the voting booth, the voter sees the text of the amendment itself; the voter does not, for example, see the differing opinions about whether the amendment, if approved, would have retroactive effect.

Perhaps it would be thought too severe a restriction to require that the amendment expressly incorporate retroactive intent. After all, if everyone received explanatory materials in the mail making clear that the amendment would retroactively validate a statute, then perhaps the relevant intention could thereby be established.

Even if the intention to retroactively validate a statute could be constructively inferred when a mass mailing has made that effect of the amendment clear, however, this would not help establish that the Hawaii amendment should have been construed to have retroactively validated the portion of the statute at issue here. The materials that Hawaiians received in the mail suggested that the amendment was to have *prospective* rather than retrospective application. Voting "yes" on the proposed constitutional amendment was explained in the following way: "A 'yes' vote would add a new provision to the Constitution that would give the Legislature the power to reserve marriage to opposite-sex couples only. The Legislature could then pass a rule that would limit marriage to a man and a woman, overruling the recent Supreme Court decision regarding same-sex couples."[17]

This explanation suggests that the amendment would confer a power on the Hawaii legislature that it then could exercise. It suggests in addition that the amendment would not retroactively validate a previous statute, since there would be no need to then pass a rule restricting marriage if the amendment's adoption would have retroactively validated that rule.

By the same token, the explanation of the *effect* of a "yes" vote suggested that it was prospective rather than retrospective. That explanation was, "People who want the proposed amendment to pass believe the Legislature, and not the Supreme Court, should decide who is eligible to marry in the State. If the proposed amendment is adopted, then it will be clear that the Legislature can legally reserve marriage for opposite-sex couples. People in support of the proposed amendment believe passing this amendment is an important step to prohibit same-sex marriage in the State."[18]

Were the amendment to retroactively validate a statute, the amendment's adoption would not merely be an important step in prohibiting same-sex marriage; it would be all that would be necessary. Whether one considers the language of the amendment itself, the official explanation of the amendment, or even the explanation of its effect that had been offered by its supporters, the amendment should have been construed as prospective only. When one considers in addition that there is a presumption of prospectivity, it is difficult to see how the Hawaii Supreme Court could have held otherwise.

SEPARATION OF POWERS

Suppose that one took seriously what the legislators believed they were doing when they proposed the amendment, as reflected by what they approved and by what they said when testifying about the bill. The bill that was approved was "an amendment to article I of the Constitution of the State of Hawaii to *clarify* that the legislature has the power to reserve marriage to opposite-sex couples."[19] By offering a clarification of the constitution, the legislature might be thought to be offering its own interpretation of the state constitution. Yet, passing such a bill to establish the "correct" interpretation of the state constitution is itself problematic. As the Hawaii Supreme Court has made clear, "the courts, not the legislature, are the ultimate interpreters of the Constitution."[20] Insofar as this was a clarification, that is, an attempt to establish the meaning of the constitution, it should have been struck down on separation of powers grounds. As the Hawaii Supreme Court has explained, "Under the separation of powers so provided, each branch is coordinate with the other, and neither may exercise the power vested in the other."[21] While separation of powers would not preclude, for example, the legislature's holding hearings to help them decide what legislative action would be appropriate to take in particular circumstances, separation of powers would preclude the legislature's making what amounted to a judicial determination of the meaning of the state constitution.

Certainly, the legislature's describing the amendment as a *clarification* need not be an interpretation of the state constitution, since it might instead be a rhetorical move to persuade voters that adopting the amendment would not radically change the existing constitution. Because rhetorical persuasion is not equivalent to constitutional interpretation, the former would neither be viewed as a usurpation of the court's role nor as a violation of separation of powers.

The claim here, of course, is not that the legislature was violating separation of powers by proposing an amendment to the state constitution. On the contrary, proposing an amendment involved the exercise of a prescribed power to change the constitution. Yet, precisely because the legislature has the power to propose changes to the constitution but does not have the power to establish its meaning, the "clarification" language is best understood as an attempt to persuade the populace to support a change rather than as a definitive interpretation of the pre-amended constitution.

OTHER LAWS MILITATING AGAINST RETROACTIVE APPLICATION

Two other Hawaii laws should have helped convince the court that the amendment should not have been construed as retroactively validating a portion of the marriage statute. Hawaii law states that the "repeal of any law shall not revive any other law which has been repealed, unless it is clearly expressed."[22] This law clearly expresses the public policy against revival of statutes, absent clear language mandating such a revival.

Suppose that Hawaii had a law reserving marriage for different-sex couples. Suppose further that this law was repealed and a different law was passed prohibiting the legislature from passing a statute reserving marriage for different-sex couples. Because of a change in the composition of the legislature, however, the law prohibiting a same-sex marriage ban was repealed. According to current Hawaii law, the repeal of the law prohibiting a same-sex marriage ban would not revive the former law reserving marriage for different-sex couples. The new legislature would have to reenact that law for it to be given effect.

Admittedly, the issue under discussion here is somewhat different from the hypothetical posed above. Here, there was no repeal of a law barring the legislature from reserving marriage for different-sex couples. Rather, assuming for the sake of argument that the state constitution precluded the legislature from reserving marriage for different-sex couples, at issue here is a constitutional amendment that repealed the previous constitutional bar prohibiting the legislature from reserving marriage for different-sex couples. Yet, presumably, just as the repeal of a statute does not revive a different statute absent language to that effect, the repeal of a constitutional provision does not revive a statute absent express language to that effect.

Another difference between the hypothetical posed above and the situation in Hawaii is that the law reserving marriage for different-sex couples was never repealed; rather, that section of the law never existed because the constitution precluded its passage. Yet, if a repealed statute cannot be revived absent express language to that effect, then certainly a section that had been unconstitutional and void and, hence, had never existed in the eyes of the law should not be considered "revived" absent specific language to that effect.

A different Hawaii law makes even clearer that the Hawaii court's ruling about retroactivity was in error. Hawaii law regarding state constitutional amendments requires that the "language and meaning of a constitutional amendment shall be clear and it shall be neither misleading nor deceptive."[23] Given the official explanation of the amendment sent to the voters (that a "Yes" vote would mean that the "Legislature could then pass a law that would limit marriage to a man and a woman"), an individual who wished the legislature to have the power to reserve marriage for different-sex couples but did not wish the amendment to retroactively validate a portion of the statute enacted prior to the amendment's adoption would have been deceived into voting for the amendment. The Hawaii court's construction of the amendment makes the explanation of the amendment sent to the voters a violation of state law. Thus, not only did such a construction ignore the standard interpretation presumptions, but it cast the validity of the ballot into question because voters had been misled about the effects of their votes.

WHAT HAPPENS WHEN A PORTION OF A STATUTE IS VOID?

The discussion here is predicated upon an assumption made by the *Baehr* court, namely, that the Hawaii legislature did not have the power to pass a statute reserving marriage for different-sex couples prior to the passage of the recent amendment. If the legislature did not have that power, then the provision reserving marriage for different-sex couples was void. The legislature's not having had the power to enact that particular provision, however, would not have made the entire marriage statute void.

The United States Supreme Court has long recognized that marriage is subject to legislative control, although the Court has also recognized that legislative powers in this area are not unlimited, since federal or state constitutional guarantees might prohibit the legislature's enactment of a particular marital regulation. Consider a state that has enacted a marital statute that is unconstitutional only in part, for example, a statute that precludes interracial marriage but does not otherwise offend constitutional guarantees. The question at hand is whether the marital statute would have to be reenacted with the unconstitutional provision excised or whether the statute (minus the unconstitutional part) would be effective without reenactment.

Several courts have addressed how a statute with one unconstitutional provision should be construed. The Supreme Court of Indiana noted, "Where only a part of a legislative act violates the Constitution and is judicially declared void, and the remainder of the act is complete in itself and capable of execution according to the legislative intent, and wholly independent of that which is judicially determined to be unconstitutional, the remaining part of the act will be sustained."[24] Thus, the marital statute would not need to be reenacted with the unconstitutional part excised in order to be in effect.

In a different case, the Supreme Court of Montana offered an analogy to make its view clear:

[W]here the lawmaking body has solemnly declared its intention as to what shall be the law upon a subject clearly within its constitutional power and authority, which enactment would have become valid except for some defect in the body of the act which could originally have been cured, the roots and the "main stock" are still alive and are grounded in fertile constitutional soil, and all that is necessary to cause the tree to flourish is scientific pruning or grafting, dependent upon whether the Legislature has said too much or too little.[25]

Here, all that would be necessary would be to "prune" the marital statute of its offending provision; the remainder would be good law and would not require reenactment to be in effect.

Finally, the Supreme Judicial Court of Massachusetts has explained that,

in the consideration of a statute where one part is unconstitutional, which is in its nature separable from other parts so that they well may stand independently of it, and there is no such connection between the valid and the invalid parts that the general court would not be expected to enact the valid part without the other, the parts of the statute not in conflict with the Constitution will be held good.[26]

Where the offending part is easily separable from the remainder, the court will view the rest of the statute as valid. Of course, if this were a different case where there were so many unconstitutional provisions that it could not reasonably be assumed that the legislature would have passed the act without those provisions, then the statute would require reenactment to be in effect.

Here, the offending provision could be "pruned" and the remainder of the Hawaii marriage statute would pass constitutional muster and thus be in effect. In other words, the Hawaii marriage act would be in force except insofar as it specified that "the marriage contract . . . shall be only between a man and a woman."[27] Thus, while Hawaii still would have had a marriage statute in effect even assuming that the provision reserving marriage for different-sex couples was unconstitutional, the constitutionally offensive provision would be deemed to be void and to have no legal effect.

Once the Hawaii legislature had the power to pass a statute reserving marriage for different-sex couples, the legislature could then amend the existing statute to include that provision. Because the previous statute would have existed as pruned, however, the legislature would need to reenact the provision restricting marriage if that restriction were to have the force of law.

Suppose that the Hawaii electorate had wanted to give the legislature the power to reserve marriage for different-sex couples but had not wanted to retroactively validate the marriage statute. What would the amendment have said? It might have said, "The legislature shall have the power to reserve marriage to opposite-sex couples, but this amendment shall not be construed to retroactively validate any statutes passed prior to the effective date of this amendment." Certainly, this would have made it even clearer to the electorate that the amendment was not to have any retroactive effect.

Yet, the issue before the court was not how the amendment could have been worded to make very clear to the electorate that the amendment would not retroactively validate a previous statute. Rather, the issue before the court was how to construe the amendment, given the standard presumption of non-retroactivity. The court's holding turned the presumption on its head. It would be as if the court had said that the amendment retroactively validated the statute reserving marriage for different-sex couples because the amendment did not include this extra provision expressly denying that the amendment was retroactive, whereas the established jurisprudence requires that the amendment not have a retroactive validating effect absent express language to the contrary.

The Hawaii Supreme Court's holding that the amendment retroactively validated the statute was especially surprising in light of the recognized test of construction in this context. The amendment stated, "The legislature shall have the power to reserve marriage to opposite-sex couples." The recognized test for retroactive validation is that the language must clearly require that result. Yet, here, to argue that the amendment retroactively validates the statute requires that non-textual elements (e.g., legislators' claims about whether it would have that effect) be allowed to trump the plain language of the amendment. To suggest that "the legislature *shall* have the power" requires or even permits retroactive validation of the statute is, at the very least, a creative reading of the plain language.

The Hawaii Constitution, related statutes, and the established case law suggest that the court's construction of the amendment as retroactively validating the Hawaii marriage statute had no basis in the jurisprudence. The statutory requirements that the constitutional question be clear and that the electorate not be deceived, coupled with the complete failure even to mention retroactivity in the amendment, suggest that either the ballot question was itself defective or that the court's holding was in error.

RECONCILING CONSTITUTIONAL PROVISIONS

When examining the Hawaii constitutional amendment, a court might have been interested in a number of issues: (1) whether the amendment retroactively validated a statute passed prior to the amendment's adoption, (2) whether the amendment's validating such a statute would violate constitutional guarantees; or (3) how the amendment should be interpreted if it seemed to contradict a different part of the state constitution. The *Baehr* court purportedly addressed the first issue, although its analysis really addressed the third issue.

A court interested in whether an amendment retroactively validated a statute would carefully examine the amendment at issue to see whether its language clearly required retroactive validation. Had the *Baehr* court performed this careful examination, it would have decided that the amendment did not retroactively validate the statute. Not only did the language of the amendment not require retroactive application, but it also could not plausibly even support such an interpretation.

While ostensibly addressing retrospective validation, the *Baehr* court actually addressed a different issue, namely, how it should read potentially conflicting provisions of a constitution. To see why the *Baehr* court was in fact addressing this issue, a little background is required.

The language of the Hawaii marriage statute reads, "In order to make valid the marriage contract, which shall be only between a man and a woman, it shall be necessary that. . . ." The question for the *Baehr* court was how to reconcile the existence of this statute, which clearly classifies on the basis of sex since it defines who may marry on that basis, with the constitutional provision barring discrimination on the basis of sex. The court looked at the amendment specifically giving the legislature the power to reserve marriage for different-sex couples and concluded that the:

marriage amendment validated H.R.S. § 572–1 by taking the statute out of the ambit of the equal protection clause of the Hawaii Constitution, at least insofar as the statute, both on its face and as applied, purported to limit access to the marital status to opposite sex couples. Accordingly, whether or not in the past it was violative of the equal protection clause in the forgoing respect, H.R.S. § 572–1 no longer is.[28]

Basically, the court looked at the amendment, which specifically permitted the legislature to reserve marriage for different-sex couples, and the state constitution, which explicitly prohibits discrimination on the basis of sex, and offered a way to reconcile the two provisions.

Consider how a court might handle two conflicting provisions of a constitution. It might say that one of the contradictory provisions is null and void because it contravenes certain basic principles. Or, it might suggest that the provisions must be interpreted to be consistent if at all possible. As the Pennsylvania Supreme Court pointed out, "because the Constitution is an integrated whole, effect must be given to all of its provisions whenever possible."[29]

The Hawaii Supreme Court in its *Baehr* opinion followed the generally accepted jurisprudence with respect to how to interpret apparently conflicting constitutional provisions, namely, reconcile them if at all possible. The only difficulty with that approach was that it had very little to do with the issue that the court was allegedly deciding, namely, whether the Hawaii amendment retroactively validated a portion of the Hawaii marriage statute.

Suppose that events had occurred much differently. The amendment was adopted and the legislature then enacted legislation reserving marriage for different-sex couples. If that legislation were then challenged, the court would have to decide whether the provision authorizing the legislature to reserve marriage for different-sex couples could be reconciled with the provision prohibiting discrimination on the basis of sex. The court might in that case have construed the two provisions as consistent and issued the ruling that in fact was offered in *Baehr*. Certainly, if the *Baehr* court had held that the two provisions were inconsistent and, further, that the provision authorizing the legislature to reserve marriage for different-sex couples were somehow unconstitutional, then the court would not have needed to address whether the constitutional amendment retroactively validated a portion of the marriage statute, since the amendment itself would then have been void. Because the court found that the constitutional provisions were consistent, however, it still had to address whether the amendment retroactively validated part of the statute.

The *Baehr* court never explicitly stated that the amendment retroactively validated the portion of the statute reserving marriage for different-sex couples. If indeed the equal protection guarantees of the pre-amended constitution precluded the legislature from restricting marriage in that way, however, and if indeed that would mean that the Hawaii marriage statute pruned of the offending provision would be in effect, then the provision would have to have been retroactively validated in order for it to have existed so that it could be taken out of the "ambit" of the equal protection clause. If that voided provision had not been retroactively validated and thus had been nonexistent, there would not yet have been anything that needed to be taken out of the clause's ambit.

It is simply unclear whether the *Baehr* court understood the implications of its own decision, because the court simply refused to address retroactivity or even the proper construction of the Hawaii constitutional provision that might have been thought to have changed the presumptions regarding retroactive validation. At some future point, however, the court may have to explain whether Hawaii's retroactivity jurisprudence is nonstandard or, perhaps, whether the court must invalidate the amendment ballot because it deceived the voters with respect to whether the amendment would retroactively validate Hawaii's marriage statute.

BAEHR SILVER LININGS—WHAT MIGHT HAVE BEEN SAID

A different way to reconcile the Equal Protection Clause of the Hawaii Constitution and the specific provision permitting the legislature to reserve marriage for different-sex couples would have been to deny that the Equal Protection Clause precluded reserving marriage for different-sex couples, either by asserting that such a classification involved an orientation- rather than a sex-based classification or by holding that even if such a classification were sex-based, it nonetheless did not offend constitutional guarantees. The Hawaii Supreme Court chose neither and instead opted to reconcile the provisions, suggesting that by removing the marriage statute from the Equal Protection Clause's ambit, the amendment created a narrow exception in the equal protection jurisprudence.

In his *Baehr* concurrence, Justice Ramil urged the court to overrule its previous *Baehr* decision. He objected to the *Baehr* plurality's use of the plain meaning rule of statutory construction, claiming that the Hawaii statute distinguished on the basis of orientation rather than gender. Justice Ramil offered the following hypothetical to illustrate his point:

[I]f a male plaintiff in this case somehow changed his gender to become a woman, but remained homosexual (i.e., lesbian), she would still be disadvantaged by the prohibition on same-sex marriage inasmuch as she would not be permitted to marry another woman. However, if that same male plaintiff somehow changed his homosexual orientation, he would not be disadvantaged by H.R.S. § 572–1 inasmuch as he would be able to marry a female.[30]

Justice Ramil concluded that the statute therefore "disadvantages homosexuals, whether male or female, on account of their desire to enter into a marriage relationship with a person of the same sex."[31]

Justice Ramil's hypothetical is unpersuasive because he so severely limits the possibilities. Suppose, for example, that the male plaintiff changed his orientation but not his sex. Suppose further that he nonetheless wanted to marry another male so that he could receive particular benefits from the state. The state would deny the marriage license, heterosexual orientation notwithstanding. Or, suppose that the plaintiff neither changed his sex nor his orientation but nonetheless wanted to marry a female so that he could receive the state benefits referred to above. In this case, he would be able to marry, same-sex orientation notwithstanding. Thus, the statute discriminates on the basis of sex, not orientation.

Justice Ramil's example obscures the effect of the statute because the individual in his hypothetical somehow changed both his sex (from male to female) and his orientation (from male to female). Yet, the way to determine whether the basis of the classification at issue is sex rather than orientation would be to hold one of those factors constant or, perhaps, to consider what would happen if the individual sought to marry someone to whom he or she was not sexually attracted. When these possibilities are considered, the meaning and effect of the statute are clarified.

The *Baehr* court reaffirmed that "rudimentary principles of statutory construction renders manifest the fact that, by its plain language, H.R.S. § 572–1 restricts the marital relation to a male and a female."[32] The separate question of whether that facial classification violated equal protection guarantees no longer had to be addressed because the new amendment took the statute out of the "ambit" of the equal protection clause of the Hawaii Constitution. Thus, the court suggested that the marriage statute now occupied a safe haven that rendered state equal protection guarantees inapplicable (at least with respect to the restriction at issue). Of course, that says nothing about federal equal protection guarantees and, if rudimentary principles of statutory construction establish that the marriage statute classifies on the basis of sex, statutes reserving marriage for different-sex couples would seem vulnerable on federal constitutional grounds.

Not only did the court reaffirm that rudimentary principles of statutory construction reveal that same-sex marriage bans classify on the basis of sex but the court also explained that "the framers of the 1978 Hawaii Constitution, sitting as a committee of the whole, expressly declared their intention that a proscription against discrimination based on sexual orientation be subsumed within the clause's prohibition against discrimination on the basis of sex."[33] Thus, even if Justice Ramil had been correct that the statute discriminated on the basis of orientation rather than sex, the statute still would have been subject to equal protection scrutiny but for the adoption of the constitutional amendment.

In one footnote, the court did several things.[34] First, it reinforced its previous holding that a statute allowing a man to marry a woman but not a man and allowing a woman to marry a man but not a woman classifies on the basis of sex. Second, the court made clear that, at least in Hawaii, discrimination on the basis of orientation is subject to the same kind of scrutiny as is discrimination on the basis of sex and, indeed, is subsumed within the latter kind of discrimination. Thus, other legislative classifications based on orientation will be subjected to strict scrutiny in Hawaii. The court's having made these points in its decision is worthy of note and praise.

RECOGNITION OF SAME-SEX MARRIAGES VALIDLY CELEBRATED ELSEWHERE

Currently, no state recognizes same-sex marriages, so it is unclear what Hawaii would do were such marriages recognized elsewhere and (1) a Hawaiian same-sex couple were to go there to marry and then return home, or (2) a same-sex couple validly married in that state were to move to Hawaii. Existing case law coupled with the legislature's *failure* to make clear that such marriages will not be recognized offer a basis for arguing that such marriages should be recognized.

The current statute reserves marriage for different-sex couples but does not specify whether same-sex marriages validly celebrated elsewhere will be recognized. Various states have made clear their intention to refuse to recognize same-sex marriages validly celebrated in other jurisdictions. Given Hawaii's *failure* to pass a similar statute and given Hawaii's case law suggesting that non-polygamous, non-incestuous marriages validly celebrated elsewhere will be recognized in Hawaii as long as those unions were contracted voluntarily,[35] there is reason to believe that same-sex marriages if validly celebrated elsewhere will be recognized locally.

By not requiring the reenactment of the marriage restriction, the *Baehr* court may have been helpful in that, otherwise, the legislature might not only have restricted marriage but might also have made clear that same-sex marriages validly celebrated elsewhere would not be recognized in Hawaii. Of course, the legislature can still do that if it so desires and, in any event, it is unclear how such a marriage would be treated were another state to recognize such marriages and were a Hawaiian same-sex couple to travel to that state to marry and then return home. Nonetheless, it is at least more likely that such a marriage would be recognized if validly celebrated elsewhere than would have been the case if a statute expressly denying such recognition had been enacted. Thus, it may be that the *Baehr* court's method of addressing and deciding the relevant issues should be viewed more positively.

CONCLUSION

The recent Hawaii constitutional amendment gave the legislature the power to reserve marriage for different-sex couples. Precisely because this amendment was power-conferring rather than substantive, however, the court should not have construed it to have retroactively validated a portion of the Hawaii marriage statute. Indeed, if the amendment is so construed, then the literature sent to the voters describing that amendment was misleading in violation of local law and, further, may have undermined the legitimacy of the amendment itself.

As H.L.A. Hart has made clear, statutes conferring powers and statutes establishing rights or disabilities are different in kind and thus an amendment doing the former should not be construed as doing the latter, absent express language to that effect. The Hawaii amendment clearly conferred a power but said nothing about validating a disability to marry and, thus, should not have been construed to have done so. By the same token, the established retroactivity jurisprudence in Hawaii and elsewhere makes clear that statutes or portions thereof will not be retroactively validated by amendment, absent express declaration to that effect. Because the amendment said nothing about retroactively validating a portion of the Hawaii marriage statute and, indeed, the explanation of the amendment mailed to the voters suggested that it would have no such retroactive validation effect, the amendment should not have been so construed, even implicitly.

The *Baehr* court's opinion is somewhat mysterious. Because it is so terse and opaque, one can only guess about whether the court understood the implications of its holding regarding retroactivity or the possible invalidity of the ballot itself. Nonetheless, some parts of the opinion were very clear. For example, it reaffirms what other courts are beginning to recognize, namely, that bans on same-sex marriages classify on the basis of sex. Indeed, appearances to the contrary notwithstanding, the opinion may eventually help to secure the recognition of same-sex marriage in Hawaii or elsewhere since the opinion suggests both that same-sex marriage bans are vulnerable on federal constitutional grounds, and that the validity of the Hawaii amendment itself is open to question.

A separate issue is how the Hawaii Supreme Court should decide the next retroactive validation question brought before it, since the court has either implicitly reversed the standard presumptions regarding retroactivity or has adopted an interpretation of the Hawaii Constitution that rejects those standard presumptions. The most likely resolution is that the court will implicitly overrule itself so that it can restore the jurisprudence that has always existed without having to revisit an issue that the court clearly finds too onerous to continue to address.

The most disappointing aspect of the *Baehr* decision was not the result per se, since it seems likely that the legislature would in fact have reenacted the legislation had the court held that doing so was necessary. Rather, it is that recognizing the personhood of individuals with a same-sex orientation is still so controversial that courts must sometimes obscure the relevant legal issues, whether consciously or unconsciously, so that they can both recognize the basic human dignity of such individuals and, at the same time, placate those committed to refusing to recognize that inherent human worth.

NOTES

1. *Great Northern Railway Company v. Sunburst Oil & Refining Company*, 287 U.S. 358, 365 (1932).

2. See *Bonds v. State Department of Revenue*, 49 So.2d 280, 282 (Ala. 1950); *State v. Yothers*, 659 A.2d 514, 520 (N.J. 1995).

3. See *Banaz v. Smith*, 133 Cal. 102, 104 (1901).

4. See *Baehr v. Miike*, 1999 Haw. LEXIS 391, at *5.

5. H.L.A. Hart, *The Concept of Law* 79 (Oxford: Clarendon Press, 1961).

6. *Id.* at 78–79.

7. *Id.* at 79.

8. *Id.* at 77.

9. Hawaii Constitution art. 18, § 9.

10. Hawaii Admission Act § 15 (1959).

11. *In re Island Airlines, Incorporated*, 361 P.2d 390, 395 (Haw. 1961).

12. *G.E.M. Sundries Company, Incorporated v. Johnson and Johnson, Incorporated*, 283 F.2d 86, 89 n.2 (9th Cir. 1960).

13. See *id.* at 89–90.

14. Hawaii Revised Statutes § 1–3 (1985).

15. *Graham Construction Supply, Incorporated v. Schrader Construction, Incorporated*, 632 P.2d 649, 653 (Haw. 1981).

16. *Robinson v. Bailey*, 28 Haw. 462, 467 (Haw. Terr. 1925).

17. Plaintiffs-Appellees' Supplemental Brief, Part II, Baehr v. Miike, 1999 Haw. LEXIS 391 (No. 20371).

18. *Id.*

19. Hawaii Session Laws House Bill 117 § 2, at 1247 (emphasis added).

20. *State v. Shak*, 466 P.2d 422, 425 (Haw. 1970).

21. *Maui County Council v. Thompson*, 929 P.2d 1355, 1357 Haw. 1997).

22. Hawaii Revised Statutes § 1–8 (1993).

23. Hawaii Revised Statutes § 11–118.5 (Supp. 1999).

24. *Keane v. Remy*, 168 N.E. 10, 14 (Ind. 1929).

25. *State v. Silver Bow Refining Company*, 252 P. 301, 304 (Mont. 1926).

26. *Lawton Spinning Company v. Commonwealth*, 121 N.E. 518, 520 (Mass. 1919).

27. See Hawaii Revised Statutes. § 572–1 (Supp. 1999).

28. *Baehr v. Miike*, 1999 Haw. LEXIS 391, at 6.

29. *Cavanaugh v. Davis*, 440 A.2d 1389, 1382 (Pa. 1982). The North Dakota Supreme Court made a similar point. See *Pelkey v. City of Fargo*, 453 N.W.2d 801, 804 (N.D. 1990).

30. *Baehr*, 1999 Haw. LEXIS 391, at *8 n.1 (Ramil, J., concurring).

31. *Id.* at *8 n.1.

32. *Id.* at *6.

33. *Id.* at *6 n.1.

34. See *id.* n.1.

35. See, for example, *Republic v. Li Shee*, 12 Haw. 329 (Haw. 1900).

Chapter Six

Toleration and Same-Sex Relationships

Some commentators who disapprove of same-sex marriages or civil unions claim that the state should not legally recognize such relationships because the state's doing so would endorse rather than merely tolerate them. These theorists explain the difference between endorsement and toleration by pointing to the endorsement test in Establishment Clause jurisprudence or by discussing the difference between constitutionally protected activity on the one hand and activity subject to statutory regulation on the other. Yet, the existing Establishment Clause jurisprudence in particular and the Court's constitutional jurisprudence more generally suggest that the state is precluded from expressing approval of some citizens to make other citizens feel like outsiders. Further, commentators' claims to the contrary notwithstanding, the difference between legislative permission and constitutional protection does not support the state's refusal to recognize same-sex unions but instead helps illustrate why such unions must not only be recognized but also be afforded constitutional protection.

ON TOLERANCE AND ENDORSEMENT

Theorists suggest that same-sex relationships should not be legally recognized by the state because doing so would imply some sort of approval of those unions. Yet, that thesis is incorrect both because legal recognition does not imply approval and because, even if it did, that would not be a reason to refuse to recognize such relationships. Indeed, the thesis that states should or even may refuse to recognize same-sex unions simply because it disapproves of them ignores and, in fact, contradicts the developing right to marry jurisprudence.

THE BACKGROUND MARRIAGE JURISPRUDENCE

Some commentators suggest that the state should not express approval of same-sex unions by legally recognizing them because such a recognition would confer on such unions "a legally preferred status."[1] This argument implies that (1) the state endorses those marriages that it recognizes, and (2) the bare desire not to endorse a union suffices as a justification for a state's refusing to recognize it. Neither thesis is correct or even plausible, although these theses might have been thought persuasive had they been offered at an earlier time in our constitutional history. In 1877, the United States Supreme Court suggested in *Pennoyer v. Neff* that the state "has absolute right to prescribe the conditions upon which the marriage relation between its own citizens shall be created, and the causes for which it may be dissolved"[2] and, eleven years later, suggested in *Maynard v. Hill* that "[m]arriage, as creating the most important relation in life, as having more to do with the morals and civilization of a people than any other institution, . . . [is] subject to the control of the legislature."[3] Further, during that same period, various state supreme courts made clear their understanding that the state has almost unlimited discretion with respect to which marriages it will recognize.

Often, the issue arose in the state courts in the form of a challenge to a state's anti-miscegenation statute. For example, *Kinney v. Commonwealth* involved an interracial couple, domiciled in Virginia, who had married in the District of Columbia in accord with local law. The Virginia Supreme Court of Appeals had to determine the validity of the marriage because Kinney had been charged with and convicted of lewd association and cohabitation, a conviction that could only stand if in fact he were not legally married to Mahala Miller, the woman with whom he was cohabiting in Virginia and whom he had married in D.C. The court affirmed the conviction after having explained that "[m]arriage, the most elementary and useful of all, must be regulated and controlled by the sovereign power of the state."[4] Because the state did not recognize the validity of his marriage, Kinney's conviction for nonmarital cohabitation could stand.

The Indiana Supreme Court expressed a similar view when that state's interracial marriage prohibition was challenged. In *Gibson v. State*, the court upheld the state's anti-miscegenation statute, explaining that the "right in the States to regulate and control, to guard, protect, and preserve this God-given, civilizing and christianizing institution [marriage] is of inestimable importance, and cannot be surrendered, nor can the States suffer or permit any interference therewith."[5] The supreme courts of

Georgia and Tennessee also found that their respective state legislatures had the power to preclude interracial marriage.[6]

In 1967, the United States Supreme Court made clear in *Loving v. Virginia* that the states do not have the power to prohibit interracial marriage, even if the states disapprove of such marriages and, eleven years later, made clear in *Zablocki v. Redhail* that states have only limited discretion with respect to their marriage regulations even when race is not at issue. It was quite clear in *Zablocki* and *Loving* that the states did not approve of the marriages at issue. Nonetheless, state disapproval notwithstanding, the individuals' rights to marry were recognized. Indeed, the fact that Virginia and Wisconsin were constitutionally required to recognize the marriages at issue, disapproval of those unions notwithstanding, indicates both that mere disapproval of a union will not suffice as a justification for refusing to allow individuals to marry and that the analysis offered by these commentators is fundamentally mistaken.

ON ENDORSING MARRIAGES

Suppose that the United States Constitution precluded states from being forced to "endorse" marriages of which they did not approve. Even were that so, a separate issue requiring analysis would involve determining when states had put their seal of approval on particular unions. Merely because a state had recognized a marriage would not entail that the state had endorsed that marriage. For example, when the United States Supreme Court made clear that states had to recognize interracial marriages, those states that had prohibited such marriages did not suddenly change their views and endorse them, notwithstanding that the states were now required to allow such unions to be celebrated. Indeed, South Carolina and Alabama seemed to have kept their anti-miscegenation laws on the books for their "expressive" value, notwithstanding that the laws prohibiting such unions have been unenforceable since *Loving*.[7]

Individuals might disagree about the expressive content of an unenforceable anti-miscegenation statute that remains on the books. Some would claim that it expresses societal disapproval of interracial marriage, while others would claim that it expresses racism or, perhaps, provincial attitudes indicating that the state would not be a good place in which a business should locate or expand. Regardless of which expressive content is most plausibly ascribed when a state keeps such a law on the books, it is quite clear that South Carolina and Alabama could hardly be said to have been giving interracial unions their stamp of approval over the past thirty years. The actions of South Carolina and Alabama suggest at least two weaknesses in the argument that states should not endorse same-sex marriages by recognizing them: (1) claims to the contrary notwithstanding, states can legally recognize unions without endorsing them, and (2) if states are not permitted to refuse to recognize interracial marriages, even if in fact they disapprove of such unions, it is not at all clear why the disapproval of same-sex unions justifies a refusal to recognize those unions.

TOLERATION VERSUS ACCEPTANCE

Part of the disagreement over whether states should recognize same-sex unions involves differing analyses concerning whether toleration and endorsement are compatible. Commentators disagree about whether an individual who is tolerant of another's practices implicitly disapproves of those practices or, instead, has no implicit position about those practices whatsoever. Yet, even were it clear what an *individual* would be saying were she merely to tolerate another's beliefs or practices, that would not establish what the *state* would be saying were it tolerant of different groups. Whether or not one assumes that the "tolerant" individual implicitly disapproves of those whom she tolerates, one should not make such an assumption about the tolerant state.

Michael Walzer suggests that individuals who "make room for men and women whose beliefs they don't adopt, whose practices they decline to imitate," that is, who have the virtue of tolerance, have that quality "without regard to their standing on the continuum of resignation, indifference, stoical acceptance, curiosity, and enthusiasm"[8] of the beliefs or practices at issue. Thus, according to Walzer, individuals may appropriately be said to be tolerant even if in fact they have no objections to and in fact approve of the attitudes or practices of which they are tolerant.

Other commentators offer a different view. For example, Bernard Williams distinguishes between indifference and tolerance. He points out that if a same-sex relationship arouses no hostile reaction, that might be due to indifference rather than tolerance. While this lack of reaction might be thought to exemplify the practice of tolerance, Williams would hesitate to call these people "tolerant" if they had ceased to think the behavior wrong. Strictly speaking, he is tempted to call a group tolerant only when it "puts up with"[9] the other, differing group. Thus, on his view, tolerance is not only to be distinguished from endorsement but also from indifference, and "toleration" should only be used when the object of toleration elicits disapproval.

Steven Smith's analysis is similar to Williams's: Smith suggests that one can tolerate only that of which one disapproves. He offers an example to illustrate his point, suggesting that while a community might tolerate prostitution or pornography, it would not tolerate honesty, compassion, or artistic achievement.[10] Yet, Smith's analysis is less persuasive than first appears. For example, it would be perfectly coherent for someone to say that a community not only tolerates but positively encourages a particular quality, for example, honesty. It is not as if "tolerates" would have been used incorrectly or improperly there.

As a separate point, Smith may have been misled by his own examples. Consider a community that tolerates different religious or political views. The community is presumably *not* saying that it *disapproves* of those religious or political views, even if it would in fact disapprove of prostitution or pornography. Thus, while a community might disapprove of *some* of its objects of toleration, that same community might approve of or be indifferent toward other objects of its toleration.

In *Webster's Third New International Dictionary*, the definition for "tolerate" includes both "to permit the existence or practice of: to allow without prohibition or hindrance: make no effort to prevent" and "to endure with forbearance or restraint: put up with: bear."[11] The former definition suggests nothing about the tolerant individual's attitudes, since she or he might make no effort to prevent the expression of attitudes of which she or he disapproves or, for that matter, approves. The latter definition suggests some sort of disapproval, since one would not need to "put up with" attitudes with which one agreed. Thus, there would seem to be at least two senses of "tolerance": a broader sense that does not imply any particular attitude toward that which is tolerated and a narrow sense that implies disapproval.[12]

Arguably, an individual who *merely* tolerates another might be inferred to be "putting up with" that person and, in addition, not to be giving that person "equal concern and respect." Yet, even if that is so, it is unclear whether such an inference is justified because of the word "tolerate" or, instead, because of the word "merely." Arguably, use of the words "merely tolerates" implies disapproval or perhaps indifference, which would not have been implied by use of the word "tolerates" alone.

Even if a *person's* tolerating something or someone else implies indifference or disapproval, a separate question is whether a *state's* tolerating particular religions or races, for example, implies disapproval of those races or religions. Whether or not it is appropriate to infer the narrow sense of "tolerate" when describing the attitude of an individual who (merely) tolerates others, the broad sense of "tolerate" both is and should be used when the state is tolerating someone or something. A state that tolerated but disapproved of particular races or religions would hardly be thought particularly tolerant, and the same might be said of a state that tolerated but disapproved of some of its citizens on the basis of their sexual orientation.

Two different issues should not be conflated. Certainly, it is correct to suggest that individuals working to secure rights for lesbians, gays, bisexuals, and transgendered people do not wish to be treated as second class citizens nor merely to be tolerated. Further, acceptance might be distinguished from tolerance, which itself might be distinguished from indifference. That said, it is mistaken to claim that the legal recognition of same-sex marriages would imply acceptance,[13] at least insofar as one would thereby be implying that the recognition of such unions would indicate or perhaps automatically bring about that acceptance.

As an examination of the recent history of the anti-miscegenation laws of South Carolina and Alabama reveals, racial acceptance should not be assumed merely because a state recognizes interracial marriages. This is true both because recognition of interracial marriage occurred before everyone accepted such unions and because the recognition of those unions did not suddenly cause people to discard their biased attitudes. Although the refusal to recognize interracial marriage involved invidious racial discrimination, the removal of those bans did not suddenly extirpate the prejudicial attitudes that motivated such bans.

In *Loving,* the Court recognized that Virginia's anti-miscegenation law was a manifestation of the state's preference for some of its citizens over others. This attempt by the state to indicate its preference for some of its citizens over others was a reason to *invalidate* the statute. Though the Court would have struck down the statute, "even assuming an even-handed state purpose to protect the 'integrity' of all races,"[14] it was clear that the Court was especially offended by the racial classifications that directly subverted the Fourteenth Amendment's underlying principle of equality. Thus, while the Court clearly understands the difference between toleration and preference, the Court has not endorsed the preference model for determining which marriages should be recognized, commentators' claims to the contrary notwithstanding. Indeed, it is especially ironic that commentators want to use the endorsement test in Establishment Clause jurisprudence as the appropriate model for determining the kinds of preferences the state may manifest, since that model undermines the very position that these commentators propose.

ESTABLISHMENT CLAUSE JURISPRUDENCE

Professor Wardle points out that states universally distinguish between tolerance and preference, citing the endorsement test in Establishment Clause jurisprudence to establish that point.[15] Yet, even a brief consideration of that jurisprudence helps to establish why the state should rather than should not recognize same-sex unions.

In *Lynch v. Donnelly,* the Court suggested that the Constitution requires accommodation of all religions and forbids hostility toward any. Justice O'Connor made clear in her *Lynch* concurrence, however, that accommodation is not the equivalent of endorsement. "Endorsement sends a message to nonadherents that they are outsiders, not full members of the political community, and an accompanying message to adherents that they are insiders, favored members of the political community."[16] The Court will pay close attention to make sure that a challenged governmental practice has neither the purpose nor the effect of endorsing religion. Further, in this jurisprudence, the issue is not whether the state has "endorsed" rather than, for example, merely "preferred" one religion over another. As the Court has made clear, "Whether the key word is 'endorsement,' 'favoritism,' or 'promotion,' the essential principle remains the same."[17]

Commentators are correct to suggest that there is an important difference between permitting and endorsing a practice. However, they draw exactly the wrong inference from that acknowledged distinction. The state should tolerate and even accommodate different religions but must not, in fact, endorse one over another or even religion over nonreligion. Just as the endorsement test in Establishment Clause jurisprudence precludes the state from treating nonadherents of a particular faith as outsiders who are not full members of the community, an endorsement test should preclude the state from denying individuals the right to marry merely because it wants to tell those individuals that they are outsiders who are not full members of the community.

ON DIFFERENT CLASSES OF CITIZENSHIP

It might be argued that worries about the state's endorsing or preferring some groups over others are relevant in the context of religion but not in other contexts. Such a view is mistaken, even if one brackets the claim that animus against lesbian, gay, bisexual, or transgendered people might be religiously based. There is a long tradition establishing that the state is precluded from making individuals into second-class citizens.

In *Burton v. Wilmington Parking Authority*, the Court held that the state could not lease public property to a restaurant that refused to serve individuals because of their race, since the state would thereby be a party to making such individuals second-class citizens. While the Equal Protection Clause does not reach *private* wrongful conduct, the State is not entitled to make such distinctions among its citizens. Further, the Court has made clear that this equal protection limitation includes attempts by states to harm on the basis of orientation. Thus, in *Romer v. Evans*, the Court suggested that because the state constitutional amendment at issue "classifie[d] homosexuals not to further a proper legislative end but to make them unequal to everyone else,"[18] the amendment was unconstitutional.

Certainly, the claim is not that the state is precluded from making any distinctions among its citizens. The Equal Protection Clause does not require that all persons be treated identically, since "the machinery of government would not work if it were not allowed a little play in its joints."[19] Yet, precluding the state from targeting a class to make them unequal to everyone else can hardly be said to be so limiting as to impose a strait jacket on the state.

Commentators are correct to suggest that there is an important difference between toleration or accommodation on the one hand and endorsement on the other. As Establishment Clause jurisprudence makes clear, the state should not be implying that certain citizens are outsiders who are not full members of the community. The same point has been made in other contexts as well: The state must not create classifications to indicate that certain citizens are "second-class" or are unequal to everyone else. Thus, a state's refusing to recognize same-sex marriages because it wants to communicate that gays, lesbians, bisexuals, and transgendered people are second-class citizens thereby provides a reason to *strike* rather than uphold the legislation at issue.

CONSTITUTIONAL PROTECTION VERSUS LEGISLATIVE CREATION

Even if one rejects that the endorsement test analogy supports the claim that the state should refuse to recognize same-sex unions, one might be tempted to accept a different rationale that has been offered to support that contention. Commentators suggest that some activities or relationships are prohibited, some permitted, and some afforded protection. Those in the latter group are "preferred," and, these commentators suggest, same-sex relationships should at best be permitted but should not be afforded this special "preferred" status.

ON PERMITTING VERSUS PROTECTING

Bruce Hafen distinguishes between three different categories of conduct: "(1) protected conduct (such as political speech), which is protected by a preferred constitutional right; (2) permitted conduct (such as driving a car), which is the subject neither of constitutional protection nor of unusual prohibitions; and (3) prohibited conduct (such as robbery), which is forbidden by a criminal sanction."[20] He argues that there is a significant difference between protected and permitted conduct, even bracketing the content of the conduct. Thus, suppose that there are two societies. In one, a particular conduct is protected, and in another that very same conduct is merely permitted. Although one would not be able to distinguish between the contents of the conduct permitted in the two societies, the conduct in the first society would have a preferred status, if only because the legislature in the second, but not in the first, society could easily criminalize the conduct at issue sometime in the future.

In *Trop v. Dulles*, the Court discussed the use of denationalization as a punishment. The Court pointed out that such a punishment strips a citizen of his status in the national and international political community.

Stripping him of that status would not be a physical punishment, and a country might, in fact, accord such an individual some rights. Nonetheless, the enjoyment of those rights might be terminated at any time, and the individual's very existence would be "at the sufferance of the country in which he happens to find himself."[21]

The *Trop* Court was suggesting that denationalization was an extreme punishment, which violated the Eighth Amendment barring cruel and unusual punishment, notwithstanding that the denationalized citizen might in fact enjoy many of the same rights and privileges that others enjoyed. Precisely because those rights and privileges could be withdrawn at any time, the denationalized citizen would be in a precarious position. Such a citizen might always fear, for example, that because of a change in the political climate, he or she might suddenly be deprived of the rights that he or she had previously enjoyed.

In his concurrence in *Wieman v. Updegraff,* Justice Black discussed the First Amendment right of free expression. He pointed out that individuals are guaranteed an undiluted right to express themselves on questions of public interest and made clear that this "means that Americans discuss such questions as of right and not on *sufferance* of legislatures, courts, or any other governmental agencies."[22]

The difference between having a right protected by the Constitution and having a privilege on sufferance of the legislature does not involve the content of the liberty at issue. Justice Black's point is that the liberty of free expression is greatly diminished if one has that liberty only on sufferance and not as a matter of constitutional right, even if the liberty accorded as a matter of sufferance would permit one to do as much as would a similar liberty accorded as a matter of constitutional right.

Professor Hafen illustrates the difference between constitutionally protected and statutorily permitted conduct by suggesting that sexual relations within marriage are protected, whereas sexual relations outside of marriage are either prohibited or merely permitted. Part of his point was to suggest that when a judge strikes down a statute prohibiting particular conduct on constitutional grounds, the conduct moves from the prohibited to the protected category, whereas when a legislature decriminalizes conduct, the conduct moves from the prohibited to the permitted category. Although the conduct will be permissible whether the statute was repealed or instead struck down as unconstitutional, those engaging in the conduct might feel much more secure if it were constitutionally protected rather than merely legislatively permitted.

HAFEN'S TRI-PARTITE ANALYSIS APPLIED TO RELATIONSHIPS

Commentators have applied Hafen's analysis to types of personal relationships.[23] They suggest that same-sex relationships should at best be placed in the "permitted" category, whereas different-sex marriages are and should be placed in the preferred category. They then argue that same-sex marriage proponents are seeking "special" treatment when attempting to have something currently in the permitted category instead included within the preferred category. There are a number of reasons, however, why this analysis is faulty.

Same-sex marriage proponents are only seeking the same privileges that others have. It is hardly a request for "special treatment" in any common sense of the term when individuals are merely "struggl[ing] to change a social order that ha[s] consistently treated them as second class citizens" and are seeking "only the equal respect and equal treatment to which they [are] constitutionally entitled."[24]

Commentators are correct to talk about marriage as a preferred relationship. The right to marry is an extremely important right and, as the Court has made clear, "fundamental rights may not be submitted to vote; they depend on the outcome of no elections."[25] The issue at hand is not whether marriage will remain "preferred" but who will be entitled to marry.

Some commentators deny that the issue is who should be allowed to marry, claiming that lesbians and gays, like everyone else, can marry; they simply cannot marry someone of their own sex. One could easily imagine the analogous argument having been made when interracial couples wished to marry. Thus, the would-be marrieds had the right to marry; they simply did not have the right to marry someone of another race. This argument is no more persuasive in the context under discussion here than it was when rejected in the interracial marriage context. Indeed, commentators seem not to appreciate that the analogs of their arguments might have been offered by those seeking to preclude the recognition of interracial marriage. Interracial marriage opponents would note that some states permitted interracial marriage and others did not and would argue that the fact that such relationships were permitted would not have made them "preferred." These commentators might further claim that interracial marriage proponents were confusing tolerance with preference.[26]

There are other respects in which the analogs of these arguments might have been used to advantage by those supporting anti-miscegenation laws. In response to the claim that interracial marriage bans manifested impermissible bias, these commentators might have claimed that society has acted upon a long-standing moral consensus that conceives of marriage as a unique two-person community of individuals of the same race. The interracial marriage opponent might have continued: "To say that other kinds of relationships are not within [southern] society's concept of marriage is not an expression of intolerance or animosity. One kind of relationship gets the benefit of a moral preference, and all others receive tolerance."[27] That these kinds of arguments were rejected in the context of interracial marriage suggests that they should not be given credence in this context either.

The interracial marriage opponent described above, like the same-sex marriage opponents discussed here, has confused types of *relationships* with types of *people*. A society might decide to give one relationship (marriage) preference over other kinds of relationships (nonmarital cohabitation) without at the same time endorsing the view that certain classes of individuals will be barred from enjoying that preferred status. Thus, the arguments of the interracial and same-sex marriage opponents are unpersuasive for the same reason: they have confused giving preference to a status with giving preference to particular people.

Proponents of interracial or same-sex marriages are not denying that marriage enjoys a preferred status and thus hardly are confusing toleration with preference. Instead, they are merely suggesting that the state is not allowed to designate certain people as second-class citizens by refusing to permit them to marry.

Professor Duncan offers some consolation to those same-sex couples who have been denied the right to marry. After all, he suggests, individuals "may enter into committed same-sex relationships, perhaps even with benefit of clergy, and consider themselves married. In this latter case, although same-sex couples are denied the legal and public status of married persons, they are free to live with and love whomever they wish."[28] Yet, the state would hardly be free to preclude interracial marriage as long as it permitted those thus deprived "to live with and love whomever they wish[ed]."

THE HAFEN ANALYSIS APPLIED TO MARRIAGE

Couples who are permitted to live together but not to marry are at a disadvantage, at least in part, because they have been denied the legal and public status of married persons. Suppose, however, that the legislature creates a special status for certain couples called "civil unions," which by statute confers all of the benefits of marriage. Even if one brackets the presumed stigma attached to the legislature's having set up a different status that mirrors marriage but does not have that name, there is an additional difficulty, namely, that all of the benefits of civil unions could disappear were the legislature to have a change of heart and repeal the legislation.

Professor Hafen's analysis suggests why marriage would be preferable to civil unions, even if each status accorded the same benefits. Marriage is constitutionally protected, whereas civil unions would be at the sufferance of the legislature subject to repeal with a change in legislative composition or sentiment.

Suppose that a state legislature were to follow Vermont's lead and create a civil union status, which entitles same-sex couples to all of the rights and responsibilities of marriage. Even were the rights and responsibilities identical to those that would be conferred by marriage, that *status* would nonetheless be significantly inferior because it had been legislatively conferred rather than constitutionally protected. Thus, same-sex marriage opponents' views notwithstanding, Professor Hafen's analysis shows why same-sex unions must be constitutionally protected rather than accorded recognition on sufferance of the legislature. It certainly does not show why such unions should not be recognized at all, just as it does not show why states would be permitted to prefer intra-racial marriages over interracial unions.

CONCLUSION

Some same-sex marriage opponents argue that same-sex unions should not be legally recognized because the state would thereby be endorsing such unions. Yet, this is unpersuasive both because legal recognition does not entail endorsement and, even if it did, this would not be a reason to refuse to recognize such unions, since such unions promote the same kinds of state interests that different-sex unions promote and thus should be endorsed by the state.

Commentators sometimes cite the endorsement test of Establishment Clause jurisprudence to support their claim that the state distinguishes between endorsement and toleration. Though they are correct that the state recognizes the distinction, they are incorrect to believe that their position is thereby supported, since the endorsement test is used to determine which state practices are *impermissible* because of preferring some citizens over others.

Some theorists cite Hafen's analysis distinguishing between preferred and nonpreferred activities in an attempt to show why same-sex unions should not be recognized. Yet, they misapply his analysis, since it might be used to distinguish between marriage and other types of cohabitation but *not* to distinguish between those who will be allowed to enjoy a particular status and those who will not. Indeed, commentators' claims notwithstanding, the Hafen analysis does not establish why the state should refuse to recognize same-sex marriages any more than it establishes why the state should refuse to recognize interracial marriages. On the contrary, the analysis instead establishes why both interracial and same-sex marriages should be recognized as a matter of constitutional right rather than mere legislative sufferance.

These same-sex marriage opponents are correct that the endorsement test of Establishment Clause jurisprudence and the Hafen analysis regarding tolerated and preferred activities are important in the same-sex marriage debate. These commentators fail to appreciate, however, that the very arguments upon which they rely support rather than undermine the state's recognizing same-sex unions and in fact help to show why these commentators' positions are simply unsupportable in light of current law.

NOTES

1. See Lynn D. Wardle, "Legal Claims for Same-Sex Marriage: Efforts to Legitimate a Retreat from Marriage by Redefining Marriage," 39 *South Texas Law Review* 735, 752 (1998). See also Richard F. Duncan, "Homosexual Marriage and the Myth of Tolerance: Is Cardinal O'Connor a 'Homophobe'?" 10 *Notre Dame Journal of Law, Ethics and Public Policy* 587, 593 (1996) ("the demand for same-sex marriage laws is a call not for tolerance but for approval, encouragement and preferred status. . . . A tolerant society might decide that homosexual behavior, although permitted between consenting adults, should nevertheless be discouraged or at least deprived of public encouragement.")

2. *Pennoyer v. Neff*, 95 U.S. 714, 734-35 (1877). See also Atherton v. Atherton, 181 U.S. 155, 163 (1901) ("The state, for example, has absolute right to prescribe the conditions upon which the marriage relation between its own citizens shall be created, and the causes for which it may be dissolved.")

3. *Maynard v. Hill*, 125 U.S. 190, 205 (1888).

4. *Kinney v. Commonwealth*, 71 Va. (30 Grattan) 858, 869 (1878).

5. *Gibson v. State*, 36 Ind. 389, 403 (1871).

6. See *Scott v. State*, 39 Ga. 321, 324 (1869) ("The Legislature certainly had as much right to regulate the marriage relation by prohibiting it between persons of different races as they had to prohibit it between persons within the Levitical degrees, or between idiots."); *Lonas v. State*, 50 Tenn. (3 Heiske) 287, 310 (1871).

These police powers of the state extend to every conceivable subject, where the good order, the domestic peace, the private happiness or public welfare of the people demand legislation. Unless that legislation is inhibited in the fundamental law, no State has acquitted itself of the duties of government without it. We hold that such legislation is not, never has been, and never should be, prohibited to the States, in reference to the intermarriage of the races.

7. The South Carolina and Alabama Constitutions were amended in 1998 and 2000 respectively to remove their anti-miscegenation provisions.

8. Michael Walzer, *On Toleration* 11 (New Haven: Yale University Press, 1997).

9. Bernard Williams, "Toleration: An Impossible Virtue?" in David Heyd ed. *Toleration: An Elusive Virtue* 18, 19 (Princeton: Princeton University Press, 1996).

10. Steven D. Smith, "The Restoration of Tolerance," 78 *California Law Review* 305, 306 (1990).

11. See *Webster's Third New International Dictionary* 2405 (1981).

12. *See* George Fletcher, "The Instability of Tolerance," in *Toleration: An Elusive Virtue* 158, 169 (David Heyd ed. 1996) ("Among those more tolerant of homosexuality, the problem is distinguishing among the sentiments of indifference, acceptance, and tolerance in the narrow sense.")

13. *Id.* The claim here is not that Professor Fletcher is against such acceptance, *see id.* ("I confess to a certain amount of sympathy for this push toward acceptance rather than tolerance or indifference toward homosexuality"), but merely that recognition of same-sex unions should not be thought to establish general acceptance and should not be put off until there is that general acceptance.

14. *Loving,* 388 U.S. at 11 n.11.

15. Lynn D. Wardle, "A Critical Analysis of Constitutional Claims for Same-Sex Marriage," 1996 *Brigham Young University Law Review* 1, 58 n.257.

16. *Lynch v. Donnelly,* 465 U.S. 668, 673 (1984).

17. *County of Allegheny v. American Civil Liberties Union,* 492 U.S. 573, 593 (1989). See also Capitol Square Review and Advisory Board v. Pinette, 515 U.S. 753, 763–64 (1995).

We must note, to begin with, that it is not really an "endorsement test" of any sort, much less the "endorsement test" which appears in our more recent Establishment Clause jurisprudence, that petitioners urge upon us. "Endorsement" connotes an expression or demonstration of approval or support. The New Shorter Oxford English Dictionary 818 (1993); Webster's New Dictionary 845 (2d ed. 1950). Our cases have accordingly equated 'endorsement' with 'promotion' or 'favoritism.'" (citing *Allegheny,* 492 U.S. at 593).

18. *Romer v. Evans,* 517 U.S. 620, 635 (1996).

19. *Bain Peanut Company v. Pinson,* 282 U.S. 499, 501 (1931).

20. Bruce C. Hafen, "The Constitutional Status of Marriage, Kinship, and Sexual Privacy; Balancing the Individual and Social Interests," 81 *Michigan Law Review* 463, 546 (1983).

21. *Trop v. Dulles* 356 U.S. 86, 101 (1958).

22. *Wieman v. Updegraff,* 344 U.S. 183, 194 (1952) (Black J., concurring) (italics added).

23. Richard F. Duncan, "Homosexual Marriage and the Myth of Tolerance: Is Cardinal O'Connor a 'Homophobe'"? 10 *Notre Dame Journal of Law, Ethics and Public Policy* 587, 593 (1996); Lynn D. Wardle, "A Critical Analysis of Constitutional Claims for Same-Sex Marriage," 1996 *Brigham Young University Law Review* 1, 58.

24. *See Federal Trade Commission v. Superior Court Trial Lawyers Association,* 493 U.S. 411, 426 (1990).

25. *Santa Fe Independent School District v. Doe,* 530 U.S. 290, 304–05 (2000) (citing *West Virginia Board of Education v. Barnette,* 319 U.S. 624, 638 (1943)).

26. Lynn D. Wardle, "Legal Claims for Same-Sex Marriage: Efforts to Legitimate a Retreat from Marriage by Redefining Marriage," 39 *South Texas Law Review* 735, 751 (1998).

27. Richard F. Duncan, "The Narrow and Shallow Bite of *Romer* and the Eminent Rationality of Dual-Gender Marriage: A (Partial) Response to Professor Koppelman," 6 *William & Mary Bill of Rights Journal* 147, 159 (1997).

28. Richard F. Duncan, "Homosexual Marriage and the Myth of Tolerance: Is Cardinal O'Connor a 'Homophobe'"? 10 *Notre Dame Journal of Law, Ethics and Public Policy* 587, 598 (1996).

Chapter Seven

Marriage, Religion, and Free Exercise

Reactions to Vermont's recognition of civil unions have ranged across a wide spectrum. Some suggest that Vermont has not gone far enough, since the state might instead have permitted same-sex couples to marry; others suggest that the state has struck exactly the right balance by affording same-sex couples the rights and responsibilities of marriage while at the same time reserving marriage for different-sex couples; and still others suggest that the state has taken steps that will lead to the destruction of marriage and the family. This range of reactions was not unexpected, and any other state considering the creation of civil union status should expect an equally broad range of views among its citizens, although the percentage of citizens holding one view rather than another would presumably vary from state to state.

There is no single explanation for the vastly differing reactions to same-sex unions, although it is safe to assume that those responses are based in part on differing views regarding the nature, meaning, and purposes of marriage. These views differ radically, both within and across perspectives. Thus, not only might Vermont's recognition of same-sex unions contradict the teachings of some religions regarding permissible and impermissible relationships, but the teachings of some religions contradict the teachings of other religions on that subject. Recognizing that there is this diversity of opinion both within and across perspectives is important, both because it undercuts the legitimacy of the claim that the same-sex marriage issue is basically a debate between religious and secular groups and because this diversity of opinion may affect the relevant legal analysis.

THE LEGAL DEFINITION OF MARRIAGE

Any analysis of civil union status can be offered only after certain related issues are considered: (1) Do same-sex couples meet the legal definition of marriage and, if not, what implications does this have? and (2) Could the legal functions and purposes of marriage be served even if both parties are of the same sex and, if so, what implications does this have?

A state's definition of marriage might be found in its statutes or in its case law. A number of states have enacted statutes making clear that a marriage contract will be valid only if it is made between a man and a woman, although those statutes do not specify whether such marriages will be invalid because of how marriage is *defined* or instead for some other reason. Consider the Minnesota statute which reads, "Marriage, so far as its validity in law is concerned, is a civil contract between a man and a woman . . ."[1] or the Georgia statute which reads, "Marriages between persons of the same sex are prohibited in this state."[2] Though both states refuse to permit same-sex marriages to be celebrated locally, it is not at all clear that either state claims that such unions are precluded by definition rather than are simply prohibited by law.

The Georgia and Minnesota statutes might be contrasted with the Louisiana statute, which reads, "Marriage is a legal relationship between a man and a woman that is created by civil contract."[3] Rather than declare that certain individuals are prohibited from marrying or, perhaps, that they will be unable to enter into a valid marital contract, the latter provides a definition of marriage that, by its very terms, makes same-sex couples ineligible.

At least one question raised by these different ways of precluding same-sex marriages is whether a legislature's enacting one statute rather than another would have different legal ramifications. For example, it might be thought that a definition rather than a mere prohibition somehow represents the nature of things and thus is immune from constitutional attack. This nature-of-things argument has indeed been offered by the courts. Thus, when upholding the denial of a marriage license to two women in *Jones v. Hallahan,* the Kentucky Supreme Court suggested that the "appellants [were] prevented from marrying, not by the statutes of Kentucky or the refusal of the County Court Clerk of Jefferson County to issue them a license, but rather by their own incapability of entering into a marriage as that term is defined."[4] Here, the court implied that Kentucky *could not* have recognized a marriage of same-sex partners even if the legislature had thought it appropriate to do so, for example, because that would contradict Natural Law. Had the Kentucky court not believed the legislature somehow precluded from passing such a statute, the court would have admitted that the statutes of Kentucky (rather than the individuals' sexes) had prevented these individuals from marrying and then would have engaged in the relevant constitutional analysis to determine whether that exclusion was permissible in light of state and federal constitutional guarantees.

Perhaps this sort of mistake was understandable in the 1970s, since *Baehr v. Lewin* had not yet been decided. In *Baehr,* a plurality of the Hawaii Supreme Court suggested that the state's marital statute prohibiting same-sex partners from marrying was subject to constitutional scrutiny, explicitly recognizing that the definitional argument is "circular and unpersuasive."[5] Indeed, had Hawaii not changed its state constitution by referendum in 1998, it seems likely that Hawaii would now recognize same-sex marriages. The same might be said of Alaska.

Surprisingly, an analysis similar to the Kentucky Supreme Court's was offered in 1995 even after the *Baehr* decision had been handed down. In his concurring and dissenting opinion in *Dean v. District of Columbia,* Judge Terry suggested:

But if two people are incapable of being married because they are members of the same sex and marriage requires two persons of opposite sexes, . . . then I do not see how it makes any difference that the District of Columbia, or any agency of its government, discriminates against these two appellants by refusing to allow them to enter into a legal status which the sameness of their gender prevents them from entering in the first place.[6]

What the Kentucky Supreme Court, Judge Terry, and various commentators fail to appreciate is that the plaintiffs would have been able to marry, sameness of their sexes notwithstanding, had the respective legislative bodies amended the relevant statutes. The sameness of the parties' sexes, like the ages of minors or particular individuals' relations of affinity or consanguinity, was a bar to marriage precisely because the relevant statutes had made it a bar. A separate question involves whether or not the particular limitations are justified, but that will not be answered by simply pointing out that a prohibitory definition is included within the statute.

The use of definitions above is to be distinguished from the use of definitions in *Littleton v. Prange,* in which a Texas appellate court noted, "Marriage is tightly defined in the United States: 'a legal union between one man and one woman.'" [7] Here, however, the court was not claiming that a state could not recognize same-sex marriages. On the contrary, the court recognized that a state could, although the court cautioned that "even if one state were to recognize same-sex marriage, it would not need to be recognized in any other state, and probably would not be."[8] Although interstate recognition is a separate issue requiring its own analysis, the *Littleton* court at least implicitly understood that definitions could not be used to immunize legislative decisions.

THE NATURE AND PURPOSES OF MARRIAGE
FROM A LEGAL PERSPECTIVE

Merely because marital statutes incorporating definitions are not immune from constitutional scrutiny does not mean that they are impermissible. Rather, they must be examined in light of the implicated state and individual interests to see whether they in fact pass constitutional muster. Thus, the claim here is not that all marital regulations are arbitrary and should be rejected. As the Court recognized in *Zablocki v. Redhail,* reasonable marital regulations may legitimately be imposed if they do not significantly interfere with the right to marry. Rather, the claim here is merely that each marital regulation should be examined to determine whether "it is supported by sufficiently important state interests and is closely tailored to effectuate only those interests."[9]

The reason that marital prohibitions must be examined closely is that marriage involves such an important right, which serves a variety of societal and individual purposes. Marriage provides a setting in which children might be produced and raised and, given the lesbian and gay baby boom, this is an important reason to *recognize* same-sex unions. Marriage also provides stability for adults, making them happier and more productive, which is good both for society and for the individuals involved. Yet, if recognizing same-sex marriages would promote societal and individual interests, then the state must have important interests that would be undermined by recognizing same-sex unions in order for such a refusal to be justified.

THE LACK OF UNANIMITY REGARDING
SAME-SEX MARRIAGE

When discussing the religious view of marriage, two different issues must be addressed: (1) Is it true that marriage from a religious perspective precludes same-sex unions? and (2) Were that so, what implications for the law would flow from that common religious view regarding which marriages are precluded? Views to the contrary notwithstanding, (1) there is no universal religious view on the nature of marriage even if one focuses solely on whether same-sex marriages are permissible, and (2) even were this claimed consensus to exist, it would not have the implications that are claimed by same-sex marriage opponents.

The claim that no religion (or country, for that matter) recognizes same-sex unions simply is not tenable. *Some* rather than all religions refuse to recognize same-sex unions, and Quakers, Unitarians, Buddhists, Reconstructionist Jews, and Reform Jews might all celebrate same-sex unions.

Commentators offer an inaccurate picture when suggesting that the same-sex marriage debate is between those who would respect religious views and those who would not. It cannot truthfully be claimed that the state refusal to recognize same-sex marriage somehow supports the sanctity of marriage from "the" religious view or even that the state's considering the recognition of such unions is clearly a slap in the face of anyone religious. Rather, the most that can be claimed is that the state position supports the religious dictates of *some* but not all religions.

Given the claimed neutrality of the United States with respect to the religions, much less the claimed neutrality between religion and non-religion, it simply will not do to say that because the recognition of same-sex marriages would not be compatible with the views of *some* religions the state must therefore refuse to recognize such unions. On the contrary, the Court has made quite clear that the "Free Exercise Clause simply cannot be understood to require the Government to conduct its own internal affairs in ways that comport with the religious beliefs of particular citizens."[10] Even if the religious sentiments of some would be offended, for example, by recognizing civil unions or same-sex marriages, that alone would not suffice to justify the state's refusal to recognize those unions.[11] Indeed, even the granting of benefits (and using taxes to pay for those benefits) could not successfully be challenged by claiming that one's religion would not support that use of taxes. As the Supreme Court has explained, "The tax system could not function if denominations were allowed to challenge the tax system because tax payments were spent in a manner that violates their religious belief."[12]

In *Dean v. District of Columbia,* the trial court suggested that the Establishment Clause is not violated merely because a law happens to coincide with the tenets of some or all religions. Such a statement is unobjectionable. Murder, for example, is both religiously and legally proscribed. The court made clear, however, that it was far more deferential to particular religious views than such an observation might imply, suggesting that the Establishment Clause is not violated by a same-sex marriage ban because "[n]o religion is advanced by a refusal to . . . [recognize such unions], since said refusal applies equally to same-sex applicants who are atheists, agnostics or believers, and no one is thereby coerced in the slightest to alter his or her convictions."[13] Such a standard allows far too much. For example, it would permit public schools to have students elected to offer nondenominational prayers at football games, since all students at the school—whether atheists, agnostics, or believers—might potentially be selected to give the address, all attending the game—whether atheists, agnostics, or believers—would get to hear such prayers, and no one would be coerced into altering his or her convictions. Yet, the Supreme Court has made clear that such a system would violate the Establishment Clause.[14]

The *Dean* trial court was willing to uphold legislative action that was merely motivated by religious convictions. The court was perfectly comfortable with the notion that the District of Columbia marriage ban might have been motivated by the belief that same-sex marriage was morally repugnant, even if that belief were of religious origin. After all, the court suggested, when one engages in the correct due process inquiry, one sees that the relevant issue is not "the fundamental nature of an abstract 'right to marry,' but rather, whether the Constitution confers a fundamental right upon persons of the same sex to marry one another."[15] Because of this "correct" framing of the question, the court held that the legitimate interest in promoting religious morality sufficed to justify the ban.

Ironically, the *Dean* trial court cited *Loving* to support its position. Yet, if the *Loving* Court had examined not "the fundamental nature of an abstract 'right to marry,' but rather whether the Constitution confers a fundamental right upon persons *of different races* to marry one another" and had, in addition, consulted the history and traditions of this country to provide an answer, the Court would never have suggested that Virginia's anti-miscegenation statute violated due process guarantees. If belief that the relationship was morally repugnant was all that was necessary to justify Virginia's anti-miscegenation statute, assuming that the recognition of the particular union at issue was not deeply rooted in the nation's history and tradition, then the *Loving* Court would have issued a much different opinion. After all, many in Virginia at the time thought interracial marriages morally repugnant. Further, several states prohibited interracial marriage the year that *Loving* was decided, and thus it would have been easy to establish that the recognition of such unions was not firmly rooted in the nation's history and traditions.

The argument of this chapter, however, is based on the First rather than the Fourteenth Amendment. Further, the analysis here is to be distinguished from other lines of argument that have been offered in the literature regarding the relationship between religious beliefs on the one hand and the imposition of legal disabilities on lesbians, gays, bisexuals, and transgendered people on the other.

Some commentators and judges suggest that adverse treatment on the basis of orientation is a product of religious bias, and that laws passed because of a religious view about the alleged immorality of same-sex relations do not pass constitutional muster unless the state has an independent and legitimate reason to have that regulation. Here, the claim is not that all religions are biased, especially considering that there is no uniform religious view regarding the permissibility of same-sex relations, but is merely that the willingness of some religious groups to recognize same-sex marriage has constitutional import.

Another view to be distinguished from the position offered here is that a proper understanding of the freedom of conscience includes a freedom from moral slavery that would protect the right to same-sex marriage.[16] Here, the claim does not involve the more robust notion of liberty of conscience that is implied there, but the weaker notion of freedom of conscience that merely includes existing religious beliefs and practices.

THE LEGAL IMPLICATIONS OF RELIGIOUS CONSENSUS ABOUT MARRIAGE

Some commentators imply that *all* religions preclude same-sex couples from marrying and that religions merely disagree about the *justification* for prohibiting same-sex marriage. One religion might say that same-sex individuals cannot marry because they cannot produce a child through their union; another might say that such individuals cannot form a union which would reflect "the icon of man and woman destined from the first book of revelation as partners in procreation, mutual commitment, and an ordered pair for procreation and rearing of children";[17] still another might suggest that such unions are precluded because of the required complementarity of the partners; and still others might offer some other reasons. Regardless of the differing justifications for the ban, however, the religions are allegedly presenting a united front with respect to the view that such unions should be prohibited, and thus the debate surrounding same-sex unions might be characterized as pitting religion against the secular state.

Even were there this unanimity among the religions, it is not at all clear what implications would follow. Presumably, those claiming this consensus would not be arguing, for example, that any marriage recognized by a religion should be recognized by the state, since they then would be suggesting that polygamous unions should be recognized. Nor would they be suggesting that any unions not recognized by *any* religion should not be recognized by the state. Thus, were it true that no religion would recognize the marital unions of atheists, this presumably would not be a reason for the state to refuse to recognize such unions.

The point here, of course, is not to suggest that religions in fact agree on the impermissibility of same-sex marriages, since that is false. Rather, the point is merely that even were all of the religions to agree that same-sex marriages should not be recognized, that alone would not justify the state's refusal to do so.

The *Dean* trial court upheld the same-sex marriage ban at issue, believing it irrelevant that the prohibition might have been based upon the legislators' religious and moral beliefs. Yet, it is simply unclear whether religious moral views, especially the moral views of some rather than all religions, will, without more, suffice to justify legislation as a general matter, much less justify the legislation at issue here.

In *Bowers v. Hardwick,* the Court suggested that the presumed religious moral views of the Georgia populace sufficed to provide a rational basis for the state's statute *criminalizing* sodomy. In *Romer v. Evans,* however, that same presumed "rational" disapproval of sodomy did not suffice to justify the imposition of *civil* penalties against lesbians, gays, and bisexuals, prompting some commentators to suggest that *Romer* effectively overruled *Bowers.*

Justice Scalia argued in his *Romer* dissent that if "it is constitutionally permissible for a State to make homosexual conduct criminal, surely it is constitutionally permissible for a State to enact other laws merely disfavoring homosexual conduct."[18] Although his argument did not win the day in *Romer,* a separate question is whether his analysis and implicit ordering are correct. If *Romer* merely involved laws disfavoring same-sex conduct and such laws are more constitutionally palatable than laws making same-sex conduct criminal, then *Romer* would seem to significantly undermine the *Bowers* holding. Thus, the question at hand is whether the contrapositive of Justice Scalia's position is true: because it is not constitutionally permissible for a state to enact laws "merely disfavoring" same-sex relations as Colorado tried to do in *Romer,* the state is also prohibited from making adult same-sex consensual conduct criminal. If Justice Scalia's analysis is correct, then *Bowers* has been effectively overruled.

THE CONSTITUTIONAL IMPLICATIONS OF THE RELIGIOUS IMPORT OF MARRIAGE

That some religions sanctify same-sex unions establishes that there is no religious unanimity with respect to whether such unions should be celebrated. Yet, there is another aspect of this willingness to recognize such unions that has not been given adequate attention, namely, that the religious significance of marriage has constitutional import and that this is a reason that same-sex marriages should be legally recognized.

The United States Supreme Court has recognized the religious significance of marriage. Indeed, when the Court was explaining why the interest in marriage is fundamental in *Turner v. Safley,* the Court noted that "many religions recognize marriage as having spiritual significance; for some . . . , therefore, the commitment of marriage may be an exercise of religious faith as well as an expression of personal dedication."[19]

The *Turner* Court did not suggest that marriage would have religious significance only if a duty to marry had been imposed by that religion, and *Turner* makes clear that the state would be remiss for imposing unnecessary burdens on marriage even without, for example, an explicit religious duty to tie a marital knot. One would not have understood this aspect of Supreme Court right-to-marry jurisprudence from reading the Eleventh Circuit decision of *Shahar v. Bowers.*

In *Shahar,* the court upheld the State Attorney General's rescinding a job offer to Robin Shahar because she had married her same-sex partner in a religious ceremony. The court downplayed the importance of her having married her partner in such a ceremony because her religion did not impose a *duty* upon her to marry. One can imagine the reactions if a court were to try to justify a job offer rescission by pointing out that (1) a member of a different-sex couple had married someone of whom the public did not approve, and (2) the person's religion (Reconstructionist Judaism, Catholicism, or whatever) did not impose a duty on her to marry.

The point here should not be misunderstood. The claim here is not that Shahar was being penalized *because* she was engaging in a practice promoted by her religion. The same result presumably would have occurred were Shahar and her partner to have taken part in a ceremony that was not religiously endorsed. Further, the claim here is not that the result would have been different had there been a religiously imposed duty to marry. Even were there such a duty, this would not have guaranteed that the right to marry would be respected. Rather, the point is that the decision was rife with rationalizations that would have been rejected out of hand had they been offered in most other contexts.

Supposedly, had Shahar taken the job, there would have been a lack of "public confidence" in her ability to perform that job.[20] Yet, as Judge Birch pointed out in dissent, the same "reasonable concerns" might have disqualified an unmarried person from working for the State Attorney General if that person were dating, since that person might have been presumed to be unable to enforce Georgia's fornication law. Indeed, there is reason to doubt the State Attorney General's sincerity concerning public confidence in law enforcement, given his admission of a long adulterous affair in violation of Georgia law. Further, as if to add insult to injury, Georgia's sodomy law was declared unconstitutional a year after the Eleventh Circuit decision was issued,[21] undercutting even further the rationale for Shahar's firing.

One confusing issue that was raised in *Shahar* involves the conditions under which religious considerations can permissibly motivate behavior by a state representative. Consider *Church of the Lukumi Babalu Aye, Incorporated v. City of Hialeah,* in which the Court struck down a prohibition of animal sacrifice precisely because the state was trying to restrict religious practices. The Court noted that the "principle that government may not enact laws that suppress religious belief or practice is so well understood that few violations are recorded in our opinions."[22] When explaining why the statute at issue offended the constitutional protection for free exercise of religion, the Supreme Court pointed to statements by council members that the practice violated Biblical teachings, and that this religion was "a sin, 'foolishness,' 'an abomination to the Lord,' and the worship of 'demons.'"[23] It would not have been a surprise if Shahar's religious practices had elicited similar reactions.

Of course, the mere fact that the practices of Santeria violated the religious beliefs of the council members did not preclude the state from regulating those practices. The Court has made clear that merely because a religion has a particular practice does not entail that the state must permit that practice. For example, the Court has upheld the permissibility of prohibiting polygamy, notwithstanding the former acceptance of that practice by the Church of Latter Day Saints. As the Court pointed out in *Reynolds v. United States,* a religious acceptance of a wife's jumping on her deceased husband's funeral pyre would not entail that the state would have to permit that practice. Thus, as suggested in *Bowen v. Roy,* the Court has "long recognized a distinction between the freedom of individual belief, which is absolute, and the freedom of individual conduct, which is not absolute."[24]

When upholding the constitutionality of polygamy prohibitions, the Court has offered a variety of reasons, some helpful and others not. For example, the *Reynolds* Court pointed out, "Polygamy has always been odious among the northern and western nations of Europe, and, until the establishment of the Mormon Church, was almost exclusively a feature of the life of Asiatic and of African people."[25] Yet, this is hardly a reason to prevent a practice, since there might be a variety of Asian or African practices that would be beneficial to emulate. The *Davis* Court came closer to giving a reason when it suggested that polygamy tends to "destroy the purity of the marriage relation, to disturb the peace of families, to degrade woman, and to debase man."[26] Here, the Court might have had in mind that polygamy would have a destabilizing effect if, for example, a husband secured a second wife without the consent of his first wife.

THE SUBSTANTIAL THREAT PRINCIPLE

When attempting to justify the permissibility of prohibiting polygamy, the *Reynolds* Court did more than merely discuss the practices of northern and western European nations; it, in addition, suggested that polygamy is incompatible with democracy. That thesis has received support in the secondary literature and has been cited approvingly by Justice Souter in his *Hialeah* concurrence in which he suggested that *Reynold*'s claim that "polygamy leads to the patriarchal principle, and . . . fetters the people in stationary despotism" is "consistent with the principle that religious conduct may be regulated by general or targeting law only if the conduct pose[s] some substantial threat to public safety, peace or order."[27]

The substantial threat principle is important to consider because it limits the conditions under which the state can prohibit religious practices. That principle suggests that a religious practice of recognizing same-sex marriage should be prohibited only if it can be shown to pose that level of danger to the public welfare. Further, it will not do to argue that because polygamy may be prohibited, same-sex marriages may be prohibited too, since the former may well be viewed as more harmful than the latter.[28] Indeed, once Vermont has had a few years' experience with civil unions without falling apart, it will be even clearer that the state would not be endangered were same-sex marriages recognized.

The point here is not to debate whether polygamy promotes despotism, is a substantial threat to the public welfare, or even whether it may be prohibited by the states without offending constitutional guarantees. For purposes here, the important point is that in recent times when courts have examined the constitutionality of polygamy restrictions, they have not simply said, for example, that marriage is by definition the union of one man and one woman and thus polygamy may of course be prohibited without offending constitutional guarantees. Rather, the courts have instead closely examined the restriction to see whether it passes constitutional muster, recognizing that because the right to marry is of fundamental importance, the state must establish that its prohibition of polygamy is narrowly tailored to promote compelling state interests. Thus, a Utah federal district court held that the state had a compelling interest in prohibiting plural marriages and, further, that the prohibition of such unions was narrowly tailored to promote that state interest.[29]

It is possible that a court imposing the compelling interest test might in fact find that same-sex marriage bans are constitutionally permissible. There is reason to doubt such a claim, however. For example, a Hawaii court examined that state's marital law in light of this very demanding test and held that the state law failed to meet the relevant standard. An Alaska court reached the same conclusion.[30]

Commentators might point out that as of this date neither Alaska nor Hawaii recognizes same-sex marriage. Yet, that is not because the courts misapplied the relevant tests but instead because the state constitutions upon which those decisions were based were themselves changed so that the same-sex marriage prohibitions themselves became immune from state constitutional challenge.

Consider *Baker v. State* in which the Vermont Supreme Court held that same-sex couples could not be deprived of the rights and obligations of marriage. That ruling was based on a standard that is much less strict than the one described above. These decisions at least suggest that a law banning same-sex marriage would not survive constitutional scrutiny were the analysis usually imposed for marital restrictions in fact employed.

In *Employment Division, Department of Human Resources of Oregon v. Smith,* the Court suggested that " the First Amendment bars application of a neutral, generally applicable law to religiously motivated action . . . [only when] the Free Exercise Clause in conjunction with other constitutional protections"[31] have been implicated. The issue under discussion here does not only involve the Free Exercise Clause but, in addition, the right to marry or perhaps the right to intimate association. Indeed, it has been suggested that the *Smith* hybrid rule does much less work than some on the Court seem to think[32] and that the Free Exercise Clause "is best understood as an affirmative guarantee of the right to participate in religious practices and conduct without impermissible governmental interference, even when such conduct conflicts with a neutral, generally applicable law."[33] When one further considers that, as Justice O'Connor has suggested, "the First Amendment was enacted precisely to protect the rights of those whose religious practices are not shared by the majority and may be viewed with hostility,"[34] the Free Exercise claim that same-sex marriages must be permitted is more difficult to dismiss than is generally appreciated.

VERMONT'S CIVIL UNION STATUTE

The Vermont legislature's decision to recognize civil union status was reached only after the Vermont Supreme Court had at least implicitly suggested that it would recognize same-sex marriages if the state did not recognize some sort of status that would afford same-sex couples the rights and obligations of marriage. When creating the special civil union status, the legislature made quite clear that civil unions were not marriages. Notwithstanding that declaration, there was a backlash by those objecting to the creation of this status, although it seems safe to say that there would have been an even greater backlash had the legislature instead amended that state's marriage laws to permit same-sex couples to marry.

Two of the candidates in the 2000 presidential election publicly endorsed the notion of civil unions for same-sex couples, while at the same time suggesting that marriage should be reserved for different-sex couples. Given that those contracting civil unions have the same rights and obligations as do those contracting marriages, an explanation is needed as to why a separate status should be created. Such an explanation would presumably have at least two components: (1) why such a status should be created rather than, for example, creating no such status at all, and (2) why a separate status should be created when the marriage laws could instead easily be modified to include same-sex couples.

REASONS TO ACCORD MARRIAGE-LIKE RIGHTS
AND OBLIGATIONS

There are a number of reasons why such a status might be conferred. It might be in response to a recognition by a court that equal protection guarantees require at the very least that such a status be conferred. It might also involve the recognition by a state legislature that same-sex couples have the same needs and interests as do different-sex couples and that the state should provide a status which would help fulfill those needs and protect those interests. According to these kinds of analyses, the status would be afforded because of the individual needs, desires, and interests that were implicated.

Or, a much different analysis might also be offered. Such a status might be created and conferred out of a recognition that the *societal* interests served by the state's recognizing such a status for different-sex couples— providing a setting for the raising of the young; providing a method whereby the distribution of assets will be organized should the relationship end; supporting an institution whereby individuals might be happier and more productive, thereby benefiting society as a whole as well as the individuals themselves—are also served by recognizing such a status for same-sex couples. According to this kind of analysis, recognition of a marriage-like status for same-sex couples would promote the general welfare.

The recognition that similar societal interests would be served by affording legal recognition of same-sex unions at least implicitly recognizes that the same-sex couples upon whom that status might be conferred are similar in important ways to different-sex couples. Were the couples so different that the relevant interests would not be served by affording that status, then there presumably would be little reason to afford that status.

One of the reasons that there has been a partial transformation in the debate regarding lesbian/gay/bisexual/transgender rights is that the rights sought would not even be desirable were the stereotypes of lesbian/ gay/bisexual/transgendered people accurate. For example, were it true that "those" people only sought anonymous sexual encounters and were not interested in having meaningful long-term relationships, it would not make sense to seek the right to marry except perhaps as a way of achieving other goals. The same might be said of parental rights. Were gay/ lesbian/bisexual/transgendered people not having and raising children and not wanting to have children to raise, the desire to have parental rights recognized and respected would be hard to fathom except perhaps instrumentally.

At the same time that the presidential candidates were claiming that gay/lesbian/bisexual/transgendered individuals should have a status affording them all of the rights and obligations of marriage, they also were asserting that marriage should be reserved for different-sex couples. The question then becomes why a "separate but equal" status should be conferred.

THE MEANING OF CIVIL UNIONS

While transgendered/bisexual/lesbian/gay people are viewed as less foreign than they were once thought to be, it is clear that the creation of civil unions—a "separate but equal" status—communicates at least two additional messages. First, it suggests that same-sex relationships are not as good as different-sex relationships. Indeed, same-sex marriage opponents do not even attempt to mask their view that society must not view same-sex unions as on a par with different-sex unions. Second, it suggests that same-sex unions are somehow an affront to religious principles, notwithstanding that some religions recognize such unions. The very term *"civil* union" suggests that though the union may be recognized by the state, it certainly should not be recognized as having any spiritual significance. Indeed, the language describing the process by which these unions are recognized says a great deal, since different-sex couples' marriages are "solemnized" and same-sex couples' civil unions are "certified."[35]

CONCLUSION

No state currently recognizes same-sex marriages, notwithstanding the state and individual interests that would be promoted by such a recognition. Some suggest that same-sex marriage is anathema to those who are religious. Given that some religions sanctify such unions, however, the most that can be said is that same-sex marriage is anathema to some but not other religions.

The fact that some religions recognize such unions has much more import than merely undermining the claimed consensus view that such unions should not be permitted. In addition, a strong argument can be made that, at least for some couples, such unions must be recognized because of the Free Exercise guarantees of the Federal Constitution. Were the appropriate level of scrutiny employed to determine whether the state could justify interfering with this religious practice, the state would never be able to establish that such a ban is justified.

The creation of civil unions is important for a variety of reasons, since the recognition of such a status at the same time suggests that individuals with a same-sex orientation are not as different as they were once thought to be and that unions for same-sex couples serve many of the same state and individual interests that are served by marriage for different-sex couples. Yet, the creation of this separate status also makes clear that society believes that same-sex couples do not deserve the same status and respect as do other members of the community.

One issue is whether it is permissible for the state to impose a stigma on one group out of deference to the religious or non-religious sensibilities of another. Scholars will debate that point. A different issue is whether the state can interfere with a religious practice like marriage without a showing of the substantial harm that would likely be caused without such a prohibition. The state has not yet offered justifications for its same-sex marriage bans that have survived even heightened scrutiny and thus it is unlikely that the test normally imposed for violations of Free Exercise would permit the state to maintain such a ban.

The separate status of civil unions and, even more so, the refusal to give legal recognition to same-sex relationships communicate an attitude of inequality that would be viewed as intolerable in most other contexts. One can only guess how long this double standard will remain, although if events of the last few years are any indication, it may remain for a much shorter period than would have been imaginable a mere decade ago.

NOTES

1. Minnesota Statutes Annotated § 517.01.
2. Georgia Statutes 19–3–3.1(a). See also Alabama Code 1975 30–1–19(b) ("A marriage contracted between individuals of the same sex is invalid in this state."); Arizona Revised Statutes 25–101(c) ("Marriage between persons of the same sex is void and prohibited."); Arkansas Code Annotated 9–11–109(b) ("A marriage between persons of the same sex is void."); Hawaii Revised Statutes 572–1.6(b) ("A marriage between persons of the same sex is void."); Kentucky Revised Statutes 402.020 (1) ("Marriage is prohibited and void: . . . (d) Between members of the same sex."); Maine Statutes Tit. 19A § 701 (5) ("Same sex marriage prohibited. Persons of the same sex may not contract marriage."); Michigan Statutes § 551.1 ("A marriage contracted between individuals of the same sex is invalid in this state."); Minnesota Statutes Annotated § 517.03(a) ("The following marriages are prohibited: (4) a marriage between persons of the same sex."); Montana Statutes 40–1–401 (1) ("The following marriages are prohibited: (d) a marriage between persons of the same sex."); South Carolina Statutes 20–1–15 ("A marriage between persons of the same sex is void ab initio and against the public policy of this State."); Utah Statutes 30–1–2 ("The following marriages are prohibited and declared void: . . . (5) between persons of the same sex."); Virginia Statutes 20–45.2 ("A marriage between persons of the same sex is prohibited.")
3. Louisiana Statutes Annotated-Century Code art. 86.
4. *Jones v. Hallahan*, 501 S.W. 2d, 588, 589 (Ky. 1973).
5. *Baehr v. Lewin*, 852 P.2d 44, 61 (Haw.), reconsideration granted in part, 875 P.2d 225 (Haw. 1993).
6. *Dean v. District of Columbia*, 653 A.2d 307, 361 (D.C. App. 1995) (Terry, J., concurring and dissenting). See also *Dean v. District of Columbia*, 1992 WL 685364, *3 (D.C. Super.) ("it is the definition of marriage itself, not the 'sexual orientation' of the plaintiffs herein, which stands as a bar to their obtaining a marriage license").
7. *Littleton v. Prange*, 9 S.W.3d 223, 226 (Tex App. 1999).
8. *Id.*
9. *Zablocki v. Redhail*, 434 U.S. 374, 388 (1978).
10. *Bowen v. Roy*, 476 U.S. 693, 699 (1986).
11. See *Lyng v. Northwest Indian Cemetery Protective Association*, 485 U.S. 439, 452 (1988).

A broad range of government activities—from social welfare programs to foreign aid to conservation projects—will always be considered essential to the spiritual well-being of some citizens, often on the basis of sincerely held religious beliefs. Others will find the very same activities deeply offensive, and perhaps incompatible with their own search for spiritual fulfillment and with the tenets of their religion. The First Amendment must apply to all citizens alike, and it can give to none of them a veto over public programs that do not prohibit the free exercise of religion. The Constitution does not, and courts cannot, offer to reconcile the various competing demands on government, many of them rooted in sincere religious belief, that inevitably arise in so diverse a society as ours.

12. *United States v. Lee*, 455 U.S. 252, 260 (1982).

13. *Dean v. District of Columbia*, 1992 WL 685364 (D.C. Super.), *7.

14. See *Santa Fe Independent School District v. Doe*, 530 U.S. 290 (2000) (striking down such a practice as a violation of the Establishment Clause).

15. *Id.* at *1.

16. For an extensive development of this view, see generally David A.J. Richards, *Women Gays, and the Constitution* (Chicago: University of Chicago Press, 1998). Richards has been described as offering "the most sustained and thoughtful exposition of this position." See Michael W. McConnell, "The Origins and Historical Understanding of Free Exercise of Religion," 103 *Harvard Law Review* 1409, 1492 (1990).

17. See Rev. Raymond C. O'Brien, "Single-Gender Marriage: A Religious Perspective," 7 *Temple Political & Civil Rights Law Review* 429, 445 (1998).

18. *Romer v. Evans*, 517 U.S. 620, 641 (1996) (Scalia, J., dissenting).

19. *Turner v. Safley*, 482 U.S. 78, 96 (1987).

20. See *Shahar v. Bowers*, 114 F.3d 1097, 1110 (11th Cir. 1997). See also Cynthia J. Frost, "*Shahar v. Bowers:* That Girl Just Didn't Have Good Sense!," 17 *Law & Inequality* 57, 76–77 (1999) ("The court also determined that the Attorney General was not unreasonable to believe that Shahar's presence on his staff could damage the Department's credibility with the public.")

21. See *Powell v. State*, 510 S.E.2d 18 (Ga. 1998).

22. *Church of the Lukumi Babalu Aye, Incorporated v. City of Hialeah*, 508 U.S. 520, 523 (1993).

23. *Id.*

24. *Bowen v. Roy*, 476 U.S. 693, 699 (1986).

25. *Reynolds v. United States*, 98 U.S. 145, 164 (1878).

26. *Davis*, 133 U.S. at 341.

27. *Church of the Lukumi Babalu Aye, Incorporated v. City of Hialeah*, 508 U.S. 520, 569 (1993) (Souter, J., concurring in part and concurring in the judgment).

28. See *Romer v. Evans*, 517 U.S. 620, 651 (1996) (Scalia, J., dissenting) ("Has the Court concluded that the perceived social harm of polygamy is a 'legitimate concern of government,' and the perceived social harm of homosexuality is not?") and *id.* (Scalia, J., dissenting) ("I strongly suspect that the answer to the last question is yes").

29. See *Potter v. Murray City*, 585 F. Supp. 1126 (D. Utah 1984).

30. See *Baehr v. Miike*, CIV. No. 91-1394, 1996 WL 694235 (Haw. Cir. Ct. Dec. 3, 1996); *Brause v. Bureau of Vital Statistics*, 1998 WL 88743 (Alaska Super.).

31. *Employment Division, Department of Human Resources of Oregon v. Smith*, 494 U.S. 872, 881 (1990).

32. See *Church of the Lukumi Babalu Aye, Incorporated v. City of Hialeah*, 508 U.S. 520, 567 (1993) (Souter, J., concurring in part and concurring in the judgment).

If a hybrid claim is simply one in which another constitutional right is implicated, then the hybrid exception would probably be so vast as to swallow the *Smith* rule, and, indeed, the hybrid exception would cover the situation exemplified by *Smith* since free speech and associational rights are certainly implicated in the peyote ritual. But if a hybrid claim is one in which a litigant would actually obtain an exemption from a formally neutral, generally applicable law under another constitutional provision, then there would have been no reason for the Court in what *Smith* calls the hybrid cases to have mentioned the Free Exercise Clause at all.

See also Michael W. McConnell, "Free Exercise Revisionism and the *Smith* Decision," 57 *University of Chicago Law Review* 1109, 1122 (1990) ("Why isn't *Smith* itself a 'hybrid' case? Whatever else it might accomplish, the performance of a sacred ritual like the ingestion of peyote communicates, in a rather dramatic way, the participants' faith in the tenets of the Native American Church.")

33. See *City of Boerne v. Flores*, 521 U.S. 507, 546 (1997) (O'Connor, J., dissenting).

34. *Employment Division, Department of Human Resources of Oregon v. Smith*, 494 U.S. 872, 902 (1990) (O'Connor, J., concurring in the judgment).

35. Michael Mello, Essay, "For Today, I'm Gay: The Unfinished Battle for Same-Sex Marriage in Vermont," 25 *Vermont Law Review* 149, 251 (2000) ("The bill also distinguished between the terminology for the rites and rituals that symbolize the two classes of unions, heterosexual and homosexual. Marriages of heterosexuals are 'solemnized.' Unions of homosexuals would be 'certified' by judges or clergy members.")

Chapter Eight

Understanding *Loving* and Equal Protection Guarantees

Loving v. Virginia has played a central role in recent cases in which same-sex marriage bans have been challenged. Though *Loving* involved a challenge to marital regulations on the basis of race rather than sex, its holding and analysis are strongly suggestive that same-sex marriage bans also offend constitutional guarantees. Recognizing the rhetorical force that the decision has in the context under discussion here, same-sex marriage opponents have been attempting to rework *Loving* in ways that are neither in accord with the decision itself nor with subsequent decisions in the field.

Some judges and commentators argue that *Loving* provides no support for the claim that the Constitution protects the right of same-sex couples to marry. Their analyses, however, tend to involve such strained and implausible interpretations of the decision and have such unpalatable results that these analyses bolster rather than undermine the very position that they are designed to refute. In addition, these analyses almost systematically either ignore or mischaracterize subsequent developments in the right to marry jurisprudence and subsequent explanations offered by the Court of what *Loving*, itself, means. While the Court has not made clear whether the right to marry includes the right to marry a same-sex partner, the Court has made clear that the right to marry is not nearly as limited as these commentators imply.

These disagreements about how to interpret the *Loving* line of cases implicate a variety of issues including fundamental questions about what the equal protection guarantees of the United States Constitution protect and about what kinds of state interests must be asserted or established if those protections are to be overridden. At stake here is not only whether same-sex marriages are protected by the Constitution; rather, the outcome of these disagreements will help to shape the constitutional protections that all citizens enjoy.

LOVING AND THE RIGHT TO MARRY

Loving v Virginia has recently received increased scholarly attention in part because it helped to change an unconscionable state policy and in part because of two court decisions suggesting that same-sex marriages might be constitutionally protected. The interpretations of *Loving* offered in the secondary literature differ in important ways. The merits of these views can only be assessed after a consideration of (1) the facts of the case, and (2) the jurisprudence regarding the power of the states to decide (a) the conditions under which their domiciliaries might marry, and (b) whether to recognize a marriage validly celebrated in another jurisdiction.

Loving v Virginia involved an interracial couple domiciled in Virginia, Mildred Jeter and Richard Loving, who were validly married in the District of Columbia and who then moved back to Virginia to live. The Lovings were charged with and convicted of violating Virginia's anti-miscegenation law. They each received a suspended sentence, contingent on their leaving the state and not returning together for twenty-five years. They moved to Washington, D.C. About four years later, they challenged Virginia's statutory scheme prohibiting and punishing interracial marriage.

The statutory scheme at issue in *Loving* involved (1) a statute making it a crime for an interracial couple domiciled in Virginia to leave the state to marry, intending to return to Virginia to live, (2) a statute making it a crime for a white person in the state to marry someone who was not white, and (3) a statute establishing that interracial marriages would be treated as null and void. The Lovings' convictions were based on the evasion statute and on the statute criminalizing the attempt to marry a partner of a different race. The United States Supreme Court reversed those convictions, reasoning that "restricting the freedom to marry solely because of racial classifications violates the central meaning of the Equal Protection Clause."[1] The Court suggested that under the United States Constitution "the freedom to marry, or not marry, a person of another race resides with the individual and cannot be infringed by the State."[2]

THE IMPLICATIONS OF *LOVING*

Loving raises a variety of questions. For example, under what conditions, if any, can a state preclude two individuals from marrying? Certainly, *Loving* does not establish that the Constitution precludes states from enacting any marital regulations whatsoever. Further analysis of the decision is required before its implications for the same-sex marriage debate can be made clear, although the analyses of *Loving* that some commentators offer obscure rather than illuminate the implicated issues. For example, some writers seem to focus on Virginia's criminalization of the Lovings' marriage, as if the decision should merely be understood to invalidate statutes that criminalize attempts to marry a partner of a different race. Such a reading, however, can make no sense of the *Loving* Court's point that restricting marriage on the basis of race violates the central meaning of the Equal Protection Clause. On the contrary, the reading that these commentators offer would suggest that states can restrict the right to marry solely on the basis of race as long as they do not in addition adopt criminal statutes to help assure that such restrictions are observed.

Suppose that one were to compare two statutory "schemes," one involving all of the criminal laws at issue in *Loving* and the other involving a statute that simply precluded individuals of different races from marrying, but neither criminalized attempts to marry someone of a different race within the jurisdiction nor criminalized attempts to do so in a different jurisdiction. Certainly, the two statutory schemes would differ in an important way—in one, a domiciliary would risk criminal penalties by attempting to marry his partner, whereas in the other the individual would "merely" be precluded from marrying the person whom he wanted to make his lifelong spouse. Yet, no reputable scholar would currently claim that *Loving* stands for the proposition that states can preclude interracial couples from marrying as long as the state does not in addition criminalize the attempt.

A variation of the above misinterpretation of *Loving* has been offered by other commentators who suggest that the Due Process Clause does not require states to recognize certain marital relationships but instead merely protects an individual from unwarranted state intervention. On this view, *Loving* would have been decided differently if only the state of Virginia had not tried to intervene by charging the Lovings for attempting to intermarry but instead had merely sent the Lovings a polite letter informing them that the state did not recognize their marriage. Yet, as the Supreme Court has made quite clear, "the right to marry is part of the fundamental 'right of privacy' implicit in the Fourteenth Amendment's Due Process Clause."[3] Thus, for example, a state that did not criminalize the attempt to marry someone of another race but merely refused to recognize such unions would nonetheless be violating the United States Constitution. Further, the Court has also made clear that although *Loving* arose in the context of a challenge to a statute barring interracial marriage, "the right to marry is of fundamental importance for all individuals."[4] Thus, in the context of marital regulation, the Due Process Clause imposes a greater obligation on the states than merely to refrain from threatening to impose criminal sanctions on certain individuals who attempt to marry; it imposes an affirmative obligation on the states not to prohibit such unions.

Some commentators attempt to distinguish between the constitutional issues posed by the refusal of some states in the 1960s to recognize interracial marriages and the constitutional issues posed by the current refusal of states to recognize same-sex marriages in the following way: they suggest that when *Loving* was decided, some but not all states permitted interracial couples to marry, whereas no state currently permits same-sex couples to marry. Yet, that point hardly establishes that the United States Constitution does not protect same-sex marriage. Indeed, in the not-too-distant future when some states recognize such marriages, commentators who currently trumpet the importance of no state's recognizing such unions will probably suddenly discover that the uniform lack of recognition is not a constitutionally significant factor after all. Rather, these commentators will instead discover the importance of allowing the states to perform their role as laboratories for experimentation, notwithstanding that the experimentation would involve "one of the vital personal rights essential to the orderly pursuit of happiness"[5] and notwithstanding that the same argument might have been made at the time *Loving* was decided in an attempt to justify permitting the states to prohibit interracial marriages.

That some but not all states permitted interracial marriages does not support the claim that interracial marriages implicate federal constitutional guarantees; on the contrary, it suggests that the United States Constitution neither requires nor prohibits the recognition of such marriages, since states were allowed to enact the marital regulations that they saw fit. Yet, as the *Loving* Court made clear, states are prohibited by the United States Constitution from preventing interracial couples from marrying, long-standing past practices involving the prohibition of such unions notwithstanding. Thus, at least for purposes of the current discussion, the important point is that, prior to *Loving,* the lack of uniformity suggested that states had the power to decide whether to permit interracial couples to marry, whereas after the decision it was clear that the states had no such power.

Indeed, it is ironic that same-sex marriage opponents admit that when *Loving* was decided some states permitted interracial marriages while others did not. Many of these same commentators suggest that same-sex marriages should not be recognized because they are not deeply rooted in the traditions of the American people or perhaps are not essential to the concept of ordered liberty. Yet, given the number of states prohibiting interracial marriage at the time that *Loving* was decided, it would seem difficult to argue that interracial marriage met those standards. As the Kentucky Supreme Court pointed out, "miscegenation was an offense with ancient roots."[6] Thus, those offering the ordered liberty or traditions tests to explain why same-sex marriages are not constitutionally protected conveniently forget that the same explanation would have justified a different result in *Loving.*

INTERSTATE RECOGNITION OF MARRIAGE

An examination of *Loving* helps illustrate the way that the interstate recognition of marriage is structured in our federalist system. To see how, it will be necessary to distinguish some of the different interstate marriage recognition issues raised by *Loving*.

Virginia's refusal to recognize the Lovings' marriage and imposition of criminal sanctions for their attempt to marry in a jurisdiction in which such unions could be legally celebrated might seem subject to legal challenge on a variety of grounds. For example, it might be thought that:

1. Virginia was precluded by the Full Faith and Credit Clause from refusing to recognize a marriage validly celebrated in another jurisdiction.
2. Virginia's imposition of criminal sanctions against the Lovings was what made the relevant statutes constitutionally offensive.
3. Virginia was precluded from preventing the Lovings from marrying without having a sufficiently compelling reason to justify that marital prohibition.

In *Loving,* there was no suggestion that Virginia was forced by the Full Faith and Credit Clause to recognize the Lovings' marriage merely because that union had been validly celebrated in the District of Columbia. Indeed, one might have expected the Court to have pursued that tack were it viable, given the Court's then-recent refusals to hold that interracial marriage bans violated the United States Constitution. For example, about a decade earlier, the Court had refused to hear a case challenging Virginia's anti-miscegenation statute, allegedly because no federal issues were implicated.[7] Further, a mere three years before *Loving* was decided, the Court explicitly refused to address whether interracial marriage bans were unconstitutional.[8] Thus, if the Court could have avoided the issue by appealing to the Full Faith and Credit Clause, one would have expected the Court to have done so.

Not only was there no suggestion that evasion statutes in general were unconstitutional, but there further was no suggestion in *Loving* that evasion statutes that impose a criminal penalty are constitutionally offensive. Although the Court reversed the conviction at issue, it did so because of the particular content of that statute rather than because such statutes as a general matter are constitutionally offensive. So, too, when the Court examined a Wisconsin statutory scheme that both limited the right to marry and imposed criminal sanctions against those seeking to evade the restriction, the Court invalidated the restriction because of its particular content rather than holding, for example, that evasion statutes were unconstitutional per se.[9]

States had, and continue to have, evasion statutes. Currently, states tend not to criminalize the attempt to evade local law by marrying elsewhere but instead "merely" refuse to recognize the marriage validly celebrated outside of the domicile. Yet, the fact that states tend not to criminalize marital evasion attempts hardly establishes that the imposition of criminal penalties for such an offense is somehow unconstitutional. Indeed, both Virginia and Wisconsin continue to have statutes that criminalize certain attempts to evade local marital law.

Traditionally, states have been given much leeway with respect to their power to set the conditions under which their domiciliaries might marry. Had the Court held that Virginia had to give full faith and credit to the marriage validly celebrated in the District of Columbia, the Court would have severely undermined the general power of the state to establish marital regulations for its domiciliaries, since Virginia domiciliaries could have avoided any local marital regulation as long as there was another state that did not impose the regulation at issue. Further, had the Court held that the Full Faith and Credit Clause required Virginia to recognize the marriage validly celebrated in the District of Columbia, the Court might also have felt obliged to hold that marriage evasion statutes are unconstitutional on the theory that what the Constitution "precludes the government from commanding directly, it also precludes the government from accomplishing indirectly."[10] Of course, this is all speculation, because the Court has never held that the domicile at the time of the marriage's celebration is forced to recognize that union as long as it is validly celebrated elsewhere. Both before and after the passage of the Defense of Marriage Act, states could refuse to recognize their domiciliaries' same-sex marriages validly celebrated elsewhere, assuming that those marriages could not have been celebrated within the domicile and assuming that the prohibition itself did not and does not offend constitutional guarantees.

In *Loving*, the Court neither cast doubt on the general power of states to determine the conditions under which their domiciliaries might marry nor cast doubt on the power of states to pass evasion statutes but instead suggested that states were prohibited from restricting marriage on the basis of race. Because the Virginia statute involved invidious racial discrimination, the Court held that the statute at issue violated the Equal Protection Clause of the United States Constitution.

TREATING THE RACES UNEQUALLY

The competing interpretations of *Loving*'s equal protection analysis emphasize different factual elements of the case or different aspects of the opinion itself. Regrettably, some interpretations focus on particular facts without regard to the role that those facts played in the opinion or in the Court's reasoning, thereby mischaracterizing both the decision itself and the part it has played in the developing right to marry jurisprudence. For example, some commentators suggest that the statute at issue in *Loving* was unconstitutional because it limited the options of white people, whereas other commentators suggest that the statute was unconstitutional because it specifically implicated race. Even on the most charitable reading of these interpretations, however, these commentators conflate what sufficed to make the statute unconstitutional with what was required to make it unconstitutional. Because of this conflation, these interpretations can neither account for the right to marry jurisprudence that has developed since *Loving* nor even the Court's own comments about what *Loving* itself represents. The best understanding of *Loving* and the right to marry jurisprudence as it has developed since then suggests that same-sex marriage bans implicate federal equal protection guarantees and that states will have great difficulty in offering the requisite justifications for those statutes.

Some commentators suggest that the statute at issue in *Loving* was unconstitutional because it more strictly limited white persons' marriage options.[11] Such an analysis is potentially misleading in a few different respects. First, insofar as this suggests that the Court's concern was that whites in particular were being treated unfairly, there is nothing in the opinion to support that view, since the Court's unfairness concern was that the statute was designed to maintain white supremacy. Second, this interpretation might be thought to imply that the Court would have upheld the statute if only the marital options of whites had been no more severely restricted than the options of members of other races, a view belied by the Court's comments in the opinion itself.

Suppose that Virginia had passed a different statute. Suppose that in an attempt to preserve racial integrity and to prevent the obliteration of racial pride, the state of Virginia had banned all interracial marriages rather than only those involving whites. One infers that these commentators would suggest that such a statutory scheme would pass constitutional muster, because the marital options of the races would have been limited equally. Yet, such a suggestion is inconsistent with the *Loving* opinion itself. First, the focus of such an analysis is on the marital options of the race rather than of the individual, thereby undercutting the *Loving* Court's recognition that the freedom to marry is a vital *personal* right. Second, the analysis cannot plausibly account for the *Loving* Court's having found the racial classifications in the statutes unconstitutional, even assuming an even-handed state purpose to protect the purity of all of the races and even assuming an equal application of the statute. Thus, those who focus on the limitations of whites' options when explaining *Loving* offer a misleading characterization in several respects.

WHICH CLASSIFICATIONS REQUIRE CLOSE EXAMINATION?

The above discussion is about *why* the statute at issue in *Loving* involved invidious discrimination rather than about whether it did. Yet, the state of Virginia denied that its marital statutes imposed unequal burdens and denied that the statutes were unconstitutional, arguing that "because its miscegenation statutes punish equally both the white and the Negro participants in an interracial marriage, these statutes, despite their reliance on racial classifications, do not constitute an invidious discrimination based upon race."[12] The Court did not dispute the state's characterization of the statute but instead rejected the notion that the mere equal application of such a statute would save it.

The Court distinguished *Loving* from other kinds of cases in which no minority was being targeted, suggesting that in the latter the relevant question is whether there is a rational basis for the classification. The *Loving* Court's approach is important to consider because it suggests the approach that should be used insofar as the constitutionality of a statute precluding same-sex marriage is at issue.

A same-sex marriage ban might be phrased in any of a number of ways. For example, a state might suggest that marriages between individuals of the same sex are invalid, that marriage between individuals of the same gender are void, or that only marriages between a man and a woman are valid. Each of these statutes classifies on the basis of sex or gender. A separate question is whether the statute involves invidious discrimination, but it at least should be clear that the above formulations are sex-based or gender-based classifications.

When commentators suggest that same-sex marriage bans do not discriminate on the basis of gender, they might mean that (a) the basis of the classification is something other than sex or gender, for example, orientation, or (b) while the basis of the classification is sex or gender, the classification is not invidious and hence should not be thought of as "discrimination." These claims must not be conflated, because they mean different things and because the test to determine whether in fact the Constitution permits the classification at issue might depend on which is being asserted.

Suppose that a different statute were at issue, namely, one that only precluded individuals with a same-sex orientation from contracting same-sex marriages. Individuals who did not have a same-sex orientation would be allowed to marry someone of the same sex and thereby, for example, receive government benefits that they would not otherwise be able to receive. Because the state would want to assure that only certain same-sex couples married, it might require each member of the couple to sign an affidavit that he or she either had a different-sex orientation or perhaps no sexual orientation.

It might seem that a state requirement of such an affidavit would itself raise serious constitutional questions. Yet, it is not as if requiring the production of an affidavit as a condition for being allowed to marry is unprecedented; Wisconsin, for example, allows first cousins to marry if either submits an affidavit signed by a physician stating that he or she is permanently sterile.[13]

The statute described above would not involve express discrimination on the basis of sex, since the explicit basis of classification would instead involve sexual orientation. Of course, that would not end the possibility of an equal protection challenge on the basis of sex. For example, if the state precluded all individuals from marrying a same-sex partner regardless of the sexual orientation of the parties, express provisions of the statute notwithstanding, then an applied challenge to the statute on the basis of sex discrimination might be appropriate. Nonetheless, a statute precluding individuals with a same-sex orientation from marrying would classify on the basis of orientation rather than sex.

A separate question is whether the state could justify permitting some but not other same-sex couples to marry. Presumably, it would not suffice as a justification were the state to suggest that it had enacted that regulation because it had wanted to punish individuals with a same-sex orientation, since the Court has already made clear that where a statute "seems inexplicable by anything but animus toward the class that it affects, it lacks a rational relationship to legitimate state interests."[14]

Many would suggest that it would be absurd to have the statute described above that allowed some but not other same-sex couples to marry, although the explanations for why that was true might vary radically. Some would claim that it makes no sense to allow any same-sex couple to marry, arguing that the purposes of marriage could not be served if the marital partners were of the same sex. Others would suggest that exactly the wrong same-sex couples would thereby have been precluded, for example, loving, committed couples who would not be marrying solely for the benefits that they might thereby receive, arguing those same-sex partners whose unions would have served the purposes of marriage would be precisely those who would have been precluded from marrying.

In any event, the same-sex marriage bans that have been enacted do not allow certain but not other same-sex couples to marry; instead, they prohibit "same-sex marriages on the part of professed or nonprofessed heterosexuals, homosexuals, bisexuals, or asexuals."[15] It is precisely because all parties, regardless of sexual orientation, are prohibited from marrying someone of the same sex that the *Baehr* plurality held that the Hawaii statute "on its face and as applied, regulates access to the marital status and its concomitant rights and benefits on the basis of the applicants' sex."[16]

Some commentators contend that notwithstanding that a same-sex marriage ban facially discriminates on the basis of sex, it nonetheless involves a reasonable orientation-based distinction. They seem not to appreciate that given that such a statute nonetheless precludes a man from marrying another man and a woman from marrying another woman without regard to the sexual orientations of the parties, the statute is not narrowly tailored. They also seem not to appreciate how the constitutionality of such a statute is undercut if the very reason that such marriages are precluded involves a desire to impose a burden on and maintain the inferiority of a particular class, namely, those with a same-sex orientation.

When holding that the state's same-sex marriage ban implicated equal protection guarantees, the *Baehr* plurality did not hold that the classification at issue was invidious or unconstitutional. Instead, it remanded the case to give the state an opportunity to establish that the statute was justified by compelling state interests and that the statute was narrowly drawn to promote those interests. By remanding the case, the *Baehr* plurality made clear that the fact that the state had chosen to enact a statute containing a sex-based classification did not establish that the statute was constitutionally infirm. That issue was left for a trial court to determine. Nonetheless, the plurality's holding that the statute involved a sex-based classification was significant because the state was thereby required to carry a heavy burden of justification when making its argument at the trial court level.

When a sex-based classification is under examination, several issues must be addressed, including (1) whether burdens are imposed on one sex that are not imposed on the other, and (2) even if not, whether the statute is closely tailored to promote sufficiently important state interests. Thus, even if it could be established that a particular sex-based classification did not impose an unfair burden on one of the sexes, that would not suffice to establish the constitutionality of the classification.

Commentators suggest that same-sex marriage bans treat men and women alike: a man is not allowed to marry another man and a woman is not allowed to marry another woman. Yet, this hardly establishes that such a classification passes constitutional muster, just as the analogous claim in *Loving*—that blacks were not allowed to marry whites and whites were not allowed to marry blacks—did not establish that the Virginia statute passed constitutional muster.

There has been some confusion about the point that just as the equal treatment of the races did not constitutionally immunize an interracial ban, so, too, the equal treatment of the sexes would not constitutionally immunize a same-sex marriage ban. The claim is not that *Loving* establishes that the civil right to marriage must be afforded to same-sex couples, since that case did not involve a challenge to a same-sex marriage ban and thus of course is not authority for that proposition. Thus, because *Loving* involved a race-based marital classification, the case does not limit the state's power to prohibit any person from entering into a same-sex marriage, just as it does not limit the state's power to prohibit any person from entering into a marriage with someone of a different religion. Yet, the fact that a case is not authority for a particular proposition hardly establishes that it is not relevant or in fact very persuasive. For example, *Loving* strongly suggests that a law barring marriages between individuals of different religions would be unconstitutional, since religion is also a suspect classification.

It is not suggested above that the state's burden in justifying a marital statute involving a sex-based classification would be as great as it would be were the statute to involve a race- or religion-based classification. Sex- or gender-based classifications must be subjected to heightened scrutiny, a level of scrutiny that is lower than that which is employed for classifications involving race or religion but higher than that which is employed where economic regulations are at issue. Nonetheless, heightened scrutiny imposes a difficult burden on parties who seek to defend a sex-based classification. As the Supreme Court has made clear, "Parties who seek to defend gender-based government action must demonstrate an 'exceedingly persuasive justification' for that action."[17]

THE *LOVING* ANALOGY

Same-sex marriage opponents seem not to appreciate that many of the arguments offered in support of such bans might analogously have been made in *Loving*. For example, some commentators imply that because same-sex couples seek to secure their marriage rights through the courts rather than simply allow the legislatures to make the relevant decisions, these couples are disingenuous in their claims of wanting to be treated as (merely) equal citizens. After all, it is argued, by attempting to get the courts to recognize a right to marry, these couples are attempting to foreclose an important public debate.

Yet, first, there is no reason to think that such recognition would in fact close off debate. For example, *Roe v Wade* has hardly foreclosed debate about abortion. Second, even were debate thereby foreclosed, that hardly should suffice as a reason to preclude individuals from having their rights recognized in court. Presumably, these commentators would not have claimed that the Lovings (1) should not have gone to court but instead should only have tried to persuade the Virginia legislature to allow them to marry, or (2) were seeking special rights by seeking to have their right to marry vindicated in the courts.

Further, these commentators would never claim that the *Loving* Court should have reached the opposite conclusion so as not to foreclose public debate, notwithstanding that the state of Virginia offered a political process argument, claiming that the Supreme Court should "defer to the wisdom of the state legislature in adopting its policy of discouraging interracial marriages."[18] The Court wisely rejected the state's argument, even though doing so overrode the will of the people.

When attempting to establish that what is at issue in the same-sex marriage controversy is different from what was at issue in the interracial marriage controversy, commentators sometimes understate the strength of the opposition to interracial marriage that existed at the time *Loving* was decided. For example, some suggest that in *Loving*, public morality triumphed over bigotry, as if interracial marriage were in accord with the public morality of the time. Yet, polls in the *1990s* indicated that a substantial number of white Americans disapproved of interracial marriages, and it is clear that attitudes toward intermarriage had become substantially more favorable over the intervening decades. Thus, a very significant percentage of whites disapproved of such marriages when *Loving* was decided. It is neither clear that public morality at the time permitted such marriages nor, for that matter, that the current opposition to same-sex marriage cannot be attributed to bigotry. The point here of course is not to suggest that *Loving* should have been decided differently if in fact interracial marriages contravened the existing public morality. On the contrary, this is to suggest that public morality is not the appropriate test to decide something that involves such a fundamental interest as the right to marry.

Some commentators reject the comparison between interracial marriage and same-sex marriage because, allegedly, this involves a comparison between classifications based on race on the one hand and based on same-sex conduct on the other. Yet, such commentators do not seem to appreciate the force or possible application of their own arguments. For example, Virginia might have claimed that it had no interest in punishing anyone because of his or her race. On the contrary, Virginia was merely trying to prevent certain kinds of sexual behaviors, namely, interracial sexual relations, and precisely because behaviors rather than immutable characteristics were at issue its anti-miscegenation statute was constitutionally permissible.

These commentators only create more difficulties for themselves when arguing that the analogy is inapt because racial classifications are logically irrelevant to legitimate social polices but that sexual behavior choices are of legitimate social concern, especially where marriage is involved. First, such a claim invites the obvious rejoinder that sexual classifications are usually irrelevant to legitimate social policies, that they are not of legitimate concern where marriage is involved, and that the whole purpose of the Court's employing heightened scrutiny when such classifications are at issue is to make sure that they indeed are promoting legitimate state purposes. Second, the state of Virginia might have agreed wholeheartedly and then claimed that because it was merely trying to preclude personal behavioral choices, especially where the institution of marriage was involved, its statute precluding interracial marriage should have been upheld.

Allegedly, same-sex marriage bans are permissible because they are related to one of the fundamental purposes of marriage laws, namely, the regulation of sexual behavior, and because they are related to the protection of family, the basic unit of society. Yet, these are exactly the kinds of arguments that Virginia might have offered. One need only consider how Florida defended its anti-miscegenation statute that punished interracial fornication more severely than intra-racial fornication. The state claimed merely to want to uphold sexual decency, a characterization with which the Supreme Court refused to quarrel. Presumably, Virginians shared the view of Floridians that interracial sexual behavior was indecent whether within or outside of marriage, and both Virginia and Florida might have claimed that their interracial marriage bans were merely protecting their citizens' understandings of the "proper" family.

Perhaps the most useful argument for the state of Virginia would have been the claim that distinctions based on relations are different from distinctions based on immutable traits and thus that sexual activity is more open to regulation than are classifications like race or sex. According to that analysis, neither heightened nor strict scrutiny is appropriate where marital relations, rather than human traits, are being regulated. Yet, if indeed same-sex marriage bans, properly understood, do not discriminate on the basis of sex because they instead classify on the basis of behavior or relations, then Virginia presumably should have argued that interracial marriage bans, properly understood, should not be thought to discriminate on the basis of race but instead on behavior or relations. Were there merit in these analyses, they would cast a whole new light on how *Loving* should have been decided.

TRANSGENDER MARRIAGES

Statutes banning same-sex marriages have become even harder to defend in light of marriages involving some but not other transgendered individuals. Consider *Littleton v. Prange,* in which a Texas appellate court had to decide whether to recognize the marriage of a post-surgical transsexual. The court first had to decide whether to define Christie Littleton's sex in light of her male chromosomes, her sexual identification, her physical appearance (she had undergone surgery to make her physical self correspond with her sexual identity), or in terms of all of these and perhaps other factors. The court held that according to Texas law sex was defined in terms of the individual's chromosomes and thus that Christie was a male and her marriage to another male was void.

A few points might be made about the decision. First, according to this understanding of Texas law, postsurgical transsexuals will be somewhat limited in whom they can marry. Christie, who self-identifies as and looks like a woman, could have married another woman or could have married another transsexual who had had corrective surgery to make his physical self correspond with his male sexual identity. Bracketing for a moment those marriages that are between two postoperative transsexuals, the Texas law would seem to *promote* same-sex marriage, at least insofar as one considers the views of the parties themselves or society at large. A postoperative transsexual who looks and feels like a woman will only be able to marry a woman, and a postoperative transsexual who looks and feels like a man will only be able to marry a man. Indeed, after the *Littleton* decision, a man-to-woman transsexual married a woman in Texas. Because the state's definition of sex is based on the individual's chromosomes, the postoperative transsexual was a man in the eyes of the state, notwithstanding that person's physical appearance and perceived sexual identity.

It is not at all clear what justification can be offered for permitting these marriages but not marriages between two individuals who look and feel like women, in the case that neither is a transsexual. The claim here of course is not that such couples are indistinguishable. (In one but not the other, the chromosomes of the parties are, presumably, XX and XY.) Rather, the claim is that it is not at all clear why this is a relevant or important distinction upon which the ability to marry should be based.

It should not be thought that only Texas has opted for this way of defining an individual's sex. A court in Ohio declined to require the issuance of a marriage license to a postoperative male-to-female transsexual who wished to marry a man. The court held that this individual, who looked, acted, and felt like a woman, was nonetheless a man because of that person's chromosomes.[19]

A few points might be made about states defining sex in terms of an individual's chromosomes. First, doing so seems arbitrary because it does not take into account (1) the individual's own view about his or her sexual identity, (2) his or her physical appearance, or (3) society's view about the person's sexual identity. Second, the criterion is not as helpful as might originally be thought. For example, it would be unclear how an individual with XXY chromosomes should be defined. If the person were not classified as a male (because of the two X chromosomes) and were not classified as a female (because of the Y chromosome), then it is not clear who that person could marry. Although other criteria could be used in that case, for example, physical appearance or self-identification, it is not clear why those criteria should *only* be used when an individual had XXY chromosomes.

Of course, other criteria would pose potential problems as well. For example, were the person's current physical state to play an important role, then a few questions would have to be answered. How should individuals who have the sex organs of both sexes be classified? Would the postoperative transsexual have had his or her sex changed, or would that person merely have had his or her physical self finally reflect the sex that the person had always been? If the latter, how should the sex of the preoperative transsexual be defined? Would it matter if that person decided never to undergo surgery?

If the classification might change depending on whether the person has had surgery, then other problems might arise. Consider a male-to-female transsexual, Alex, who wishes to marry a woman, Carol. In a state with marital restrictions based on sex, Alex might be permitted to marry Carol as long as he does so before rather than after surgery. Further, were they to marry and were Alex then to have the surgery, the state would have to decide whether the couple could remain married, assuming that constitutional guarantees would not be violated by voiding such a marriage.

Some states permit postoperative transsexuals to have their birth certificates amended to reflect their sexual identity.[20] A state permitting such an amendment would have to decide whether to look at the amended birth certificate or the original one for purposes of determining who that person might marry (assuming that the state had marriage restrictions based on sex). In *Littleton,* an amended birth certificate had been issued, but the Texas Appellate Court held that the relevant statute had not permitted that document to be amended. At least in part because her original birth certificate was used to indicate her sex, Littleton's marriage was viewed as a nullity.

Suppose that the law had been different and had said that postoperative transsexuals could have their birth certificates changed to reflect their sexual identity and that the person's sex would be determined in light of the *amended* certificate for purposes of determining who that individual might marry. The postoperative transsexual would then be permitted to marry either a man or a woman. A postoperative male-to-female transsexual who wanted to marry a man would have the birth certificate amended to reflect her sexual identify and that same person might elect *not* to have the certificate changed were that person's partner a woman.

The point here, of course, is neither to suggest that postoperative transsexuals should be forced to have their birth certificates changed nor that such individuals should not be permitted to have them changed but merely that the current system seems irrational. What legitimate state interest could be served by saying that two individuals could marry but only if one of the individuals has (or does not have) the birth certificate amended? Neither the public's perception of the couple nor the individuals' perceptions of themselves would depend upon whether the birth certificate had been amended, since the public in general presumably would not know about the certificate one way or the other, and the individuals themselves would have their own views regardless of what the birth certificates said or did not say.

It simply will not do to say that it does not matter how these issues are resolved because the real goal is to make sure that same-sex couples will be unable to marry (where neither member of the couple is a transsexual.) This would not count as an acceptable justification. As the *Romer* Court made clear, a classification is unconstitutional if it is designed not to further a proper legislative end but to make lesbians, gays, and bisexuals unequal to everyone else.

The difficulty highlighted by state regulations regarding transgender marriages is not merely that it is not obvious where the lines should be drawn regarding who may marry whom. Rather, it is that no matter where the line is drawn, some individuals will be denied the fundamental right to marry for a reason that simply cannot withstand scrutiny.

CONCLUSION

Same-sex marriage opponents offer several arguments in their attempts to show why former interracial marriage bans are not even analogous to current same-sex marriage bans. Protestations to the contrary notwithstanding, however, many of the arguments offered to establish the permissibility of same-sex marriage bans might have been analogously offered by the state of Virginia to justify its own interracial marriage ban.

That these arguments might have been used analogously to support anti-miscegenation laws should not be thought to establish that such theorists do or even would have supported such bans. On the contrary, it seems clear that these theorists find interracial bans so obviously wrong and same-sex marriage bans so obviously right that they cannot even see the ways in which their current arguments against same-sex marriage were once used to support statutes like the one at issue in *Loving*.

Loving is important for a variety of reasons. It makes clear how distinctions can be invidious, notwithstanding their popular acceptance, and why a state's prohibition of something as fundamental as the right to marry should be examined closely to make sure that the reasons articulated are both legitimate and important. When something like the ability to reproduce through the union of the parties is required for some to marry, is ignored when others wish to marry, and is a disqualifying condition when still others wish to marry, it should be clear that a fundamental interest is being denied for specious reasons. Although *Loving* does not establish that the right to marry a same-sex partner is constitutionally protected, it and the subsequent right to marry cases establish the necessity of closely examining the articulated state interests allegedly justifying such a marital prohibition. It is difficult to understand how the reasons thus far articulated to justify same-sex marriage bans could ever withstand the requisite scrutiny. Indeed, the utter speciousness of the reasons offered by many commentators allegedly justifying same-sex marriage bans only serves to bolster the view that the state has no important, legitimate interests in depriving an entire group of such a fundamental right.

One aspect of the same-sex marriage debate that is underappreciated is that it has important implications for right to marry jurisprudence more generally. For example, some same-sex marriage opponents suggest that *Loving* merely stands for the proposition that interracial marriages cannot be criminalized. According to this view, a state is permitted not only to deny the legal and public status of marriage to interracial couples but to prevent them from living together. The state would simply enforce its statutes prohibiting non-marital cohabitation, as long as the state does not criminalize the attempt to marry someone of another race. Needless to say, this is a radical reworking of the right to marry jurisprudence which is supported neither by *Loving* itself nor by the subsequent right-to-marry jurisprudence.

Transgender marriages make even clearer that current marital restrictions on the basis of sex are not rationally related to legitimate state purposes. There is no rational basis behind the current system and the obvious difficulties in basing something as fundamental as the right to marry on arbitrary definitions of sex or on who may appropriately marry whom beg to be closely examined. A close examination of these statutes would reveal that they cannot meet the requirements of the Federal Constitution.

NOTES

1. *Loving v. Virginia*, 388 U.S. 1, 12 (1967).
2. *Id.*
3. *Zablocki*, 434 U.S. at 384.
4. *Id.*
5. *Loving*, 388 U.S. at 12.
6. *Commonwealth v. Wasson*, 842 S.W.2d 487, 497 (Ky. 1992).
7. See *Naim v. Naim*, 350 U.S. 985 (1956).
8. See *McLaughlin v. Florida*, 379 U.S. 184, 196 (1964).
9. See *Zablocki v. Redhail*, 434 U.S. 374 (1978).
10. *Rutan v. Republican Party of Illinois*, 497 U.S. 62, 78 (1990).
11. See, for example, Jay Alan Sekulow and John Tuskey, "Sex and Sodomy and Apples and Oranges—Does the Constitution Require States to Grant a Right to Do the Impossible?" 12 *Brigham Young University Journal of Public Law* 309, 324 (1998).
12. *Id.*
13. See Wisconsin Statutes § 765.03 (1993).
14. *Romer v. Evans*, 517 U.S. 620, 644 (1996).
15. See *Baehr v. Lewin*, 852 P.2d 44, 71 (Haw. 1993) (Heen, J., dissenting).
16. *Id.* at 64.
17. *United States v Virginia*, 518 U.S. 515, 531 (1996).
18. *Id.* at 8.
19. See *In re Ladrach*, 513 N.E.2d 828 (Ohio Misc. 1987).

20. See Arizona Revised Statutes § 36–326(A)(4) ("A sworn statement from a licensed physician in good standing that he has performed a surgical operation or a chromosomal count on a person and that by reason of this operation or count the sex of the person has been established as different from that in the original document. The state registrar may reserve the right to require further proof if deemed necessary, or to seek independent professional evaluation of the evidence offered before creating a new certificate."); Georgia Code Annotated § 31–10–23(e) ("Upon receipt of a certified copy of a court order indicating the sex of an individual born in this state has been changed by surgical procedure and that such individual's name has been changed, the certificate of birth of such individual shall be amended as prescribed by regulation."); Louisiana Revised Statutes Annotated § 40:62(A) ("Any person born in Louisiana who has sustained sex reassignment or corrective surgery which has changed the anatomical structure of the sex of the individual to that of a sex other than that which appears on the original birth certificate of the individual, may petition a court of competent jurisdiction as provided in this Section to obtain a new certificate of birth."); Mississippi Code Annotated § 41–57–21 ("Where there has been a bona fide effort to register a birth and the certificate thereof on file with the office of vital records does not divulge all of the information required by said certificate, or such certificate contains an incorrect first name, middle name, or sex, then the state registrar of vital records may, in his discretion, correct such certificate upon affidavit of at least two (2) reputable persons having personal knowledge of the facts in relation thereto."); North Carolina General Statutes § 130A–118(b)(4) ("A written request from an individual is received by the State Registrar to change the sex on that individual's birth record because of sex reassignment surgery, if the request is accompanied by a notarized statement from the physician who performed the sex reassignment surgery or from a physician licensed to practice medicine who has examined the individual and can certify that the person has undergone sex reassignment surgery.")

Chapter Nine

Threats to the Right to Privacy

The right to privacy includes the right to make important decisions regarding marriage, family, and children. There is some controversy, however, regarding the degree to which substantive due process rights protect individuals with a same-sex orientation. Taking their cue from the United States Supreme Court's decision in *Bowers v. Hardwick,* many jurists and commentators suggest that the right to privacy does not protect the right of same-sex couples to marry, establish families, or have children. Yet, appearances to the contrary notwithstanding, *Bowers* suggests that the right to privacy may well protect such families and, further, that those courts in states with more robust right to privacy protections than are contained within the Federal Constitution might have great difficulty in explaining why their own substantive due process guarantees do not include the right to marry a same-sex partner.

THE IMPLICATIONS OF *BOWERS* FOR THE RIGHT TO MARRY A SAME-SEX PARTNER

In *Bowers,* the United States Supreme Court refused to recognize a fundamental right to engage in homosexual sodomy, instead upholding a Georgia sodomy law criminalizing both same-sex and opposite-sex sodomitical relations. Jurists and commentators have suggested that the Court's unwillingness to recognize a constitutional right to have consensual, sodomitical relations strongly suggests that the right to marry a same-sex partner does not fall within the substantive due process protections of the Fourteenth Amendment of the United States Constitution. It is not clear that such a conclusion is warranted, however, because the

Court was not sufficiently explicit about why the right to privacy did not include consensual sodomy.

It may seem strange to suggest that the *Bowers* Court was not sufficiently explicit about why sodomy was not protected by the right to privacy, since the Court offered several justifications for its holding, any one of which would seem to have sufficed. For example, the Court suggested that "to claim a right to engage in such conduct [sodomy] is 'deeply rooted in this Nation's history and tradition' or 'implicitly in the concept of ordered liberty' is, at best facetious,"[1] implying that unless a practice or activity could plausibly be described in those terms, it would not be included within the right to privacy. The difficulty with this justification was not that the Court was wrong to conclude that the protection of sodomy was not deeply rooted in this nation's history and tradition, but merely that the Court might have made the same point about contraception, abortion, and interracial marriage, and each of those is nonetheless protected by the right to privacy. Thus, although the Court was no doubt correct that sodomy has been criminalized historically, it is not at all clear that the point establishes that sodomitical relations are not protected by the Constitution.

The *Bowers* Court rejected the claim that the Georgia sodomy statute was invalid as a majoritarian attempt to impose particular moral values on a disfavored minority, pointing out that the law is constantly based on moral choices. The Court further pointed out that if all laws representing moral choices were unconstitutional, it would be forced to invalidate a whole host of laws. Yet, the claim was not that *any* statute promoting morality must be struck down—statutes prohibiting murder serve legitimate, nonmoral ends and thus are permissible—but merely that statutes that promote no legitimate nonmoral ends and which are perhaps designed to punish a disfavored minority, should be struck down.

The *Bowers* Court accepted that consensual sodomy was a victimless crime but then suggested that, after all, other "victimless" crimes are permissibly criminalized. The Court's argument was unpersuasive, however, since its examples—the possession of drugs, guns, and stolen property—were hardly victimless crimes. The Court further undermined its own persuasiveness when suggesting that it could not distinguish between adultery and sodomy, as if the promise-breaking and breach of trust likely involved in the former but not the latter provide no relevant basis for differentiation.

As a separate point, were the Court serious when implying that the right of privacy would not protect practices that society viewed as immoral, the Court would have some difficulty in explaining why abortion, contraception, and interracial marriage were all protected by the right to privacy, notwithstanding their being or having been viewed as immoral. Thus, while numerous reasons were offered to reject that sodomy was protected by the right to privacy, many of those reasons were specious and, further, would not account for why those practices already recognized as protected by the right to privacy are in fact protected.

The *Bowers* Court suggested that the right to privacy did not include consensual sodomy because there was no evidence of any connection between that activity on the one hand and family, marriage, or procreation on the other. If that is the reason, however, then *Bowers* does not preclude the Court's recognizing that the right to privacy protects the right to marry a same-sex partner. Although the Court might plausibly deny a connection between a one-night stand (which happened to involve sodomitical relations) on the one hand and marriage and family on the other, the Court could not plausibly deny a connection between same-sex unions on the one hand and marriage and family on the other. Exactly what is at issue in the same-sex marriage debate is whether same-sex couples will be able to form a legally recognized marriage or family, and thus this *Bowers* line of argument supports rather than undermines that the right to privacy protects same-sex marriage.

A separate question is whether connection to marriage and family in fact is the relevant criterion. If, instead, the relevant question is whether the activity or status at issue is fundamental to concepts of personhood, then both same-sex marriages and adult, consensual, non-marital, sexual activity should be recognized as protected by the right to privacy. Arguably, the latter is the appropriate criterion and, thus, the claim here is neither that *Bowers* was rightly decided nor that *Bowers* should not have been litigated, but merely that the jurisprudence articulated in *Bowers* does not undermine the claim that the Federal Constitution protects the right to marry a same-sex partner.

DIFFERENT UNDERSTANDINGS OF *BOWERS*

Notwithstanding that the right to marry a same-sex partner might be protected by the right to privacy even if the right to commit sodomy is not, a variety of commentators have suggested that *Bowers* is incompatible with a federally recognized right to same-sex marriage. The arguments that *Bowers* precludes such a recognition might helpfully be separated into three different categories. The first concerns itself with the language of the opinion, suggesting that same-sex marriage does not meet the relevant test for determining whether the activity at issue is protected by the right to privacy. The second concerns itself with the substance of the decision, suggesting that because sodomy is illegal and because same-sex couples would presumably be having sodomitical relations if permitted to marry, the right to privacy obviously cannot include the right to marry a same-sex partner. The third concerns itself with the tone rather than the language or substance of the opinion, suggesting that even if *Bowers* does not substantively preclude same-sex marriage, the attitude manifested by the Court in that opinion indicates the Court's understanding that the Constitution permits the imposition of burdens on individuals with a same-sex orientation that could not be imposed on other groups.

Some commentators examining the language of *Bowers* suggest that same-sex marriage cannot be included within the right to privacy because such unions are not deeply rooted in the history and traditions of the country. Ironically, when explicating the history and traditions test, these theorists seem not to appreciate the implications of their own positions. For example, they suggest that the history and traditions test protects interracial marriage, because marriage and family are deeply embedded in the country's history and traditions even if interracial marriages in particular are not, seeming not to appreciate the force of the analogous argument that might be made about same-sex marriages: even if same-sex marriages are not deeply rooted in this nation's history and tradition, marriage and family are, and thus same-sex unions might nonetheless be protected. Indeed, an Alaska trial court has already recognized that the historic place in our hierarchy of values occupied by marriage and family may well entail that same-sex unions are constitutionally protected.[2]

Other commentators consider the substance of *Bowers* and suggest that because sodomy is permissibly criminalized, same-sex marriage is obviously not constitutionally protected. Yet, this argument is unpersuasive for a few different reasons. First, as a practical matter, most states do not criminalize sodomy, so it is unclear why any of those states would nonetheless be permitted to claim that permitting sodomitical relations so strongly offends public policy that same-sex unions cannot be legally recognized. Second, most states with sodomy statutes criminalize both same-sex and different-sex sodomy. If indeed a state criminalizing same-sex sodomy could not recognize same-sex marriage as a fundamental right, then a state criminalizing different-sex sodomy presumably could not recognize different-sex marriage as a fundamental right. Yet, the latter contention is absurd, since the Court has recognized that marriage is a fundamental right, and that right is no less fundamental in states that criminalize different-sex sodomy.

The reason that the existence of a sodomy statute does not preclude the recognition that the right to marry a different-sex partner is fundamental is *not* that married individuals do not engage in sodomitical relations. On the contrary, they do, but their right to do so probably is protected by the Federal Constitution. Indeed, since *Griswold v. Connecticut,* in which the Court explained that the Constitution bars states from searching for contraceptives in "the sacred precincts of marital bedrooms,"[3] it has not been at all clear that the Constitution permits states to criminalize consensual, marital, sodomitical relations.

It might be argued that same-sex and different-sex couples differ because the former can *only* have sodomitical sexual relations, whereas the latter can have sodomitical and non-sodomitical relations. Yet, such a claim is incorrect, at least insofar as sodomy is defined as including only oral and anal sexual relations. Same-sex couples can engage in non-sodomitical relations, although not in penile-vaginal relations.

Suppose, however, that sodomitical relations are defined as all non-penile-vaginal sexual relations. Even if the difficulties in formulating such a definition could be avoided, for example, so that kissing one's partner on the mouth would not count as sodomy, it would seem at the very least question-begging to have changed the definition of sodomy so that same-sex couples could now be said to be unable to engage in non-sodomitical sexual behaviors. In any event, different-sex couples would not be barred from marrying even if they could *only* have sodomitical relations or perhaps could not have sexual relations at all. It thus seems plausible to believe that the sodomy justification for same-sex marriage bans is pretextual.

Precisely because it is likely that marital, consensual, sodomitical relations are protected by the Federal Constitution, those states that have sodomy laws have created exceptions for married couples either through their legislatures or their courts. Were same-sex marriages recognized, sodomitical relations within marriage would presumably not be subject to the statutory prohibition and, in any event, would likely be protected by the Federal Constitution. Thus, whether or not *Bowers v. Hardwick* is still good law, same-sex sodomy *within marriage* would presumably not be subject to criminal penalty, and the existence of sodomy statutes would have no effect on whether there is a fundamental right to marry a same-sex partner.

Commentators who claim that the permissibility of sodomy statutes established the permissibility of same-sex marriage prohibitions seem to forget recent constitutional history. In *McLaughlin v. Florida*, the state of Florida argued that its punishing interracial coupling more severely than intra-racial coupling was reasonably related to its goal of preventing inter-racial marriage. The Supreme Court rejected that argument, suggesting that each statute had to be examined on its own merits and that "the State's policy against interracial marriage [can] . . . be as adequately served by the general, neutral, and existing ban on illicit behavior as by a provision . . . which singles out the promiscuous interracial couple for special statutory treatment."[4] The Court struck down the Florida statute at issue without expressing an opinion about whether Florida's interracial marriage ban was itself constitutional. By doing so, the Court emphasized that statutes regulating marriage and statutes regulating non-marital sexual relations implicate different issues and thus their constitutionality may hinge on different factors.

The *McLaughlin* Court did not even hint that a statute regulating non-marital relations would be unconstitutional, "dealing as it does with illicit extramarital and premarital promiscuity."[5] Rather, the Court established that special penalties could not be imposed on unmarried, interracial couples having sexual relations, conveniently ignoring that, because interracial couples could not marry in Florida, they could only have "nonmarital" relations if they were to have sexual relations at all. The Court did not strike down interracial marriage bans until three years later, although the opportunity to do so had been presented in the mid-1950s.

It is perhaps underappreciated that miscegenation might refer to interracial coupling or to interracial marriage. Former laws prohibiting interracial coupling are analogous to current laws prohibiting same-sex sodomy, since in each case special penalties were or are being imposed as a way of burdening disfavored groups. Because such laws target specific groups, they may be constitutionally offensive even if the general behavior that they seek to regulate is permissibly proscribed.

Former laws prohibiting interracial marriage are analogous to current laws prohibiting same-sex marriage, since in each case individuals are being prevented from marrying their would-be spouses, notwithstanding the clear public policy reasons supporting the recognition of such unions. Indeed, many of the specious arguments currently offered in an attempt to justify same-sex marriage bans echo the specious reasons formerly offered in attempts to justify interracial marriage bans.

Here, the issue is whether a state with a sodomy statute could thereby justify its same-sex marriage ban. As suggested both by the *McLaughlin* Court's requirement that Florida's interracial fornication and marriage statutes be examined separately, each needing to be justified on its own merits, and by the *Griswold* Court's recognition of marital privacy, the permissibility of a sodomy statute hardly establishes that same-sex marriage is not protected by the right to privacy.

Were the issue presented before the Court today, the current Supreme Court would presumably say that while interracial marriage bans are unconstitutional, statutes banning nonmarital, intra-racial and interracial coupling are not so protected, although the state is of course precluded from punishing the latter more severely than the former. So, too, the Court might say, even if statutes banning same-sex marriage are unconstitutional, statutes prohibiting sodomy (especially if not distinguishing between same-sex and opposite-sex couples) might nonetheless be upheld. The historical treatment of interracial coupling and marriage and the current treatment of same-sex coupling and marriage are much more analogous than some commentators seem willing to admit.

Still other commentators address the tone of the *Bowers* opinion, suggesting that even if the substance of the opinion has no implications for same-sex unions, the tone of the opinion indicates that individuals with a same-sex orientation are not protected by the Federal Constitution. That kind of analysis is more difficult to critically evaluate, since at least two issues would have to be addressed: (1) whether in fact individuals with a same-sex orientation are not entitled to all of the protections taken for granted by many people; and (2) if in fact not all protections are applicable, which are not or perhaps under what conditions those protections are inapplicable. Using the tone analysis, one simply cannot even know which kinds of arguments could be successfully marshaled to show that rights had been violated in a particular case, especially when the implication is that a different standard is applicable without a specification of what that higher standard is or how it differs from the standards against which others are judged.

Consider Judge Reinhardt's dissenting opinion in *Watkins v. United States Army,* in which he suggested that *Bowers* must be read either as "about 'sodomy,' and heterosexual sodomy is as constitutionally unprotected as homosexual sodomy, or it is about 'homosexuality,' and there are some acts which are protected if done by heterosexuals but not if done by homosexuals."[6] He regretfully concluded that it was about the latter, believing that the "anti-homosexual thrust of *Hardwick,* and the Court's willingness to condone anti-homosexual animus in the actions of the government, are clear."[7]

SCALIA ON *BOWERS*

It is not difficult to understand how someone might infer that *Bowers* relegated those individuals with a same-sex orientation to second-class citizen status, since at least some members of the current Court seem to interpret *Bowers* that way. For example, in his dissent in *Romer,* Justice Scalia suggested that the issue in *Romer*—whether the electorate could constitutionally preclude lesbians, gays, and bisexuals from receiving the kinds of protections that other groups in the state were already receiving—was already settled by *Bowers.* Yet, it was not obvious why *Bowers*—a case involving the constitutionality of Georgia's sodomy statute criminalizing both same-sex and different-sex sodomitical relations—would be dispositive of the question at issue in *Romer,* since Colorado had been one of the first states to repeal its own sodomy statute and was not attempting to recriminalize that activity. Thus, were *Bowers* "merely" holding that same-sex sodomitical relations were not protected by the right to privacy, one could not thereby infer that the Constitution therefore permitted homosexuality to be singled out for disfavorable treatment.

When the *Bowers* Court pointed out that sodomy was a criminal offense at common law, the Court failed to mention that both heterosexual and homosexual sodomy had been proscribed. That there was such a prohibition does not justify selecting same-sex sodomitical relations for special

adverse treatment, since the prohibition applied to all sodomitical relations, regardless of the sexes or the marital status of the parties involved.
Nonetheless, Justices Scalia, Thomas, and Rehnquist construe *Bowers* and
the Constitution as targeting those with a same-sex orientation, notwithstanding that the common law targeted not persons but a practice.

THE IMPLICATIONS OF CRIMINALIZABILITY

Justice Scalia has suggested that the very possibility that sodomy
statutes may be passed without offending the Federal Constitution gives
the states great leeway with respect to how they treat those with a same-
sex orientation. In *Romer v. Evans,* Justice Scalia claimed, "If it is constitutionally permissible for a State to make homosexual conduct criminal,
surely it is constitutionally permissible for a State to enact other laws
merely disfavoring homosexual conduct."[8] Thus, a state would not *in fact*
have to criminalize same-sex relations to make it permissible to pass other
laws adversely impacting lesbians and gays; the mere possibility would
suffice.

Perhaps it will be thought that this is an unfair interpretation of Justice
Scalia's position. Yet, Justice Scalia argued that Colorado's Amendment
2 was justified as an expression of hostility to homosexual conduct, notwithstanding Colorado's having been one of the first states to repeal its
sodomy law and notwithstanding the Amendment's not having been limited to sodomy but instead having targeted "homosexual, lesbian, or bisexual orientation, conduct, practices, or relationships."[9]

Several points should be made about the breadth of Amendment 2. Even
had it "merely" been limited to same-sex conduct and practices, it presumably would have included a number of activities that do not involve
sodomy, for example, handholding, embracing, kissing, etcetera, since
these might also qualify as same-sex practices. But the Amendment was
much broader than that, since it also targeted orientation and relationships, too. The *Romer* majority recognized that the broad language of the
Amendment could effect a "[s]weeping and comprehensive . . . change"[10]
in the law. Yet, Justice Scalia saw nothing wrong with this broad sweep,
characterizing the Amendment as "a modest attempt by seemingly tolerant Coloradans to preserve traditional sexual mores against the efforts of
a politically powerful minority to revise those mores through the use of
the laws."[11]

Justice Scalia's characterization was surprising on several counts. For
example, the "modest" attempt was described by the majority as "unprecedented in our jurisprudence."[12] The Court further made clear that it was
not within this country's constitutional tradition to enact laws of this sort.
Although Justice Scalia claimed in dissent that "[n]o principle . . . imagined by this Court in the past 200 years prohibits what Colorado has done

here,"[13] he later implied in a dissenting opinion that *Romer* involved a fairly standard application of electoral process jurisprudence.[14]

Justice Scalia referred to lesbians, gays, and bisexuals as a "politically powerful minority," notwithstanding (1) the outcome of the referendum vote, and (2) the fact that numerous groups had been included in anti-discrimination ordinances in the cities of Denver, Boulder, and Aspen. Given that such ordinances often include a whole host of classifications, for example, race, color, creed, religion, ancestry, national origin, sex, age, marital status, physical handicaps, affectional or sexual orientation, family responsibility, or political affiliation, being included is hardly an indication of overwhelming power.

Justice Scalia's comments in dissent in *Romer* might be contrasted with his comments in dissent in *Board of Education of Kiryas Joel Village School District v. Grumet*. In *Grumet*, the Court held that New York's setting up a special school district for members of the Satmar religious sect was a violation of the Establishment Clause. Justice Scalia wrote, "The Court today finds that the Powers That Be, up in Albany, have conspired to effect an establishment of the Satmar Hasidim."[15] He then suggested that it was absurd to think that "the Satmar had become so powerful, so closely allied with Mammon, as to have become an 'establishment' of the Empire State."[16]

Needless to say, the *Grumet* majority had neither said nor implied that the New York legislature had been commandeered by the Satmar Hasidim. Justice Scalia's comments were especially surprising because he would seem to be the most likely individual currently on the Court to have made such a charge. One characterizing gays and lesbians as politically powerful when, after all, slightly over 53 percent of the Colorado electorate voted *for* Amendment 2 might wrongly be tempted to think a small group very powerful indeed if legislation were passed benefiting them. The point here of course is not to suggest that the Satmar Hasidim controlled the New York legislature but, rather, that Scalia's suggesting that Amendment 2 proponents were a tolerant group engaging in a modest attempt to defend themselves against a powerful "Kulturkampf" enemy speaks more about Justice Scalia's own particular views concerning lesbians, gays, bisexuals, and transgendered people than it speaks to realistic assessments of power concentrations.

ON BURDENING THOSE WITH A PARTICULAR ORIENTATION

Justice Scalia is remarkably willing to uphold legislation that imposes burdens on the basis of orientation, notwithstanding the unacceptable legal positions that are thereby at least implicitly adopted. One infers from Justice Scalia's comments not only that much same-sex conduct is an acceptable stand-in for same-sex sodomy but that, "where criminal sanctions are not involved, homosexual 'orientation' is an acceptable stand-in for homosexual conduct."[17] Lest one not understand just how broad that latter stand-in category is, Justice Scalia explains that an orientation merely involves one's having a tendency or desire to engage in a particular activity. Thus, anyone who engages in or desires to engage in same-sex practices or conduct is potentially subject to the Amendment's reach.

Suppose that one accepts the *Bowers* rationale that sexual practices whose proscriptions have "ancient roots" may be criminalized. This would mean that states could criminalize heterosexual sodomy, adultery, and fornication, as well as interracial marriage and marital sodomy. Further, because any of these could be criminalized, Justice Scalia's analysis suggests that the Constitution would permit anyone who would even have a desire to commit any of those to be subject to having unwanted burdens imposed upon him or her.

It would be true but irrelevant to point out that the fact those practices were once criminalized hardly establishes that they are not now constitutionally protected. Such a criticism involves a rejection of the criterion that was implicitly offered for determining the constitutionality of particular practices and might cast doubt on the vitality of *Bowers*. Indeed, such a point might imply that the Court should engage in the kind of reasoned judgment in light of the existing jurisprudence that the plurality endorsed in *Planned Parenthood of Southeastern Pennsylvania v. Casey* but that Justice Scalia rejected.

Nonetheless, suppose that one limits one's focus to practices that the Court has not (yet) declared protected by the right to privacy, for example, adultery and fornication. Some estimate that the percentage of the population engaging in such practices is very high, although those estimates are controversial. Yet, Justice Scalia's comments suggest that not only those committing adultery and fornication but also those who have a tendency or desire to do so may permissibly have burdens imposed upon them. The potentially burdened group would include, for example, those who had lusted in their hearts for someone to whom they were not married, even if the lusting individuals had never in fact acted on those inclinations. Thus, according to this theory, anyone who desired to have premarital or extramarital sexual relations would be tempted to commit a criminalizable (even if not criminalized) act and would be subject to disadvantageous treatment should the state deem the imposition of such treatment appropriate.

Some who might be subject to having these burdens imposed upon them might claim never to have even been tempted to have premarital or extramarital sex. Justice Scalia would presumably suggest that those individuals might bring an as-applied challenge to the statute envisioned here. In response to the claim that individuals should not be disadvantaged on the mere presumption that they would engage in these criminalizable if not criminalized activities, Justice Scalia might suggest, as he did in *Romer*, that because no criminal penalty was at issue, sexual desires would be an acceptable stand-in for conduct.

In his *Romer* dissent, Justice Scalia made clear his belief that it is permissible for a state to pass an amendment which withdraws from lesbians, gays, and bisexuals, but no others, specific legal protections from the injuries caused by discrimination, and which forbids reinstatement of these protections, because the state could (even if, in fact, it did not) have a law criminalizing sodomy. Yet, the fact that the state did not have such a law presumably indicates that it did not believe the conduct at issue sufficiently worrisome to merit criminal sanctions. Were the state in fact to have criminalized the activity, one might expect Justice Scalia to have been willing to give the state even more leeway to impose burdens on people who had a desire to commit the activity in question.

While Colorado does not have a law criminalizing sodomy, it does have a law prohibiting adultery. One wonders what civil penalties against possible adulterers Justice Scalia would be willing to countenance and what kinds of showings of propensities or desires he would constitutionally require before such penalties could be imposed. After all, it might be argued, sexual desires for the object of one's lust can be strong and, even if that person is a non-spouse, might well be irrepressible. Since no criminal penalties would be at issue, Justice Scalia would presumably suggest that the state would not need to wait until the individual had in fact acted on his or her adulterous desires for these burdens to be imposed.

The analysis of *Bowers* offered by Justice Scalia would, if taken seriously, establish the constitutional permissibility of a state's imposing a whole range of burdens on individuals with an "orientation" to commit fornication or adultery. The Court would never accept that such statutes would be constitutionally permissible, and it seems likely that the commentators who accept Scalia's analysis in *Romer* do so only insofar as it "justifies" imposing burdens on a particular, politically unpopular group.

MARITAL VERSUS NONMARITAL ACTS

Were the Court to have adopted Justice Scalia's position on Colorado's Amendment 2, one might have accepted Judge Reinhardt's analysis of *Bowers* in which he suggested that the Court believes that individuals with a same-sex orientation are not entitled to the same protections that others receive. The Court rejected Justice Scalia's analysis in *Romer*, however, and did not even mention *Bowers* in that opinion. This could be because the Court was overruling *Bowers* sub silentio or because the Court did not believe *Bowers* to be on point, perhaps reading (or limiting) the decision to be only about what it purported to be about, namely, whether the right to privacy guaranteed in the Federal Constitution includes the right to commit sodomy.

Even before *Bowers,* several courts had suggested that the right to privacy protects marital but not nonmarital sodomy. Bracketing whether distinguishing between marrieds and unmarrieds this way is rationally supportable or, instead, a violation of equal protection guarantees, this way of interpreting *Bowers* and the right to privacy jurisprudence would less readily support the claim that it is permissible to impose burdens on individuals with a same-sex orientation just because the electorate desires to make them unequal to everyone else. Though the reading of *Bowers* suggested here neither makes the decision a well-reasoned opinion nor even a respectable one, it would nonetheless remove some of the taint from one of the Court's more embarrassing recent decisions.

THE FUNDAMENTAL INTEREST IN MARRIAGE

The Court has declared that the "right to marry is of fundamental importance for all individuals" and has "routinely categorized the decision to marry as among the personal decisions protected by the right to privacy."[18] While the Court has recognized that "reasonable regulations that do not significantly interfere with decisions to enter into the marital relationship may legitimately be imposed,"[19] the Court has also warned that "[w]hen a statutory classification significantly interferes with the exercise of a fundamental right, it cannot be upheld unless it is supported by sufficiently important state interests and is closely tailored to effectuate only those interests."[20] Entirely precluding same-sex couples from marrying does more than significantly interfere with their marital decision-making.

Justice Powell recognized that the Court's right-to-marry jurisprudence might force society to modify some of its existing practices. In his concurrence in *Zablocki v. Redhail,* he suggested that the Court's willingness to "subject all state regulation which 'directly and substantially' interferes with the decision to marry in a traditional family setting to 'critical examination' or 'compelling state interest' analysis"[21] might well have implications for how the state may regulate same-sex relations.

The *Zablocki* Court suggested that it "would make little sense to recognize a right of privacy with respect to other matters of family life and not with respect to the decision to enter the relationship that is the foundation of the family in our society."[22] That suggestion, however, has been misinterpreted by some of the lower courts. For example, the *Baehr* plurality suggested that the *Zablocki* Court's linking between the right to marry on the one hand and the fundamental rights of procreation, childbirth, abortion, and child rearing on the other is the assumption that the one is simply the logical predicate of the others. Yet, given that same-sex couples are having and raising children and given this logical connection between marriage on the one hand and having and raising children on the other, one would have thought that the *Baehr* court would have felt logically compelled to recognize the right to marry a same-sex partner.

Zablocki's providing strong support for the right to marry a same-sex partner is even easier to see if one considers it in light of *Meyer v. Nebraska,* in which the Court recognized that the Due Process Clause protects the "right of the individual . . . to marry, establish a home, and bring up children,"[23] implying both that these rights are all fundamental and that they are equally important. Given that lesbian and gay parents, like other parents, have the fundamental right to make decisions regarding their children and given that the right to marry is on the same level of importance as the right to make decisions regarding one's children, *Meyer* and *Zablocki* both provide strong support for the constitutional right of lesbians and gays to marry their same-sex partners. As the *Zablocki* Court impliedly recognized, the alternative "would make little sense."[24] Of course, *Zablocki* did not establish the right to a same-sex marriage, since the Wisconsin regulation instead involved a different marital restriction, but the *Zablocki* Court's reasoning is nonetheless highly instructive.

Courts have long recognized that the state has a "compelling interest in encouraging and fostering procreation of the race and providing status and stability to the environment in which children are raised."[25] Yet, this interest would not support preventing same-sex couples from marrying, given that they are having and raising children. On the contrary, this would support the right to marry a same-sex partner, since that would lend status and stability to the environment in which the children might be raised.

When commentators seek to establish why same-sex couples should not be allowed to marry, they sometimes point to the need that children have for a long-term, stable environment. Of course, this is a reason that same-sex marriages should be recognized, unless one adds an additional condition, namely, that the long-term, stable environment must involve both of the children's biological parents. Since children need a long-term stable environment even if that setting does not involve both of their biological parents, however, there is no legitimate reason to add such a qualifier.

The state has an interest in having children raised in a loving home where they might flourish, even if only one or perhaps neither parent is biologically related to the children. Indeed, when the *Loving* Court suggested that marriage is "fundamental to our very existence and survival,"[26] there was no indication in the opinion that the survival of the race was somehow dependent on children being raised by both of their biological parents. Were that the case, one would expect that adoption laws would be quite different from what they in fact are. Not only would states not treat the adoptive parent as the legal equivalent of the biological parent, but states would take a much more active role in discouraging adoptions.

The *Bowers* rationale does not undermine the right to marry a same-sex partner as long as the test articulated—promotion of marriage and family—is the relevant test. If the test is whether the activity or practice is implicit within the concept of ordered liberty or whether it is deeply rooted in this nation's history and tradition or is such that its non-protection would violate the collective conscience of the people, then many of those practices already recognized as falling within the right to privacy are nonetheless at risk. Even the right of marrieds to use contraception arguably does not meet those tests. If the test for whether something is included within the right to privacy must account for those practices recognized as protected by that right and not merely for those practices not so recognized, the right to privacy might well protect the right to marry a same-sex partner, *Bowers* notwithstanding.

Other commentators offer a different reason that the inability of same-sex couples to produce a child through their union is allegedly relevant to whether they should be allowed to marry. Some suggest that although such unions can involve the same permanence, commitment, and exclusivity as different-sex marital unions, they nonetheless cannot create new life. Because of the alleged sterility of such unions, the state would have no interest in protecting the sexual union of such couples.

At the very least, this is a surprising argument, since it implies that the sole reason that the state has a stake in the sexual union of couples is that the couple might thereby produce children. Yet, the state would also have a stake in the couple's sexual union insofar as that might help them stay together, which would provide stability both for the individuals themselves and for any children that they might be raising. Further, such an argument suggests that there is nothing in a marriage outside of the potentially procreative sexual union in which the state has a stake. Yet, that argument fails to include some of the state's other interests in marriage, for example, the interest in its citizens being happy and productive members of society, and the state's promoting marriage furthers that interest regardless of whether that family unit involves any children.

As a separate point, the mere lack of a stake in the sexual union would hardly be a reason to *prohibit* the union. More would have to be shown, for example, that the state somehow has an important interest in prohibiting individuals from marrying who could not produce children through their union. Yet, if that really were an important state interest, one would expect the state to require that individuals be able and willing to procreate before allowing them to marry, for example, by submitting the requisite affidavits. One would never expect a state to impose as a condition of marriage that the couple not be able to procreate. Yet, states do not require the production of such an affidavit, and further, several states will only allow first cousins to marry if they can establish their inability to produce children through their union.

Some commentators seem intent on establishing why different-sex marriages are better than same-sex marriages or, perhaps, why heterosexuality is better than homosexuality. Yet, this is an approach that is clearly wrong-headed. First, it seems plausible to suggest that different-sex marriages would be better for some people and that same-sex marriages would be better for others. Even bracketing which kind of marriage or relationship is "better," it would hardly make sense to preclude individuals from marrying because their marriage would not be optimal. For example, financial difficulties can play an important role in causing marital break-ups, and thus it might seem that indigent individuals might not have "optimal" marriages. Yet, in *Boddie v Connecticut*, the Court struck down Connecticut's restriction of the ability of indigents to get a divorce, at least in part because that would prevent them from remarrying. Further, the *Zablocki* Court struck down Wisconsin's imposition of a financial litmus test for those who wish to marry, notwithstanding that such marriages might not be "optimal" and notwithstanding the state's legitimate and substantial interest in promoting the welfare of out-of-custody children. Marriage involves too important an interest to be denied to all who would not have "optimal" marriages, even if there were objective criteria to determine which unions would qualify.

Suppose that it were true in some objective sense that families with children were somehow better than families without children and thus that childless marriages would not be optimal. This would hardly be a reason to prohibit the latter, and were this any other context such a claim would never be advanced. One can imagine the outcry were someone to introduce legislation limiting marriage only to those who could and would have children.

SEXUAL ACTIVITY OUTSIDE OF MARRIAGE

When discussing which sexual activities are constitutionally protected and which are not, members of the Court have suggested that neither fornication nor adultery is constitutionally protected. Merely because both of those are currently viewed as outside of the realm of privacy rights protected by the United States Constitution, however, does not establish that no constitutionally relevant distinctions can be made between the two. The Court has suggested that there is an implicit ordering that privileges marital over nonmarital acts, but also that might protect certain nonmarital acts before others. Thus, because fornication might plausibly be viewed as less destructive to marriage than adultery, fornication might be protected by the right to privacy even if adultery is not, at least according to one understanding of the principle underlying right to privacy jurisprudence. A separate question is whether the "expanded" right to privacy would include the right to marry a same-sex partner. Needless to say, however, many of the arguments in favor of including fornication would apply equally, if not more strongly, in the case of same-sex marriage, assuming for the sake of argument that the right to marry a same-sex partner is not already protected by the right to privacy.

HARLAN'S *POE* DISSENT

In his dissent in *Poe v. Ullman*, Justice Harlan outlined a way of understanding right to privacy jurisprudence that many on the Court seemed to have adopted. He suggested:

The laws regarding marriage which provide both when the sexual powers may be used and the legal and societal context in which children are born and brought up, as well as laws forbidding adultery, fornication and homosexual practices which express the negative of the proposition, confining sexuality to lawful marriage, form a pattern so deeply pressed into the substance of our social life that any Constitutional doctrine in this area must build upon that basis.[27]

It might at first seem misguided to quote from Justice Harlan's dissent in an book suggesting that same-sex marriage is protected by the right to privacy, since he groups adultery, fornication, and homosexual practices and then suggests that they are the "negative" of the legal and social context in which children are born and raised. His concern was family life, and he envisioned same-sex and nonmarital relations as outside of the family and hence outside of the sphere protected by the Constitution. Yet, his doing so may have involved a mistake of fact: he simply may not have imagined that same-sex relationships involve any more than sex and thus may not have envisioned same-sex individuals as composing families.

At least two distinct points must be made about Justice Harlan's analysis. The first point is that his right-to-privacy jurisprudence is based upon the family without a specification of how family should be defined. Regardless of whether Justice Harlan's perspective was less broad than it might have been or, perhaps, whether social practices have changed over the past forty years or so, the issue at hand involves the legal recognition of existing families. The concept of family has evolved over the past several decades to include additional groups of individuals who function as families. While there may be disagreements about what the outer contours of this concept should be, same-sex partners (perhaps with children whom they are raising) are close enough to the core definition of family that there should be no question that they should be included. Unless the Court is going to "close [its] . . . eyes to the basic reasons why certain rights associated with the family have been accorded shelter under the Fourteenth Amendment[ ] . . . , [the Court cannot] . . . avoid applying the force and rationale of these precedents to the family choice involved in this case."[28] It has already been established that the "Constitution protects the sanctity of the family precisely because the institution of the family is deeply rooted in this Nation's history and tradition,"[29] and, as an Alaska trial court has suggested, "just as the decision to marry and raise a child in a traditional family setting is constitutionally protected as a fundamental right, so too should the decision to choose one's life partner and have a recognized nontraditional family be constitutionally protected."[30]

The second point is that Justice Harlan did not suggest that the right to privacy must be limited to family but merely that the doctrine must be built upon that basis. It would be quite compatible with his articulated view to expand right to privacy protections as long as family matters were at its core. As to how far these protections should be expanded, this is an issue that state courts are attempting to address in light of their own constitutional rights to privacy protections. For example, courts have been trying to address whether the right to privacy includes the right of unmarried adults to engage in consensual sexual relations with other unmarried adults (fornication) or the right of a married individual to have consensual sexual relations with someone other than his or her spouse (adultery).

CRIMINAL VERSUS CIVIL PENALTIES

The question of immediate concern in this section is whether the right to privacy protects the right to commit fornication or adultery. Even before that is addressed, however, a separate issue must be briefly discussed, if only so that different issues will not be conflated. Regardless of how much the constitutional right to privacy includes, the state should neither be criminalizing fornication nor adultery. Even if one rejects the claim that adultery is a violation of private rather than public morality and instead believes adultery a violation of both, there are numerous reasons that it should nonetheless not be criminalized. For example, limited public resources are better spent in enforcing other laws. It is not even clear that society thinks adultery appropriately punished, since such laws are rarely if ever enforced.

It might be argued that even if adultery laws are not enforced, an important message is communicated about society's views as long as laws prohibiting that conduct remain on the books. It is simply unclear, however, what message is communicated by unenforced laws. Perhaps the message is that society disapproves of adultery, although the failure to prosecute might also suggest that society believes adultery permissible or, at the very least, not particularly offensive. Further, yet another message might be communicated: by having laws remain on the books even though those laws are rarely if ever enforced, society may communicate that it does not believe that its own laws must be taken seriously. Thus, by having unenforced laws on the books, society may promote a lack of respect for those laws in particular or for law more generally.

As a separate matter, if the goal of laws criminalizing adultery is to promote marriage, they may in fact undermine the very goal they seek to attain. Threatened or actual imposition of criminal sanctions would seem unlikely to promote reconciliation. Further, the threat of such sanctions might also chill honest and open communication, perhaps blocking the only path that might lead to a particular marriage being saved. Thus, there seem to be a variety of reasons not to criminalize adultery. Many of these arguments would apply with equal if not greater force to fornication. Thus, regardless of whether the United States Constitution prohibits criminal sanctions for adultery or fornication, adult, consensual fornication, sodomy, and adultery should not be criminalized.

A CONSTITUTIONAL RIGHT TO COMMIT ADULTERY?

The above suggests that a legislature would be wise not to criminalize certain sexual practices. Nonetheless, a separate question is whether any or all of these practices are protected by the right to privacy. Consider the analysis offered by the Supreme Court of Texas when it was asked to consider whether adultery was protected by the right to privacy guaranteed under the Texas Constitution. The court held that adulterous relations were not protected, echoing part of Justice Blackmun's *Bowers* dissent by pointing out that "adultery often injures third persons, such as spouses and children."[31] Indeed, the court suggested that adulterous conduct "is the very antithesis of marriage and family . . . [since adultery], by its very nature, undermines the marital relationship and often rips apart families."[32]

Arguably, the Texas court was exaggerating in its description of adultery, since adultery does not by its very nature undermine marital relationships. Indeed, some claim that adulterous relationships have strengthened their marriages. Thus, perhaps the Texas court should have claimed that adultery sometimes or perhaps often destroys marriages when one of the parties has breached his or her promise to be faithful. Still, even if the court's language were too strong, its point remains. It seems reasonable to assume both that adultery sometimes destroys marriages and that adultery and fornication are distinguishable in this very respect, assuming that fornication is limited to relations between individuals who are not married to anyone.

That fornication would be less likely to destroy existing families and might indeed promote family (especially if a functional definition of family is used) might be constitutionally significant if in fact the relevant test for determining what is protected by the right to privacy involves the promotion of family rather than, for example, whether the activity is of intimate personal concern. Where the latter is the relevant test, however, a different analysis will be required if, indeed, courts nonetheless are not going to recognize that the right to privacy protects the right to commit adultery.

STATE CONSTITUTIONS

Over the past several years, various state courts have held that their own state constitutions have broader right to privacy protections than are contained in the Federal Constitution. Several state courts have struck down sodomy statutes on state constitutional grounds. The question at hand is what implications, if any, these rulings have for the other practices under discussion here.

In *Campbell v. Sundquist,* a Tennessee appellate court found that the right to privacy protected by the Tennessee Constitution was more robust than that provided by the Federal Constitution. The court suggested that an adult's right to engage in consensual and noncommercial sexual activities in the privacy of the home is protected by the state constitution's right to privacy.[33] In *Powell v. State,* the Georgia Supreme Court reached a similar conclusion on similar grounds, suggesting that nothing should rank as more private and more deserving of protection from governmental interference than unforced, private, adult sexual activity.[34]

Some commentators have worried that the reasoning of these and other courts would imply that adultery is also constitutionally protected, which would seem to prevent the imposition of any penalties, criminal or civil, for such behavior. At least two points should be made about such a claim. First, such a result might not be unwelcome. Criminal penalties should not be imposed for such conduct and, at least in certain kinds of situations, civil penalties should not be imposed either. For example, child custody decisions should be made in light of who would be a better parent rather than in light of who committed adultery, assuming that no nexus between the adultery and the parenting can be established.

It is simply unclear whether civil penalties for adultery are inappropriately imposed in other contexts—for example, when determining spousal support. Arguably, penalties are not appropriately imposed in that context either, since it may be difficult to establish which party is "really" at fault when one of the parties commits adultery. Further, allowing such an imposition may operate to systematically disadvantage one group: fault-based models have historically operated to disadvantage women. Thus, there are a number of reasons why it may be a bad idea to impose civil penalties on those who commit adultery.

ADULTERY AND WAIVER

One issue is whether it would be a good idea to punish adulterers either civilly or criminally. A different issue is whether a statute imposing such penalties would pass constitutional muster.

Courts recognizing that unforced, private, adult sexual activity is protected by the right to privacy might seem to have established that their state constitutions protect adultery and that only a compelling state interest could justify statutes permitting the imposition of civil penalties against adulterers. Such a conclusion may not be warranted, however. Even assuming that the right of privacy protects consensual, adult, sexual relations, it does not follow that civil penalties could not be imposed for adulterous behavior, since an individual might be said to have waived his or her right to have unforced, private, adult relations with a non-spouse when he or she took marital vows. Using the waiver analysis, civil penalties might still be imposed on the married individual having the affair.

Ironically, although a waiver theory would account for why the marital partner might be sanctioned for having committed adultery, it is not clear whether such a theory could account for why the unmarried individual would be subject to having penalties imposed for having taken part in an adulterous affair, since that individual would not have waived the relevant right by taking marital vows. It might be argued that an unmarried individual does not have a right to have sexual relations with someone who is married (who, after all, has waived his or her right to have sexual relations with a non-spouse), since the latter might be viewed as legally incapable of consenting to such relations. Consensual relations with a minor are not protected by the right to privacy, at least in part, because minors are legally incapable of consenting, and an analogous argument *might* establish why the Constitution does not protect adulterous relations between adults.

As a general matter, society has grown more willing to allow unmarried individuals to have adult, consensual, sexual relations without fear of criminal penalty. The trend in current law is not to have statutes prohibiting fornication and not to enforce those statutes that are on the books. Nonetheless, it is also true that some states have repealed their fornication statutes while retaining their adultery laws and, further, that those adultery statutes also target the unmarried individual who takes part in the affair. Thus, it may well be that society views adultery much more unfavorably than it does fornication and, at least arguably, that the Constitution permits but does not require penalties to be imposed if one engages in the former.

The discussion above is merely intended to suggest that a recognition that the right to privacy protects the right to engage in consensual adult relations would not entail that individuals would have the right to commit adultery. Even if the right to privacy is not premised on a connection to marriage and family but instead on the right to engage in consensual, adult, intimate relations, it would not therefore follow that adultery laws are therefore unconstitutional. A court basing the right to privacy on connection to family or on the intimacy and fundamental nature of voluntary, adult relations could quite consistently hold that consenting sexual relations between unmarried adults are protected by the right to privacy without also holding that the Constitution recognizes a right to commit adultery. Further, such a court might also recognize that the right to privacy protects the right to marry a same-sex partner without also including the right to commit adultery.

THE RIGHT TO PRIVACY RECONSIDERED

The current federal right to privacy jurisprudence has family concerns at its core. This alone has a variety of implications, since those who seek the right to marry a same-sex partner are often seeking legal recognition of their already existing families. Even if *Bowers* is still good law, same-sex marriage may nonetheless be constitutionally protected by the right to privacy. Indeed, the only non-specious rationale articulated in *Bowers* to determine what is protected by the right to privacy supports rather than undermines the theory that laws banning same-sex marriage violate federal constitutional guarantees.

It should be noted that fornication might include two unmarried parties having sexual relations who had lived together for several years, had had children together, and had been monogamous for that entire period. It might also include two unmarried parties who had had a one-night stand. In the former case, the couple has a marriage-like relation even if in fact the state does not give legal recognition to their relationship. In the latter, the couple has had intimate relations, even if not a long-lasting relationship. These different relationships might receive different constitutional protections, depending upon which principle determines what is protected by the right to privacy.

Regrettably, *Bowers* offers no help in figuring out which principles underlie the right to privacy because it simply refused to consider the developing right to privacy jurisprudence. That decision was a disaster, not only because the wrong conclusion was reached but also because the reasoning was so patently specious that it is difficult to know what the Court was trying to communicate in addition to its disapproval of same-sex relations. Perhaps the Court was suggesting that sexual relations are not protected by the Federal Constitution unless they are within the family context. Arguably, that view is mistaken, although a more plausible claim might be that sexual relations within a relationship are viewed as more fundamental and hence having more constitutional protection than are individual sex acts outside of a relationship. Even if acts within a relationship are considered more fundamental than acts outside of one, however, that of course does not mean that sexual activity outside of relationships should be criminalized unless they are, for example, nonconsensual, but merely that sexual activity within relationships would be accorded constitutional priority.

If, indeed, adult, consensual *relationships* are at least as fundamental as adult, consensual *relations,* then those state constitutions protecting the latter should also protect same-sex relationships. Though there are important differences between the two—legal recognition of same-sex relationships involves a public recognition of those unions whereas protecting sexual relations might "merely" mean immunizing them from criminal prosecution—the entire right to privacy jurisprudence would have to be turned on its head for nonmarital relations to be recognized as fundamental without an accompanying recognition of the right of same-sex partners to form legally recognized families. On any plausible reading of the right to privacy jurisprudence, the federal and, especially, certain state constitutional rights to privacy already include the right of same-sex couples to form the sacred personal union which is so fundamental in that jurisprudence. Any other reading would suggest that rights and activities already recognized as protected may not enjoy that status for very long.

CONCLUSION

Vermont's recognition of civil unions will be a milestone in the history of the lesbian/gay/bisexual/transgender movement to secure equal rights. Not only have more rights thereby been accorded than in any other state, but the *Baker* opinion, especially when its misunderstanding of federal law has been corrected, will provide the legal basis for challenging same-sex marriage bans in other states. Until those bans have been overturned and the Federal Defense of Marriage Act either repealed or struck down, however, same-sex couples who have rights recognized in one state will have to consider whether those rights will be respected in other states and what actions might be taken to protect those rights.

The United States Constitution protects the right of all Americans to travel through or migrate to other states. Recently, the United States Supreme Court has suggested that the right to travel is relatively robust, thereby providing yet another basis upon which the state and Federal Defense of Marriage Acts may be declared unconstitutional. Marriages that are valid in the domicile at the time of the marriage should be considered valid in all of the states. Marriage is too dear to be something that a citizen can be forced to surrender when he or she wishes to travel though or move to a state in his or her own country.

At one time, Hawaii seemed likely to be the first state to legally recognize same-sex unions. A referendum amending the state constitution dashed those hopes. Although the Hawaii Supreme Court's interpretation of that amendment provides the grounds for its invalidation, that result does not seem likely. Nonetheless, the Hawaii opinion has positive aspects as well, since it (like the *Baker* opinion) provides the legal analysis upon which federal challenges to same-sex marriage bans can be based whether in Hawaii or elsewhere.

Same-sex marriage opponents claim that same-sex marriage should not be "endorsed" by the state. Yet, the state should not be deciding which marriages are "preferred," especially when the purpose behind manifesting such a preference is to indicate that individuals with a same-sex orientation are second-class citizens and not as good as everyone else. One of the lessons of endorsement test jurisprudence is that the state should not be privileging some citizens and making other citizens outsiders in their own state and country.

At least one reason that individuals wish not to recognize same-sex unions is that such unions may offend religious sensibilities. Yet, it is not as if no religion recognizes such unions; rather, some do and others do not. To refuse to recognize such unions merely because doing so would offend the religious sensibilities of some violates the Free Exercise Clause of the United States Constitution. While religious practices can be prohibited if the state has a sufficiently important reason for doing so, no reason thus far offered would come close to sufficing as a justification.

In order to establish that same-sex marriage bans do not violate the Constitution, courts and commentators must significantly rework both privacy and equal protection jurisprudence. The interpretations of past Supreme Court cases that have been offered to make it possible to uphold such bans would, if adopted, put many of the protections currently enjoyed by Americans at significant risk. In the not-too-distant future, the United States Supreme Court will be faced with a stark choice: admitting that the Federal Constitution protects same-sex relationships or significantly cutting back on the constitutional rights and protections that have already been recognized for all Americans. One can only hope that a majority on the Court will have the impartiality, wisdom, and courage to choose the former rather than the latter.

NOTES

1. *Bowers v. Harwick*, 478 U.S. 186, 194 (1986).
2. See *Brause v. Bureau of Vital Statistics*, 1998 WL 88743, at *4 (Alaska Super. 1998).
3. *Griswold v. Connecticut*, 381 U.S. 478, 485 (1965).
4. *McLaughlin v. Florida*, 379 U.S. 184, 196 (1964).

5. *Id.* at 193.

6. *Watkins v. United States Army*, 837 F.2d 1428, 1452 (Reinhardt, J., dissenting).

7. *Id.* at 1453 (Reinhardt, J., dissenting).

8. *Romer v. Evans*, 517 U.S. 620, 641 (1996) (Scalia, J., dissenting).

9. See *id.* at 624.

10. See *id.* at 627.

11. See *id.* at 636 (Scalia, J., dissenting).

12. *Id.* at 633.

13. *Id.* at 644 (Scalia, J., dissenting).

14. See *Equality Foundation of Greater Cincinnati, Incorporated v. City of Cincinnati*, 518 U.S. 1001, 1001 (1996) (Scalia, J., dissenting) ("The consequence of its [*Romer's*] holding is that homosexuals in a city (or other electoral subunit) that wishes to accord them special protection cannot be compelled to achieve a state constitutional amendment in order to have the benefit of that democratic preference.")

15. *Board of Education of Kiryas Joel Village School District v. Grumet*, 512 U.S. 687, 732 (1994) (Scalia, J., dissenting).

16. *Id.* (Scalia, J., dissenting).

17. *Romer*, 517 U.S. at 641 (Scalia, J., dissenting).

18. *Zablocki v. Redhail*, 434 U.S. 374, 384 (1978).

19. *Id.* at 386.

20. *Id.* at 388.

21. *Id.* at 396 (Powell, J., concurring).

22. *Id.* at 386.

23. *Meyer v. Nebraska*, 262 U.S. 390, 399 (1923).

24. *Zablocki*, 434 U.S. at 386.

25. See, for example, *Adams v. Howerton*, 486 F. Supp. 1119, 1124 (C.D. Cal. 1980).

26. *Loving*, 388 U.S. at 12.

27. *Poe v. Ullman*, 367 U.S. 497, 545 (Harlan, J., dissenting).

28. *Moore v. City of East Cleveland*, 431 U.S. 494, 501 (1977) (plurality opinion).

29. *Id.* at 503 (Brennan, J., concurring).

30. *Brause v. Bureau of Vital Statistics*, 1998 WL 8743, at *6 (Alaska Super.).

31. *City of Sherman v. Henry*, 928 S.W.2d 464, 470 (Tex. 1964).

32. *Id.*

33. *Campbell v. Sundquist*, 926 S.W.2d 250, 262 (Tenn. App. 1996).

34. See *Powell v. State*, 510 S.E.2d 18, 24 (Ga. 1998). The Montana Supreme Court expressed similar sentiments. See *Gryczan v. State*, 942 P.2d 112, 123 (Mont. 1997).

Bibliography

FEDERAL COURTS

Supreme Court

Adarand Constructors, Incorporated v. Pena, 515 U.S. 200 (1995)
Allied Stores of Ohio, Incorporated v. Bowers, 358 U.S. 522 (1959)
Allstate Insurance Company v. Hague, 449 U.S. 302 (1981)
American Trucking Association, Incorporated v. Smith, 496 U.S. 167 (1990)
Arlington Heights v. Metropolitan Housing Development Corporation, 429 U.S. 252 (1977)
Atherton v. Atherton, 181 U.S. 155 (1901)
Attorney General v. Soto-Lopez, 476 U.S. 898 (1986)
Auffm'ordt v. Rasin, 102 U.S. 620 (1880)
Austin v. New Hampshire, 420 U.S. 65 (1975)
Bain Peanut Company v. Pinson, 282 U.S. 499 (1931)
Baker v. General Motors Corporation, 522 U.S. 222 (1998)
Baldwin v. Fish & Game Commission, 436 U.S. 371 (1978)
Baxtrom v. Herold, 383 U.S. 107 (1966)
Bell's Gap Railroad Company v. Pennsylvania, 134 U.S. 232 (1890)
Board of Education of Kiryas Joel Village School District v. Grumet, 512 U.S. 687 (1994)
Boddie v. Connecticut, 401 U.S. 371 (1971)
Bowen v. Georgetown University Hospital, 488 U.S. 204 (1988)
Bowen v. Roy, 476 U.S. 693 (1986)
Bowers v. Hardwick, 478 U.S. 186 (1986)
Bradley v. School Board of Richmond, 416 U.S. 696 (1974)
Bray v. Alexandria Women's Health Clinic, 506 U.S. 263 (1993)
Burlington Northern Railroad Company v. Ford, 504 U.S. 648 (1992)
Burton v. Wilmington Parking Authority, 365 U.S. 715 (1961)

Califano v. Goldfarb, 430 U.S. 199 (1977)

Capitol Square Review and Advisory Board v. Pinette, 515 U.S. 753 (1995)

Chicot County Drainage District v. Baxter State Bank, 308 U.S. 371 (1940)

Church of the Lukumi Babalu Aye, Incorporated v. City of Hialeah, 508 U.S. 520 (1993)

City of Boerne v. Flores, 521 U.S. 507 (1997)

City of Cleburne v. Cleburne Living Center, Incorporated, 473 U.S. 432 (1985)

City of New Orleans v. Dukes, 427 U.S. 297 (1976)

Civil Aeronautics Board v. Delta Air Lines, Incorporated, 367 U.S. 316 (1961)

Cleveland v. United States, 329 U.S. 14 (1946)

Colgate v. Harvey, 296 U.S. 404 (1935)

Cooper v. Aaron, 358 US 1 (1958)

County of Allegheny v. American Civil Liberties Union, 492 U.S. 573 (1989)

Craig v. Boren, 429 U.S. 190 (1976)

Crandall v. Nevada, 73 U.S. 35 (1 Wallace) (1867)

Davis v. Beason, 133 U.S. 333 (1890)

Dunn v. Blumstein, 405 U.S. 330 (1971)

Edwards v. California, 314 U.S. 160 (1941)

Eisenstadt v. Baird, 405 U.S. 438 (1972)

Employment Division, Department of Human Resources of Oregon v. Smith, 494 U.S. 872 (1990)

Equality Foundation of Greater Cincinnati, Incorporated v. City of Cincinnati, 518 U.S. 1001 (1996)

Estin v. Estin, 334 U.S. 541 (1948)

Federal Trade Commission v. Superior Court Trial Lawyers Association, 493 U.S. 411 (1990)

Ferguson v. Skrupa, 372 U.S. 726 (1963)

Florida Prepaid Postsecondary Education Expense Board v. College Savings Bank, 527 U.S. 627 (1999)

Fowler v. Rhode Island, 345 U.S. 67 (1953)

General Motors Corporation v. Romein, 503 U.S. 181 (1992)

Great Northern Railway Company v. Sunburst Oil and Refining Company, 287 U.S. 358 (1932)

Griffin v. Breckenridge, 403 U.S. 88 (1971)

Griswold v. Connecticut, 381 U.S. 479 (1965)

United States v. Guest, 383 U.S. 745 (1966)

Heller v. Doe, 509 U.S. 312 (1993)

United States v. Heth, 7 U.S. 399 (1806)

Hooper v. Bernalillo County, 472 U.S. 612 (1985)

Interstate Commerce Commission v. Brotherhood of Locomotive Engineers, 482 U.S. 270 (1987)

Jones v. Helms, 452 U.S 412 (1981)

Kulko v. Superior Court, 436 U.S. 84 (1978)

Late Corporation of the Church of Jesus Christ of Latter-Day Saints v. United States, 136 U.S. 1 (1890)

Lee, United States v., 455 U.S. 252 (1982)

Lemon v. Kurtzman, 411 U.S. 192 (1973)

Lewis v. United States, 523 U.S. 155 (1998)
Lopez, United States v. 514 U.S. 549 (1995)
Loving v. Virginia, 388 U.S. 1 (1967)
Lunding v. New York Tax Appeals Tribunal, 522 U.S. 287 (1998)
Lynch v. Donnelly, 465 U.S. 668 (1984)
Lyng v. Northwest Indian Cemetery Protective Association, 485 U.S. 439 (1988)
Massachusetts Board of Retirement v. Murgia, 427 U.S. 307 (1976)
Matthews v. Lucas, 427 U.S. 495 (1976)
Maxwell v. Bugbee, 250 U.S. 525 (1919)
Maynard v. Hill, 125 U.S. 190 (1888)
McGowan v. Maryland, 366 U.S. 420 (1961)
McLaughlin v. Florida, 379 U.S. 184 (1964)
Memorial Hospital v. Maricopa County, 415 U.S. 250 (1974)
Meyer v. Nebraska, 262 US 390 (1923)
Meyers v. United States. 272 U.S. 52 (1926)
Michael M. v. Superior Court of Sonoma County, 450 U.S. 464 (1980)
Michigan v. Long, 463 U.S. 1032 (1983)
Minnesota v. Hodgson, 497 U.S. 417 (1990)
Mississippi University for Women v. Hogan, 458 U.S. 718 (1982)
Moore v. City of East Cleveland, 431 U.S. 494 (1977)
Naim v. Naim, 350 U.S. 985 (1956)
Newberry v. United States, 256 U.S. 232 (1921)
Norton v. Shelby Company, 118 U.S. 425 (1886)
Orr v. Orr, 440 U.S. 268 (1979)
Pace v. Alabama, 106 U.S. 583 (1883)
Paris Adult Theatre I v. Slaton, 413 U.S. 49 (1973)
Paul v. Virginia, 75 U.S. 168 (1868)
Pennoyer v. Neff, 95 U.S. 714 (1877)
Personnel Administrator of Massachusetts v. Feeney, 442 U.S. 256 (1979)
Phillips Petroleum Co. v. Shutts, 472 U.S. 797 (1985)
Planned Parenthood of Southeastern Pennsylvania v. Casey, 505 U.S. 833 (1992)
Poe v. Ullman, 367 U.S. 497 (1961)
Railway Express Agency, Incorporated v. New York, 336 U.S. 106 (1949)
Reynolds v. United States, 98 U.S. 145 (1878)
Roe v. Wade, 410 U.S. 113 (1973)
Rutan v. Republican Party of Illinois, 497 U.S. 62 (1990)
Romer v. Evans, 517 U.S. 620 (1996)
Rumely, United States v., 345 U.S. 41 (1953)
Saenz v. Roe, 526 U.S. 489 (1999)
Santa Fe Independent School District v. Doe, 530 U.S. 290 (2000)
Santosky v. Kramer, 455 U.S. 745 (1982)
Schneider v. Rusk, 377 U.S. 163 (1964)
Shapiro v. Thompson, 394 U.S. 618 (1969)
Shaw v. Reno, 509 U.S. 630 (1993)
Sherrer v. Sherrer, 334 U.S. 343 (1948)
Stanley v. Illinois, 405 U.S. 645 (1972)
Supreme Court v. Friedman, 487 U.S. 59 (1988)

Supreme Court v. Piper, 470 U.S. 274 (1985)
The Slaughterhouse Cases, 83 U.S. (1 Wallace) 36 (1872)
Thompson v. Thompson, 484 U.S. 174 (1988)
Toomer v. Witsell, 334 U.S. 385 (1948)
Trop v. Dulles, 356 U.S. 86 (1958)
Turner v. Safley, 482 U.S. 78 (1987)
Union National Bank v. Lamb, 337 U.S. 38 (1949)
Union Pacific Railroad Company v. Laramie Stock Yards Company, 231 U.S. 190
      (1913)
United Building & Construction Trades Council v. Mayor of Camden, 465 U.S.
      208 (1984)
United States v. (see name of opposing party)
United States Department of Agriculture v. Moreno, 413 U.S. 528 (1973)
Usery v. Turner Elkhorn Mining Company, 428 U.S. 1 (1976)
Village of Belle Terre v. Boraas, 416 U.S. 1, 8 (1974)
Virginia, United States v., 518 U.S. 515 (1996)
Wallace v. Jaffree, 472 U.S. 38 (1985)
Ward v. Maryland, 79 U.S. 418 (1870)
Washington v. Davis, 426 U.S. 229 (1976)
Washington v. Glucksberg, 521 U.S. 702 (1997)
Whitfield v. Ohio, 297 U.S. 431 (1936)
Wieman v. Updegraff, 344 U.S. 183 (1952)
Williams v. Fears, 179 U.S. 270 (1900)
Williams v. North Carolina, 317 U.S. 287 (1942)
Williams v. Rhodes, 393 U.S. 23 (1968)
Wisconsin v. Yoder, 406 U.S. 220 (1971)
Zablocki v. Redhail, 434 U.S. 374 (1978)
Zobel v. Williams, 457 U.S. 55 (1982)

Courts of Appeal

Corfield v. Coryell, 6 F. Cas. 546 (E. D. Pa. 1823)
Cotner v. Henry, 394 F.2d 873 (7th Cir. 1968)
Compassion in Dying v. Washington, 79 F.3d 790 (9th Cir. 1996), rev'd, Wash-
      ington v. Glucksberg, 521 U.S. 702 (1997)
Ex parte (see name of party)
Founding Church of Scientology of Washington, D.C. v. United States, 409 F.2d
      1146 (D.C. Cir. 1969)
G.E.M. Sundries Company, Incorporated v. Johnson and Johnson, Incorporated,
      283 F.2d 86 (9th Cir. 1960)
Kinney, *Ex parte,* 14 F. Cas. 602 (E.D. Va. 1879)
Lovisi v. Slayton, 539 F.2d 349 (4th Cir. 1976)
Shahar v. Bowers, 114 F.3d 1097 (11th Cir. 1997)
Watkins v. United States Army, 837 F.2d 1428 (9th Cir. 1988), superseded by 847
      F.2d
1329 (9th Cir. 1988), withdrawn on rehearing by 875 F.2d 699 (9th Cir. 1989)

District Court

Adams v. Howerton, 486 F. Supp 1119 (C.D. Cal 1980), affd, 673 F2d 1036 (9th Cir. 1982)

Hobbs, *In re*, 12 F. Cas. 262 (N.D. Ga. 1871)

In re (see name of party)

Potter v. Murray City, 585 F. Supp. 1126 (D. Utah 1984)

Towler v. Peyton, 303 F. Supp. 581 (W.D. Va. 1969)

STATE COURTS

Supreme Court

Adoption of Tammy, 619 N.E.2d 315 (Mass. 1993)

Akahane v. Fasi, 565 P.2d 552 (Haw. 1977)

Baehr v. Lewin, 852 P.2d 44 (Haw. 1993), reconsideration granted in part, 875 P.2d 225 (Haw. 1993)

Baehr v. Miike, 1999 Haw. LEXIS 391

Baker v. State, 744 A.2d 864 (Vt. 1999)

Banaz v. Smith, 65 P. 309 (Cal. 1901)

Bonadio, Commonwealth v., 415 A.2d 47 (Pa. 1980)

Bonds v. State Department of Revenue, 49 So.2d 280 (Ala. 1950)

Bouquet, *In re* Marriage of, 546 P. 2d 1371 (Cal. 1976)

Braschi v. Stahl Associates Company, 543 N.E.2d 49 (N.Y. 1989)

Buol, *In re* Marriage of, 705 P. 2d 354 (Cal. 1985)

Burns v. State, 48 Ala. 195 (Ala. 1872) (1872 WL 8955), overruled by Green v. State, 58 Ala. 190 (Ala. 1877) (1877 WL 1291).

Cavanaugh v. Davis, 440 A.2d 1380 (Pa. 1982)

Chiaradio, State v., 660 A.2d 276 (R.I. 1995)

City of Sherman v. Henry, 928 S.W.2d 464 (Tex. 1964)

Clay v. Buchanan, 36 S.W.2d 91 (Tenn. 1931)

Commonwealth v. (see name of opposing party)

Comstock Mill and Mining Company v. Allen, 31 P. 434 (Nev. 1892)

Dean v. District of Columbia, 653 A.2d 307 (D.C. App. 1995)

De Mello v. Fong, 37 Haw. 415 (1946)

Doria v. University of Vermont, 589 A.2d 317 (Vt. 1991)

Dubish, State v., 675 P.2d 877 (Kan. 1994)

Elliot, State v., 551 P.2d 1352 (N.M. 1976)

Evans v. Romer, 882 P.2d 1335 (Colo. 1994) (en banc), aff'd, 517 U.S. 620 (1996)

Ex rel. (see name of party)

Ford v. State, 53 Ala. 150 (Ala. 1875) (1875 WL 1112)

Fuqua v. Fuqua, 104 So.2d 925 (Ala. 1958)

Gardens at West Maui Vacation Club v. County of Maui, 978 P.2d 772 (Haw. 1999)

Gibson v. State, 36 Ind. 389 (Ind. 1871) (1871 WL 5021)

Gifford Memorial Hospital v. Town of Randolph, 118 A.2d 480 (Vt. 1955)

Godin v. Godin, 725 A.2d 904 (Vt. 1998)

Graham Construction Supply, Incorporated v. Schrader Construction, Incorporated, 632 P.2d 649 (Haw. 1981)

Grayson-Robinson Stores, Incorporated v. Oneida, 75 S.E.2d 161 (Ga. 1953)

Green v. State, 58 Ala. 190 (Ala. 1877) (1877 WL 1291)

Gryczan v. State, 942 P.2d 112 (Mont. 1997)

State v. Ikezawa, 857 P.2d 593 (Haw. 1993)

Island Airlines, *In re,* 361 P.2d 390 (Haw. 1961)

J.W.T., *In re,* 872 S.W.2d 189 (Tex. 1994)

Jawish v. Morlet, 86 A.2d 96 (D.C. App. 1952)

Jones v. Hallahan, 501 S.W.2d 588 (Ky. 1973)

Jones' Estate, *In re,* 8 A.2d 631 (Vt. 1939)

Kahalekai v. Doi, 590 P.2d 543 (Haw. 1979)

Keane v. Remy, 168 N.E. 10 (Ind. 1929)

Kinney v. Commonwealth, 71 Va. (30 Grattan) 858 (Va. 1878) (1878 WL 5945)

Kioke v. Board of Water Supply, City and County of Honolulu, 352 P.2d 835
    (Haw. 1960)

Lace v. University of Vermont, 303 A.2d 475 (Vt. 1973)

Lawton Spinning Company v. Commonwealth, 121 N.E. 518 (Mass. 1919)

Lenherr, *In re* Estate of, 314 A.2d 255 (Pa. 1974)

Levin v. Levin, 645 N.E.2d 601 (Ind. 1994)

Lonas v. State, 50 Tenn. (3 Heiske) (Tenn. 1871) (1871 WL 3597)

Marriage of (see name of party)

Maui County Council v. Thompson, 929 P.2d 1355 (Haw. 1997)

Mazzolini v. Mazzolini, 155 N.E.2d 206 (Ohio 1958)

McCarney v. Meier, 286 N.W.2d 780 (N.D. 1979)

McCollum v. McConaughy, 119 N.W. 539 (Iowa 1909)

State v. Miller, 66 S.E. 522 (W.Va. 1909)

State v. Musser, 175 P.2d 724 (Utah 1946), *vacated and remanded by* 333 U.S. 95
    (1948)

N.A.H. v. S.L.S., 9 P.3d 354 (Col. 2000)

Nakata, State v., 878 P.2d 699 (Haw. 1994)

Neal v. Brockway, 385 A.2d 1069 (Vt. 1978)

Nelson, State v., 271 N.W. 114 (Minn. 1937)

Oleson v. Borthwick, 33 Haw. 766 (Haw. Terr. 1936) (1936 WL 4404)

Onofre, People v., 415 N.E.2d 936 (N.Y. 1980)

Pelkey v. City of Fargo, 453 N.W.2d 801 (N.D. 1990)

People v. (see name of party)

Phillips v. Curiale, 608 A.2d 895 (N.J. 1992)

Pierce v. Pierce, 46 Ind. 86 (Ind. 1874) (1874 WL 5693)

Powell v. State, 510 S.E.2d 18 (Ga. 1998)

Price v. Rowell, 159 A.2d 622 (Vt. 1960)

Purvis v. State, 377 So. 2d 674 (Fla. 1979)

R.G.M. v. D.E.M., 410 S.E.2d 564 (S.C. 1991)

Republic v. Li Shee, 12 Haw. 329 (Haw. 1900) (1900 WL 2491)

Robinson v. Bailey, 28 Haw. 462 (Haw. Terr. 1925) (1925 WL 3138)

Rubano v. DiCenzo, 759 A.2d 959 (R.I. 2000)

Santos, State v., 413 A.2d 58 (R.I. 1980)

Saunders, State v., 381 A.2d 333 (N.J. 1977)

Scott v. State, 39 Ga. 321 (Ga. 1869) (1869 WL 1667)

Seneca Mining Company v. Secretary of State, 47 N.W. 25 (Mich. 1890)

Shaw v. Barrows, 359 A.2d 651 (Vt. 1976)

State v. Shak, 466 P.2d 422 (Haw. 1970)
Silver Bow Refining Company, State v., 252 P. 301 (Mont. 1926)
Sorensen, People v., 437 P.2d 495 (Cal. 1968)
State v. (see name of opposing party)
Stevenson, State *ex rel.,* v. Tufly, 22 P. 1054 (Nev. 1890)
Stowell, Commonwealth v., 449 N.E.2d 357 (Mass. 1983)
Sutton v. Warren, 51 Mass. (10 Metcalf) 451 (Mass. 1845) (1845 WL 4221)
Titchenal v. Dexter, 693 A.2d 682 (Vt. 1997)
Toncray v. Budge, 95 P. 26 (Idaho 1908)
Von Geldern, State v., 638 P.2d 319 (Haw. 1981)
Wasson, Commonwealth v., 842 S.W.2d 487 (Ky. 1992)
Women of State of Minnesota v. Gomez, 542 N.W.2d 17 (Minn. 1995)
Yamaguchi v. Queen's Medical Center, 648 P.2d 689 (Haw. 1982)

Courts of Appeal

Barlow v. Blackburn, 798 P.2d 1360 (Ariz. App. 1990)
Byrum v. Hebert, 425 So.2d 322 (La. App. 1982)
Campbell v. Sundquist, 926 S.W.2d 250 (Tenn. App. 1996)
Fisher v. Fisher, 324 N.W.2d 582 (Mich. App. 1982)
Frasher v. State, 30 Am. Rep. 131 (Tex. Ct. App. 1877)
Holden, State v., 890 P.2d 341 (Idaho App. 1995)
Hopgood v. State, 45 S.E.2d 715 (Ga. App. 1947)
Littleton v. Prange, 9 S.W.3d 223 (Tex. App. 1999)
Orange v. Rose, 295 N.Y.S.2d 782 (App. Div. 1968)
Poe, State v., 252 S.E.2d 843 (N.C. App. 1979)
Schochet v. State, 541 A.2d 183 (Md. App. 1988), overruled 580 A.2d 176 (Md. 1990)
Wagner, *In re* Estate of (Gutierrez v. Estate of Wagner), 748 P.2d 639 (Wash. App. 1987)
Webb v. Webb, 677 So.2d 630 (La. App. 1996)
Williams v. State, 494 So. 2d 819 (Ala. Crim. App. 1986)

Trial Court

Baehr v. Miike, CIV. No. 91–1394, 1996 WL 694235 (Hawaii Cir. Ct. Dec. 3, 1996).
Brause v. Bureau of Vital Statistics, 1998 WL 88743 (Alaska Super.)
Dean v. District of Columbia, 1992 WL 685364 (D.C. Super.)
State v. Lopes, No. P1/90–3789, 1994 WL 930907 (R.I. Super. Ct. Mar. 14, 1994), order quashed, 660 A.2d 707 (R.I. 1995)
Mehr, People v., 383 N.Y.S.2d 798 (1976)
S.B. v. S.J.B., 609 A.2d 124 (N.J. Super. Ct. 1992)
Storrs v. Holcomb, 645 N.Y.S.2d 286 (1996)

SECONDARY LITERATURE

Alexander, Louis A. Note. "Liability in Tort for the Sexual Transmission of Disease: Genital Herpes and the Law." 70 *Cornell Law Review* 101 (1984).

Amar, Akhil Reed. "Intratextualism." 112 *Harvard Law Review* 747 (1999).

American Law Institute. *Restatement of the Law of the Conflict of Laws*. St. Paul, MN: American Law Institute Publishers, 1934. (*Restatement (First) of the Conflict of Laws*).

——. *Restatement (Second) of the Conflict of Laws*. St. Paul, MN: American Law Institute Publishers, 1971.

Andre-Clark, Alice Susan. Note. "Whither Statutory Rape Laws: Of *Michael M.*, the Fourteenth Amendment, and Protecting Women from Sexual Aggression." 65 *Southern California Law Review* 1933 (1992).

Ante, Richard. Book Review. "Same-Sex Marriage and the Construction of Family: An Historical Perspective." 15 *Boston College Third World Law Journal* 421 (1995).

Arriola, Elvia Rosales. "Sexual Identity and the Constitution: Homosexual Persons as a Discrete and Insular Minority." 14 *Women's Rights Law Reporter* 263 (1992).

Backhouse, Constance. "The White Women's Labor Laws: Anti-Chinese Racism in Early Twentieth Century Canada." 14 *Law & History Review* 315 (1996).

Bartlett II, Philip L. Recent Legislation. "Same-Sex Marriage." 36 *Harvard Journal on Legislation* 581 (1999).

Becker, Mary. "Problems with the Privatization of Heterosexuality." 73 *Denver University Law Review* 1169 (1996).

——. "Women, Morality, and Sexual Orientation." 8 *University of California at Los Angeles Women's Law Journal* 165 (1998).

Blair, Anita K. "Constitutional Equal Protection, Strict Scrutiny, and The Politics of Marriage Law." 47 *Catholic University Law Review* 1231 (1998).

Borchers, Patrick J. "*Baker v. General Motors:* Implications for Interjurisdictional Recognition of Non-Traditional Marriages." 32 *Creighton Law Review* 147 (1998).

Boyce, Bret. "Originalism and the Fourteenth Amendment." 33 *Wake Forest Law Review* 909 (1998).

Bradley, Craig M. "The Right Not to Endorse Gay Rights: A Reply to Sunstein." 70 *Indiana Law Journal* 29 (1994).

Bradley, Gerard V. "Same-Sex Marriage: Our Final Answer?" 14 *Notre Dame Journal of Law, Ethics, & Public Policy* 729 (2000).

Brashier, Ralph C. "Children and Inheritance in the Nontraditional Family." 1996 *Utah Law Review* 93.

Brown, Jennifer Gerarda. "Sweeping Reform from Small Rules? Anti-Bias Canons as a Substitute for Heightened Scrutiny." 85 *Minnesota Law Review* 363 (2000).

Brown III, Leonard G. "Constitutionally Defending Marriage: The Defense of Marriage Act, *Romer v. Evans* and the Cultural Battle They Represent." 19 *Campbell Law Review* 159 (1996).

Bruce, Teresa M. Note. "Doing the Nasty: An Argument for Bringing Same-Sex Erotic Conduct Back into the Courtroom." 81 *Cornell Law Review* 1135 (1996).

Carter, Stephen L. "'Defending' Marriage: A Modest Proposal." 41 *Howard Law Journal* 215 (1998).

Case, Mary Ann. "Couples and Coupling in the Public Sphere: A Comment on the Legal History of Litigating for Lesbian and Gay Rights." 79 *Virginia Law Review* 1643 (1993).

Chambers, David L. "Polygamy and Same-Sex Marriage." 26 *Hofstra Law Review* 53 (1997).

Choper, Jesse H. "A Century of Religious Freedom." 88 *California Law Review* 1709 (2000).

Clarkson, Kevin G., David Orgon Coolidge, and William C. Duncan. "The Alaska Marriage Amendment: The People's Choice on the Last Frontier." 16 *Alaska Law Review* 213 (1999).

Coleman, Phyllis. "Who's Been Sleeping in My Bed? You and Me, and the State Makes Three." 24 *Indiana Law Review* 399 (1991).

Coleman, Thomas F. "The Hawaii Legislature Has Compelling Reasons to Adopt a Comprehensive Domestic Partnership Act." 5 *Law & Sexuality* 541 (1996).

Collett, Teresa Stanton. "Recognizing Same-Sex Marriage: Asking for the Impossible?" 47 *Catholic University Law Review* 1245 (1998).

Coolidge, David Orgon. "Playing the *Loving* Card: Same-Sex Marriage and the Politics of Analogy." 12 *Brigham Young University Journal of Public Law* 201 (1998).

———. "Same-Sex Marriage?: *Baehr v. Miike* and the Meaning of Marriage." 38 *South Texas Law Review* 1 (1997).

——— and William C. Duncan. "Beyond *Baker*, The Case for a Vermont Marriage Amendment." 25 *Vermont Law Review* 61 (2000).

Coughlin, Anne M. "Sex and Guilt." 84 *Virginia Law Review* 1 (1998).

Coverdale, John F. "Missing Persons: Children in the Tax Treatment of Marriage." 48 *Case Western Reserve Law Review* 475 (1998).

Cox, Barbara J. Essay. "But Why Not Marriage: An Essay on Vermont's Civil Unions Law, Same-Sex Marriage, and Separate But (Un)Equal." 25 *Vermont Law Review* 113 (2000).

Cox, Juliet A. Comment. "Judicial Enforcement of Moral Imperatives: Is the Best Interest of the Child Being Sacrificed to Maintain Societal Homogeneity." 59 *Missouri Law Review* 775 (1994).

Crawford, Earl T. "The Legislative Status of an Unconstitutional Statute." 49 *Michigan Law Review* 645 (1951).

Culhane, John G. "Uprooting the Arguments Against Same-Sex Marriage." 20 *Cardozo Law Review* 1119 (1999).

Currie, Brainerd & Herma Hill Schreter. "Unconstitutional Discrimination in the Conflict of Laws: Privileges and Immunities." 69 *Yale Law Journal* 1323 (1960).

Curtis, Michael Kent. "Resurrecting the Privileges or Immunities Clause and Revising *The Slaughter-House Cases* without Exhuming *Lochner:* Individual Rights and the Fourteenth Amendment." 38 *Boston College Law Review* 1 (1996).

Davis, Peggy Cooper. *Neglected Stories: The Constitution and Family Values.* New York: Hill and Wang, 1997.

Delchin, Steven A. Comment. "Scalia 18:22: Thou Shall Not Lie with the Academic and Law School Elite; It Is an Abomination—*Romer v. Evans* and America's Culture War." 47 *Case Western Reserve Law Review* 207 (1996).

Dickerson, A. Mechele. "Family Values and the Bankruptcy Code: A Proposal to Eliminate Bankruptcy Benefits Awarded on the Basis of Marital Status." 67 *Fordham Law Review* 69 (1998).

Donovan, James M. "DOMA: An Unconstitutional Establishment of Fundamentalist Christianity." 4 *Michigan Journal of Gender & Law* 335 (1997).

Duncan, Richard F. "Homosexual Marriage and the Myth of Tolerance: Is Cardinal O'Connor a 'Homophobe'?" 10 *Notre Dame Journal of Law, Ethics and Public Policy* 587 (1996).

———. "The Narrow and Shallow Bite of *Romer* and the Eminent Rationality of Dual-Gender Marriage: A (Partial) Response to Professor Koppelman." 6 *William & Mary Bill of Rights Journal* 147 (1997).

———. "From *Loving* to *Romer:* Homosexual Marriage and Moral Discernment." 12 *Brigham Young University Journal of Public Law* 239 (1998).

Dunlap, Mary C. "Gay Men and Lesbians Down by Law in the 1990's USA: The Continuing Toll of *Bowers v. Hardwick.*" 24 *Golden Gate University Law Review* 1 (1994).

Ellman, Ira Mark. "The Place of Fault in a Modern Divorce Law." 28 *Arizona State Law Journal* 773 (1996).

Ely, John Hart. "Choice of Law and the State's Interest in Protecting Its Own." 23 *William & Mary Law Review* 173 (1981).

Engleman, Michael R. "*Bowers v. Hardwick:* The Role of Privacy—Only Within the Traditional Family?" 26 *Journal of Family Law* 373 (1987–88).

Eskridge, Jr., William N. "Reneging on History? Playing the Court/Congress/President Civil Rights Game." 79 *California Law Review* 613 (1991).

———. Review Essay. "A Social Constructionist Critique of Posner's *Sex and Reason:* Steps Toward a Gaylegal Agenda." 102 *Yale Law Journal* 333 (1992).

———. "A History of Same-Sex Marriage." 79 *Virginia Law Review* 1419 (1993).

———. Essay. "Gaylegal Narratives." 46 *Stanford Law Review* 607 (1994).

———. "A Jurisprudence of 'Coming Out'; Religion, Homosexuality, and Collisions of Liberty and Equality in American Public Law." 106 *Yale Law Journal* 2411 (1997).

———. "Challenging the Apartheid of the Closet: Establishing Conditions for Lesbian and Gay Intimacy, Nomos, and Citizenship, 1961–1981." 25 *Hofstra Law Review* 817 (1997).

———. *Gaylaw: Challenging the Apartheid of the Closet.* Cambridge, MA: Harvard University Press, 1999.

———. "No Promo Homo: The Sedimentation of Antigay Discourse and the Channeling Effect of Judicial Review." 75 *New York University Law Review* 1327 (2000).

Fajer, Marc A. "Can Two Real Men Eat Quiche Together? Storytelling, Gender-Role Stereotypes, and Legal Protection for Lesbians and Gay Men." 46 *University of Miami Law Review* 511 (1992).

Farabee, Lisa M. Note. "Marriage, Equal Protection, and New Judicial Federalism: A View From the States." 14 *Yale Law & Policy Review* 237 (1996).

Finkelman, Paul. Book Review. "Cultural Speech and Political Speech in Historical Perspective." 79 *Boston University Law Review* 717 (1999).

Finnis, John. "Law, Sexuality and 'Sexual Orientation.'" 69 *Notre Dame Law Review* 1049 (1994).

Fisch, Jill E. "Retroactivity and Legal Change: An Equilibrium Approach." 110 *Harvard Law Review* 1055 (1997).

Fletcher, George. "The Instability of Tolerance." In David Heyd, ed., *Toleration: An Elusive Virtue* 158 Princeton: Princeton University Press, 1996.

Fried, Charles. "Philosophy Matters." 111 *Harvard Law Review* 1739 (1998).

Friedman, Andrew H. "Same-Sex Marriage and the Right of Privacy: Abandoning Scriptural, Canonical and Natural Law Based Definitions of Marriage." 35 *Howard Law Journal* 173 (1992).

Frost, Cynthia J. "*Shahar v. Bowers:* That Girl Just Didn't Have Good Sense!" 17 *Law & Inequality* 57 (1999).

Gangnes, Hilary Benson & Christopher P. McKenzie. "Does the Death on the High Seas Act Apply to Interisland Hawaii Flights?" 6 *University of San Francisco Maritime Law Journal* 533 (1994).

Gardner; Mary F. Note. "*Braschi v. Stahl Assocs. Co.:* Much Ado about Nothing?" 35 *Villanova Law Review* 361 (1990).

Garvey, John H. *What Are Freedoms For?* Cambridge, MA: Harvard University Press, 1996.

Goldstein, Anne B.; Comment, "History, Homosexuality, and Political Values: Searching for the Hidden Determinants of *Bowers v. Hardwick*." 97 *Yale Law Journal* 1073 (1988).

Graff, E.J., *What Is Marriage For?* Boston: Beacon Press, 1999.

Green, Stuart. "Why It's a Crime to Tear the Tag Off a Mattress: Overcriminalization and the Moral Content of Regulatory Offenses." 46 *Emory Law Journal* 1533 (1997).

Grey, Thomas C. "*Bowers v. Hardwick* Diminished." 68 *University of Colorado Law Review* 373 (1997).

Gutmann, Amy. "Religious Freedom and Civic Responsibility." 56 *Washington & Lee Law Review* 907 (1999).

Hafen, Bruce C. "The Constitutional Status of Marriage, Kinship, and Sexual Privacy; Balancing the Individual and Social Interests." 81 *Michigan Law Review* 463 (1983).

Harmer-Dionne, Elizabeth. Note. "Once a Peculiar People: Cognitive Dissonance and the Suppression of Mormon Polygamy as a Case Study Negating the Belief-Action Distinction." 50 *Stanford Law Review* 1295 (1998).

Harrison, John. "Reconstructing the Privileges or Immunities Clause." 101 *Yale Law Journal* 1385 (1992).

Hart, H.L.A. *The Concept of Law* Oxford: Clarendon Press, 1961.

Herman, Barbara. "Pluralism and the Community of Judgment." In David Heyd, ed., *Toleration: An Elusive Virtue* 60 Princeton: Princeton University Press, 1996.

Heyd, David, ed. *Toleration: An Elusive Virtue.* Princeton: Princeton University Press, 1996.

Hixson, Thomas S.; "Public and Private Recognition of the Families of Lesbians and Gay Men." 5 *American University Journal of Gender & Law* 501 (1997).

Hochman, Charles B. "The Supreme Court and the Constitutionality of Retroactive Legislation." 73 *Harvard Law Review* 692 (1960).

Hoffman, Jerome A. "Thinking About Presumptions: The 'Presumption' of

Agency from Ownership as Study Specimen." 48 *Alabama Law Review* 885 (1997).

Holland, Maurice J. "The Modest Usefulness of DOMA Section 2." 32 *Creighton Law Review* 395 (1998).

Homer, Steven K. Note. "Against Marriage." 29 *Harvard Civil Rights-Civil Liberties Law Review* 505 (1994).

Huff, Leslye M. "Deconstructing Sodomy." 5 *American University. Journal of Gender & Law* 553 (1997).

Isakoff, Peter D. Note. "Unconstitutional Discrimination in Choice of Law." 77 *Columbia Law Review* 272 (1977).

Jaasma, Keith. Note. "The Religious Freedom Restoration Act: Responding to *Smith*, Reconsidering *Reynolds*." 16 *Whittier Law Review* 211 (1995).

Johnson, Greg. "Vermont Civil Unions: The New Language of Marriage." 25 *Vermont Law Review* 15 (2000).

Kainen, James L. "The Historical Framework for Reviving Constitutional Protection for Property and Contract Rights." 79 *Cornell Law Review* 87 (1993).

Kang, John M. "Deconstructing the Ideology of White Aesthetics." 2 *Michigan Journal of Race & Law* 283 (1997).

Kass, Leon R. "The End of Courtship." *The Public Interest* 39, Issue 126 (1997).

Kaveny, M. Cathleen. "Cloning and Positive Liberty." 13 *Notre Dame Journal of Law, Ethics, & Public Policy* 15 (1999).

Keane, Thomas M. Note. "Aloha, Marriage? Constitutional and Choice of Law Arguments for Recognition of Same-Sex Marriages." 47 *Stanford Law Review* 499 (1995).

Kelley, William K. Review Essay. "Inculcating Constitutional Values." 15 *Constitutional Commentary* 161 (1998).

Keyes, Alan L. "How Should Society Handle Injustice?" 19 *Harvard Journal of Law & Public Policy* 645 (1996).

Kimpel, Jason D. Note. "'Distinctions without a Difference': How the Sixth Circuit Misread *Romer v. Evans*." 74 *Indiana Law Journal* 991 (1999).

King, Sondrea Joy. Note. "Ya'll Cain't Do That Here: Will Texas Recognize Same-Sex Marriages Validly Contracted in Other States?" 2 *Texas Wesleyan Law Review* 515 (1996).

Knauer, Nancy J. "Heteronormativity and Federal Tax Policy." 101 *West Virginia Law Review* 129 (1998).

Kohm, Lynne Marie. "A Reply to 'Principles and Prejudice': Marriage and the Realization that Principles Win Over Political Will." 22 *Journal of Contemporary Law* 293 (1996).

———. "Liberty and Marriage—*Baehr* and Beyond: Due Process in 1998." 12 *Brigham Young University Journal of Public Law* 253 (1998).

Kopytoff, Barbara K. and A. Leon Higginbothan, Jr. "Racial Purity and Interracial Sex in the Law of Colonial and Antebellum Virginia." 77 *Georgetown Law Journal* 1967 (1989).

Kramer, Larry. "Whose Constitution Is It Anyway?" In William B. Rubenstein, ed., *Lesbians, Gay Men, and the Law* 563. New York: New Press, 1993.

Kramer, Larry. "Same-Sex Marriage, Conflict of Laws, and the Unconstitutional Public Policy Exception." 106 *Yale Law Journal* 1965 (1997).

Krause, Harry D. "Marriage for the New Millennium: Heterosexual, Same Sex—
Or Not at All?" 34 *Family Law Quarterly* 271 (2000).

Kreimer, Seth F. "The Law of Choice and Choice of Law: Abortion, the Right to
Travel, and Extraterritorial Regulation in American Federalism." 67 *New
York University Law Review* 451 (1992).

———. "'But Whoever Treasures Freedom . . . ': The Right to Travel and Extraterritorial Abortions." 91 *Michigan Law Review* 907 (1993).

Kristen, Elizabeth. Recent Developments. "The Struggle for Same-Sex Marriage
Continues." 14 *Berkeley Women's Law Journal* 104 (1999).

Lacey, Linda J. "Mimicking the Words, But Missing the Message: The Misuse of
Cultural Feminist Themes in Religion and Family Law Jurisprudence." 35
Boston College Law Review 1 (1993).

Lamm, Jocelyn B. Note. "Easing Access to the Courts for Incest Victims: Toward
an Equitable Application of the Delayed Discovery Rule." 100 *Yale Law
Journal* 2189 (1991).

Laycock, Douglas. "Equal Citizens of Equal and Territorial States: The Constitutional Foundations of Choice of Law." 92 *Columbia Law Review* 249 (1992).

Lefler, Julie. "Shining the Spotlight on Johns: Moving Toward Equal Treatment
of Male Customers and Female Prostitutes." 10 *Hastings Women's Law
Journal* 11 (1999).

Leipold, Andrew D. "Rethinking Jury Nullification." 82 *Virginia Law Review* 253
(1996).

Lewis, Kevin H. Note. "Equal Protection After *Romer v. Evans:* Implications for
the Defense of Marriage Act and Other Laws." 49 *Hastings Law Journal* 175
(1997).

Lund, Nelson. "Retroactivity, Institutional Incentives, and the Politics of Civil
Rights." 1995 *Public Interest Law Review* 87.

Lynch, Gerard E. "Our Administrative System of Criminal Justice." 66 *Fordham
Law Review* 2117 (1998).

Macedo, Stephen; "Homosexuality and the Conservative Mind." 84 *Georgetown
Law Journal* 261 (1995).

Massaro, Toni M. "The Meanings of Shame Implications for Legal Reform." 3
Psychology, Public Policy & Law 645 (1997).

McConnell, Michael W. "Contract Rights and Property Rights: A Case Study in
the Relationship Between Individual Liberties and Constitutional Structure." 76 *California Law Review* 267 (1988).

———. "Free Exercise Revisionism and the *Smith* Decision." 57 *University of Chicago Law Review* 1109 (1990).

———. "The Origins and Historical Understanding of Free Exercise of Religion."
103 *Harvard Law Review* 1409 (1990).

Mendus, Susan. *Toleration and the Limits of Liberalism.* Atlantic Highlands, NJ:
Humanities Press International, 1989.

Moore, Allison. "*Loving's* Legacy: The Other Antidiscrimination Principles." 34
Harvard Civil Rights-Civil Liberties Law Review 163 (1999).

Murphy, Jeffrie G. "Moral Reasons and the Limitation of Liberty." 40 *William &
Mary Law Review* 947 (1999).

Murphy, Walter F. "*Slaughter-House,* Civil Rights, And Limits On Constitutional
Change." 32 *American Journal of Jurisprudence* 1 (1987).

Myers, Richard S. "Same-Sex 'Marriage' and the Public Policy Doctrine." 32 *Creighton Law Review* 45 (1998).

Neff, Brian. Comment. "Retroactivity and the Civil Rights Act of 1991: An Opportunity for Reform." 1993 *Utah Law Review* 475.

Neuman, Gerald L. "Territorial Discrimination, Equal Protection, and Self-Determination." 135 *University of Pennsylvania Law Review* 261 (1987).

Note, "Constitutional Barriers to Civil and Criminal Restrictions on Pre- and Extramarital Sex." 104 *Harvard Law Review* 1660 (1991).

O'Brien, Rev. Raymond C. "Single-Gender Marriage: A Religious Perspective." 7 *Temple Political & Civil Rights Law Review* 429 (1998).

Page, J. Drew. Comment. "Cruel and Unusual Punishment and Sodomy Statutes: The Breakdown of the *Solem v. Helm* Test." 56 *University of Chicago Law Review* 367 (1989).

Patten, James M. Comment. "The Defense of Marriage Act: How Congress Said 'No' to Full Faith and Credit and the Constitution." 38 *Santa Clara Law Review* 939 (1998).

Patton, William Wesley and Sara Latz. "Severing Hansel from Gretel: An Analysis of Siblings' Association Rights." 48 *University of Miami Law Review* 745 (1994).

Paulsen, Michael Stokes, "Medium Rare Scrutiny." 15 *Constitutional Commentary* 397 (1998).

Plave, Erica Frohman. Note. "The Phenomenon of Antique Laws: Can a State Revive Old Abortion Laws in a New Era?" 58 *George Washington Law Review* 111 (1989).

Pratt , Robert A. "Crossing the Color Line: A Historical Assessment and Personal Narrative of *Loving v. Virginia*." 41 *Howard Law Journal* 229 (1998).

Ramsey, Carolyn B. Book Review. "Sex and Social Order: The Selective Enforcement of Colonial American Adultery Laws in the English Context." 10 *Yale Journal of Law & Humanities* 191 (1998).

Rasmussen, Eric & Jeffrey Evans Stake. "Lifting the Veil of Ignorance: Personalizing the Marriage Contract." 73 *Indiana Law Journal* 453 (1998).

Recent Legislation. "Domestic Relations—Same-Sex Couples—Vermont Creates System of Civil Unions.—Act Relating to Civil Unions, No. 91, 2000 Vt. Adv. Legis. Serv. 68 (Lexis)." 114 *Harvard Law Review* 1421 (2001).

Richards, David A.J. "Sexual Preference as a Suspect (Religious) Classification: An Alternative Perspective on the Unconstitutionality of Anti-Lesbian/ Gay Initiatives." 55 *Ohio State Law Journal* 491 (1994).

———. *Women Gays, and the Constitution.* Chicago: University of Chicago Press, 1998.

———. *Identity and the Case for Gay Rights: Race, Gender, Religion as Analogy.* Chicago: University of Chicago Press, 1999.

Robb, Barbara A.. Note. "The Constitutionality of the Defense of Marriage Act in the Wake of *Romer v. Evans*." 32 *New England Law Review* 263 (1997).

Robinson, Paul H. and John M. Darley. "The Utility of Desert." 91 *Northwestern University Law Review* 453 (1997).

Rockwell, Reverend Nancy. "Lust and the Love of God." 13 *St. Louis. University Public Law Review* 427 (1993).

Rosen, Jeffrey. "Translating the Privileges or Immunities Clause." 66 *George Washington Law Review* 1241 (1998).

Rubenfeld, Jed. "The Right of Privacy." 102 *Harvard Law Review* 737 (1989).

Rubenstein, William B., ed. *Lesbians, Gay Men, and the Law.* New York: New Press, 1993.

Sapir, Gidon. "Religion and State—A Fresh Theoretical Start." 75 *Notre Dame Law Review* 579 (1999).

Schombert, Harold P. Note. "*Baehr v. Lewin:* How Far Has the Door Been Opened? Finding a State Policy for Recognizing Same-Sex Marriages." 16 *Women's Rights Law Reporter* 331 (1995).

Scoles, Eugene and Peter Hay. *Conflict of Laws.* St. Paul: West, 2d ed., 1992.

Scott, Elizabeth S. "Rehabilitating Liberalism in Modern Divorce Law. 1994 *Utah Law Review* 687.

Sekulow, Jay Alan and John Tuskey. "Sex and Sodomy and Apples and Oranges—Does the Constitution Require States to Grant a Right to Do the Impossible?" 12 *Brigham Young University Journal of Public Law* 309 (1998).

Shankman, Kimberly C. and Roger Pilon. "Reviving the Privileges or Immunities Clause to Redress the Balance among States, Individuals, and the Federal Government." 3 *Texas Review of Law & Politics* 1 (1998).

Shepherd, Lois. "Dignity and Autonomy After *Washington v. Glucksberg:* An Essay about Abortion, Death, and Crime." 7 *Cornell Journal of Law & Public Policy* 431 (1998).

Siegel, Martin J. "For Better or for Worse: Adultery, Crime and the Constitution." 30 *Journal of Family Law* 45 (1991–1992).

Simson, Gary J. "Discrimination Against Nonresidents and the Privileges and Immunities Clause of Article IV." 128 *University of Pennsylvania Law Review* 379 (1979).

Smith, Douglas G. "Natural Law, Article IV, and Section One of the Fourteenth Amendment." 47 *American University Law Review* 351 (1997).

Smith, Steven D. "The Restoration of Tolerance." 78 *California Law Review* 305 (1990).

Stein, Edward, *The Mismeasure of Desire: The Science, Theory, and Ethics of Sexual Orientation.* New York: Oxford University Press, 1999.

Strassberg, Maura I. "Distinctions of Form or Substance: Monogamy, Polygamy and Same-Sex Marriage." 75 *North Carolina Law Review* 1501 (1997).

Strasser, Mark. *Legally Wed: Same-Sex Marriage and the Constitution.* Ithaca: Cornell University Press, 1997.

———. "Sodomy, Adultery, and Same-Sex Marriage: On Legal Analysis and Fundamental Interests." 8 *University of California at Los Angeles Women's Law Journal* 313 (1998).

———. *The Challenge of Same-Sex Marriage: Federalist Principles and Constitutional Protections.* Westport: Praeger Publishers/Greenwood Publishing Group, 1999.

———. "Unity, Sovereignty, and the Interstate Recognition of Marriage." 102 *West Virginia Law Review* 393 (1999).

———. "From Colorado to Alaska by Way of Cincinnati: On *Romer, Equality Foundation,* and the Constitutionality of Referenda." 36 *Houston Law Review* 1193 (1999).

———. *"Loving, Baehr,* and the Right to Marry: On Legal Argumentation and Sophistical Rhetoric." 24 *Nova Law Review* 769 (2000).

———. "Marital Acts, Morality and the Right to Privacy." 30 *New Mexico Law Review* 43 (2000).

Stratton, Traci Shallbetter. Note. "No More Messing Around: Substantive Due Process Challenges to State Laws Prohibiting Fornication." 73 *Washington Law Review* 767 (1998).

Sunstein, Cass. "Forward: Leaving Things Undecided." 110 *Harvard Law Review* 4 (1996).

Tedhams, David P. "The Reincarnation of 'Jim Crow': A Thirteenth Amendment Analysis of Colorado's Amendment 2." 4 *Temple Political & Civil Rights Law Review* 133 (1994).

Thompson-Schneider, Donna. "The Arc of History: Or, the Resurrection of Feminism's Sameness/Difference Dichotomy in the Gay and Lesbian Marriage Debate." 7 *Law & Sexuality* 1 (1997).

Treanor, William Michael & Gene B. Sperling. "Prospective Overruling and the Revival of 'Unconstitutional' Statutes." 93 *Columbia Law Review* 1902 (1993).

Trosino, James. Note. "American Wedding: Same-Sex Marriage and the Miscegenation Analogy." 73 *Boston University Law Review* 93 (1993).

Varat, Jonathan D. "State 'Citizenship' and Interstate Equality." 48 *University of Chicago Law Review* 487 (1981).

Wagner, William Joseph. "The Contractual Reallocation of Procreative Resources and Parental Rights: The Natural Endowment Critique." 41 *Case Western Reserve Law Review* 1 (1990).

Waite, Linda J. and Maggie Gallagher. *The Case For Marriage: Why Married People Are Happier, Healthier, and Better Off Financially.* New York: Doubleday, 2000.

Wardle, Lynn D. "A Critical Analysis of Constitutional Claims for Same-Sex Marriage." *Brigham Young University Law Review* 1 (1996).

———. "Legal Claims for Same-Sex Marriage: Efforts to Legitimate a Retreat from Marriage by Redefining Marriage." 39 *South Texas Law Review* 735 (1998).

Wildenthal, Bryan H. "To Say 'I Do': *Shahar v. Bowers,* Same-Sex Marriage, and Public Employee Free Speech Rights." 15 *Georgia State University Law Review* 381 (1998).

Wilkinson, III, J. Harvie. "The Fourteenth Amendment Privileges or Immunities Clause." 12 *Harvard Journal of Law & Public Policy* 43 (1989).

Williams, Bernard. "Toleration: An Impossible Virtue?" In David Heyd, ed. *Toleration: An Elusive Virtue* 18. Princeton: Princeton University Press, 1996.

Wolfson, Evan. "Crossing the Threshold: Equal Marriage Rights for Lesbians and Gay Men and the Intra-Community Critique." 21 *New York University Review Law & Social Change* 567 (1994–1995).

Woodhouse, Barbara Bennett. "Sex, Lies, and Dissipation: The Discourse of Fault in a No-Fault Era." 82 *Georgetown Law Journal* 2525 (1994).

Zubler, Todd. "The Right to Migrate and Welfare Reform: Time for *Shapiro v. Thompson* to Take a Hike." 31 *Valparaiso University Law Review* 893 (1997).

Index

About the Author

MARK STRASSER is Trustees Professor of Law, Capital University Law School, Columbus, Ohio. He is the co-editor of *Same-Sex Marriages: A Debate* (Praeger, forthcoming), *The Challenge of Same-Sex Marriage: Federalist Principles and Constitutional Protections* (Praeger, 1999), and *Legally Wed: Same-Sex Marriage and the Constitution* (1997).